The X Window System:

A User's Guide

Other books published in this series:

Title	Author	ISBN
Using Informix-SQL	Jonathan Leffler	0-201-51240-8
Advanced Xerox Ventura Publisher 2.0	Frank Peetoom	0-201-51574-1
Getting Started with Xerox Ventura Publisher	W. van Engelen	0-201-51573-3
Turbo C 2.0	A. Schäpers	0-201-51195-9
Inside HyperCard Vol. 1	W. Kitza	0-201-51150-9
Inside Hypercard Vol. 2	W. Kitza	0-201-51330-7
Introduction to TeX	Schwarz	0-201-51141-X
Turbo Pascal 5.5	A. Schäpers	0-201-51171-1

Books to be published in this series:

Title	Author	ISBN
SQL/Oracle	Finkenzeller Kracke/Unterstein	0-201-52974-2
Introduction to SPSS/PC+ and Data Entry	Huizingh	0-201-52975-0
Using the SAS System	Maessen	0-201-52964-5
Novell Netware	Stroomberg Van Lent	0-201-51580-6

The X Window System:
A User's Guide

Niall Mansfield

Addison-Wesley Publishing Company Inc.

Reading, Massachusetts   Menlo Park, California   New York
Don Mills, Ontario   Wokingham, England   Amsterdam
Bonn   Paris   Milan   Madrid   Sydney   Singapore
Tokyo   Seoul   Taipei   Mexico City   San Juan

The publisher offers discounts on this book when ordered in quantity for special sales. For more information, please contact:
Corporate & Professional Publishing Group
Addison-Wesley Publishing Company
Route 128
Reading, Massachusetts   01867

ISBN: 0-201-56344-4
1 2 3 4 5 6 7 8 9 10   MW   9594939291

First printing, May 1991

Preface

The X Window System is a powerful portable window system for bitmapped displays, developed at the Massachusetts Institute of Technology (MIT). The X Window System (often just called **X**) runs on wide range of systems. It has become a de-facto standard because of its manufacturer independence, its portability, its versatility in handling colour, and its ability to operate transparently across a network. It is an excellent vehicle for research, because the source code is freely available. This book describes the release of **X** distributed by the **X**-Consortium at MIT, which is freely available.

This book is suitable for the absolute beginner, as well as others who want a tutorial description of the system. You don't need any previous knowledge of **X** or of any other window system, but we do assume a very slight familiarity with the Unix operating system (on which the MIT release of **X** runs).

To get the most out of the book, use it in conjunction with a system actually running **X**. However, there are many illustrations which give a feel for the system if no workstation is available immediately.

The book provides a simple tutorial introduction to **X**, so that you can start to use it quickly. It describes the facilities provided, how to use them, and how to customise them, and refers you to the reference manuals to find more detailed information when needed.

Our reason for writing this book is simple — to pass on the benefits of our experience learning the system, so that others can avoid the pitfalls and frustrations which we met. There are very few books about **X**, and the documentation provided with the system consists of technical reference manuals, which are ideal for the experienced user, but almost impossibly difficult for a newcomer to the system.

Structure of the Book

The structure of the book is determined by its scope. The material is tutorial, and develops just as you progress when you are learning the system. Accordingly, topics and concepts are introduced only as you require them, or at least are able to understand them in context.

The book is divided into four parts:-

1. **An Overview of the System.**

   - user's overview — what the system offers to you as a user, in the way of tools and facilities.

   - conceptual overview — how the system operates, and the mechanisms it uses to implement the facilities the user sees.

2. **Using the System.** How to start-up and close-down the system, how to manage your screen space (create new windows, move them around, resize them, etc.), and practical instruction on how to use the tools, demonstration programs and management software included in the system.

3. **Customising the System.** We assume that by the time you get to reading this part of the book, you have got fairly well used to the system, and are familiar with the basic operations; accordingly, the treatment is more formal, and perhaps more difficult.

   This part tells you how to find out more detail about the operation of the system (using status and information programs) and how to customise the system to your own taste. This includes setting defaults for the text font to be used, window background, foreground and border colours, as well as more complicated items such as how to program your keyboard keys, and alter mouse, bell, screen and keyboard parameters. It finishes off by combining all the aspects you've encountered into an easily maintained arrangement for managing your workstation while running under **X**.

4. **The Appendices.** These include:-

   - A guide to the documentation supplied with the system.

   - Installation instructions, plus some hints.

   - A list of all the software included in the MIT release of the system, with brief descriptions.

   - Information on how to get hold of the software.

   - A list of network services relating to **X**.

How to Use this Book

The book is organised for more or less sequential reading. A good approach is to skim through the overview (Part 1) and then read how to use the system (Part 2). After that, when you are familiar with the system, read the overview again: this time, you'll be able to grasp more of the concepts and see how some of the elements of the system impact on practical use.

When you are comfortable with the basic facilities, move on to customising the system (Part 3). The material is not difficult, but there is a lot of detail — especially details of syntax — so approach this part gradually. As you encounter new facilities, try to put them to practical use, and get accustomed to them before moving on. It is especially necessary to read this part in conjunction with the reference manuals included with the system.

Notes on X11 Release 4

While this book deals with Release 3 of X, the approach we have taken means that almost all the text still applies unaltered to Release 4. In particular, the overview of the system, how it operates, and how you customise it remain fundamentally correct. This is so for three reasons. First, perhaps the most significant change in Release 4 is performance: the new server is much faster than its Release 3 predecessor. However, apart from making the system more pleasant to use you won't see any difference.

Secondly, many of the changes introduced in Release 4 are "cosmetic", affecting only the appearance of a program but not its operation. For example, Release 4 supports non-rectangular windows: while many Release 4 programs make use of these for pushbuttons, this makes no difference to how you use the programs.

Thirdly, many other changes in Release 4 are internal to the system and only affect you if you are writing X programs. For example, the Toolkit has been changed substantially and programs using it have had to be recompiled. However, the programs' operation as seen by the user is unaltered.

The one area where you will see the Release 4 changes is the window manager. The window manager described in this book, uwm, has been replaced by twm, which has more facilities and is easier to use: for instance it attaches a "title-bar" to the top of each application window (rather like Microsoft Windows or the Macintosh does) which you can use to manipulate that window. Fortunately, the basic operation of twm is fairly well described in the reference manual page which is included in standard MIT Release 4. In addition, we are making available a detailed tutorial on how to customise twm; this is being donated to public archives, and can be obtained via email or other network access. (For details, see Appendix E).

In addition, Release 4 contains a few new programs. Some merely illustrate new features, such as oclock which is a clock with a round face instead of a rectangular one, or xgc which demos X's graphics operations. Others such as listres and xlsatoms are more likely to be of interest to programmers than users. And a handful of others improve administration (xauth) or provide information and status facilities (appres, xlsclients).

Finally, some small changes have been made to existing programs (the slide-rule option in xcalc has sadly been removed), and many more fonts are included together with a convenient tool (xfontsel) to help you choose the font you need.

In summary, most of the changes made with Release 4 do not affect how you see the system. Many others relate to facilities which you need only occasionally, and then probably only when you have become very experienced with the system; information about these is available in the appropriate manual pages. While the window manager has altered a lot, its basic operation is well described in the manual page, and other tutorial information is available across the network.

Acknowledgements

Many people have helped me, both directly and indirectly. Chronologically first is Ralph Swick at MIT, whose patient and helpful replies to queries got me over the hurdles when I started using **X** initially. Helmut Krings, of Sun Microsystems in Germany, and Carol Cook, of Sun in Mountain View, provided assistance without which this book would not have been possible.

On the production side, my colleague Paul Davis did a great deal of work providing the text-formatting macros so that camera-ready copy could be produced directly with the LaTeX typesetting program. Typing and managing the manuscript were made bearable through the use of the elegant and powerful Emacs editor, written by Richard Stallman, and distributed by the Free Software Foundation. Paul Andrews of Torch Technology kindly reviewed part of the manuscript. The index was produced with the assistance of tools developed by Pehong Chen (obtained via the LaTeX distribution). Everything connected with the book was carried out on a system running **X** itself, so sincere thanks are due to all the people at MIT – especially Bob Scheifler – who created the system, and made it available to everybody. Thanks also for their time and effort put into handling the **xpert** mailing list, which provides an invaluable forum for discussion of **X** and related issues.

Contents

PART 3 CUSTOMISING THE SYSTEM

PART 4   APPENDICES

List of Figures

Part 1

An Overview of the System

Chapter 1   A User's Overview of the X Window System

The **X** Window System is a powerful portable window system for bitmapped displays, developed at the Massachusetts Institute of Technology (MIT). The **X** Window System (from now on just called **X**) runs on a wide range of systems. It has become a de-facto standard because of its manufacturer independence, its portability, its versatility in handling colour, and its ability to operate transparently across a network. It is an excellent vehicle for research, because the source code is freely available.

X runs on Unix-based computers from Alliant, Apollo, DEC, Hewlett-Packard, IBM, and Sun, as well as on DEC's VAX/VMS, on MS-DOS and several other systems. Other manufacturers who have expressed support for **X** include AT&T, Adobe (the PostScript people), Control Data, Data General, Fujitsu, Prime, Siemens, Silicon Graphics, Sony, Texas Instruments, Wang and Xerox.

1.1   What is Special About X?

There are four features which between them account for most of the power of **X** and its popularity:

- **X** is *network transparent*: application programs can output simultaneously to displays on other machines elsewhere on a network just as easily as to displays on their own machine, as shown schematically in Figure 1.1. The communication mechanism used is language- and machine-independent – the other machines on the network don't have to be the same type or even running the same operating system. As a result, programs can use new display types without re-compilation or re-linking.

- Many different styles of user interface can be supported. The management of windows - their placement, sizing, stacking and so on - is not embedded in the system, but is controlled by an application program, which can easily

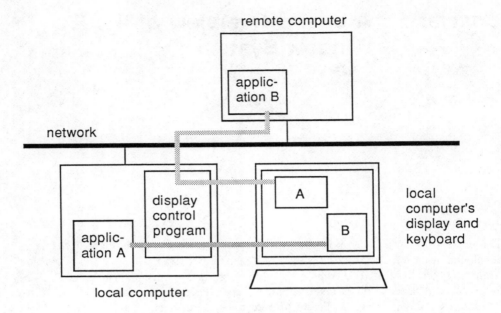

Figure 1.1 X programs can display to remote and local machines

be changed. The style of interface to individual application programs —
e.g. how you scroll text, or select an object in a window — isn't restricted
either (though that isn't as easy to change).

- **X** isn't embedded in the machine's operating system: to the operating system it is just another application program. So **X** can be ported easily to a wide range of systems.

- Windows are hierarchical: so applications can use for their own purposes most of the window-system's facilities, rather than having to invent other input or control mechanisms. (E.g. menus can be implemented by having a separate window for each selection pane).

All of these features are covered in detail in the next two chapters. But first, in the rest of this chapter we explain what a window system is, give a tiny history of **X**'s development, and go on to describe what you get in the standard release of **X** from MIT.

1.2 What is a Window System?

This section introduces a few basic ideas about window systems in general, using **X** as a specific example. If you are familiar with other window systems, you can skim through this very quickly.

X is a system for creating and managing windows on bitmapped display screens. It runs on a workstation or other form of terminal which has a bitmapped display, a keyboard, and some device that can be used to indicate particular positions or objects on the screen. **X** calls this device the "pointer"; in real life it will almost certainly be a mouse (probably with three buttons). **X** supports the usual features now expected of a windowed user interface to a computer.

Using a window system is often compared to working at a normal office desk. You have on your desktop all the papers, letters, and so on relating to the task in hand, plus other useful items (clock, diary, calculator, etc). As different parts of the task arise, you re-arrange the papers on your desk. You put the item you are concentrating on on the top of the pile, but probably refer occasionally to some of the other papers which are still visible. Later, you will put some of the papers aside temporarily, or remove them from your desk altogether.

This is a natural mode of working for people, and when they move to work on a computer, it is helpful if they can have the same sort of facilities. Unfortunately, the old-style terminal or CRT constrains you to having only a single work item on the screen at a time; only a small portion of it – about 24 lines – is visible and only textual information can be displayed; graphical items are just not handled. Window systems try to overcome this, typically giving you a larger screen, but certainly allowing you to show multiple work items simultaneously, and to display graphics and even colour.

X implements this model of working with its concept of windows. A *window* is a rectangular area of the screen, parallel to the sides of the screen. Usually, each window[1] is dedicated to a separate and independent application program. These multiple applications can output to their own windows concurrently - there isn't just one window - at a time "active" for output. **X** allows windows to overlap (as shown in Figure 1.2), and an application can continue to output to its window even if it is partially or completely covered by another window. Facilities are provided for moving windows around on the screen, making them bigger or smaller, placing them on the top or bottom of a stack of windows, and so on. Even with overlapping windows, there will be times when there are too many windows on the screen for comfort. So, in common with many other systems, **X** supports *icons*. An icon is a small picture on the screen which is a placeholder for an application window. When you *iconify* an application window, it is removed from the screen and replaced with its icon, thus freeing screen space. The reverse happens when you *de-iconify* — the icon is replaced with the original window.

Convenience functions, such as a desk-clock or diary, are *not* built into the system,

---

[1]Strictly, this ought to read "each top-level window", as **X** allows a hierarchy of windows, and a typical application window can contain many sub-windows for control, input, and display functions.

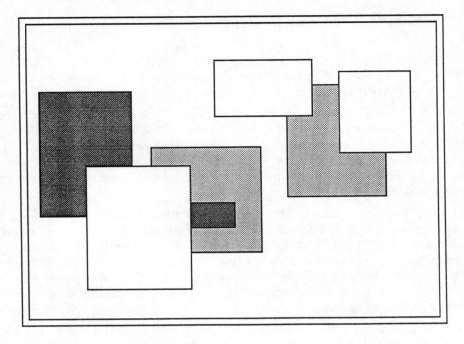

Figure 1.2 Overlapping Windows

but are provided by small programs which are separate applications.

For output, X supports a rich selection of functions for writing text and drawing graphics in windows. Multiple fonts are easily and routinely handled. There is a wide range of graphics mechanisms and methods of drawing graphics elements such as points, lines, arcs and areas. Colour is handled comprehensively. The complexity of these facilities is hidden from the user, who can use them simply and conveniently. For example, in applications, you can specify fonts by names like "*times-bold-i*" for Times bold italic, and when you want to use colours, you specify them with everyday names, like "yellow" or "navy blue".

X is equally versatile in its handling of input. X can handle different types and layouts of keyboards, and mechanisms are provided for customising the keyboard, e.g. changing it from the normal QWERTY layout to the Dvorak style, or a preferred country-specific layout. An important part of input handling is dealing with the user interface – keyboard and mouse commands telling the system how to configure the windows on the screen, and how to manipulate the contents of windows. X can support many different types of user interface, largely because the window management function isn't built into the system but is delegated to a user-level process, which can be replaced or altered. (A close analogy is the way that the command-line interpreter or *shell* in a Unix system may be replaced or altered). This flexibility in the styles of user interface which can be offered is almost unique to X.

1.3   A Brief History of X

The development of X started in 1984 at MIT's Laboratory for Computer Science, where Bob Scheifler was working on distributed systems. Around the same time Jim Gettys from DEC was working as part of Project Athena, also at MIT. Both groups had requirements for something similar – a good window system for Unix machines – and cooperative work started. From Stanford they received a copy of Stanford's own experimental window system, W. This was developed, and when it became sufficiently different that it needed to be distinguished from its parent, it was called X.

Work continued, and versions continued to be produced. (The version number was changed whenever a change was made to the software which made it incompatible with the earlier version). In mid-1985, the fundamental decision was taken that X would be made available to anybody who wanted it for just the cost of distribution. Some of the more recent milestones have been:

Version 10 : late 1985. It was around this time that people and organisations outside MIT started making real contributions to the software.

First commercial X product : DEC announced their VAXstation-II/GPX in January 1986.

Version 10, Release 3 : February 1986. (By now, X was starting to spread, and people were porting it to many new systems).

Version 10 Release 4 : November 1986

First X Technical Conference : January 1987, at MIT.

During 1986 it was clear that Version 10 could not evolve to satisfy all the requirements that were being asked of it. MIT and DEC undertook a complete redesign of the protocol. The result was X, Version 11:

Version 11 Release 1 : September 1987

Foundation of the X Consortium : the MIT X Consortium was founded to further research and development on X, and to control the standard. Currently it consists of over 30 organisations.

Second X Technical Conference : January 1988

Version 11 Release 2 : March 1988

Version 11 Release 3 : October 1988

Third X Technical Conference : January 1989

1.4 Implementations of X

Strictly, "the **X** Window System" is not a piece of software: it is a *protocol* which defines how an implementation of such a system must behave. (Just like TCP/IP, or DECnet, or IBM's SNA: all these are protocols too, describing how real pieces of software ought to function). Any system which conforms to this protocol, and which meets other criteria laid down by the **X**-Consortium can be called **X**.

For simplicity, from now on we will ignore this distinction between protocol and implementation: whenever we refer to **X**, we just mean a full and proper implementation of the system.

1.5 The MIT Release of X

MIT distributes a complete release of **X** for a wide range of computers. The current release (Version 11 Release 3) contains support for the following systems:

- Apple A/UX

- Apollo Domain/IX

- 4.3+tahoe

- Digital Equipment Corporation Ultrix

- Hewlett Packard HP-UX

- IBM AOS

- Sun Microsystems SunOS

These are the systems supported in the MIT release – there are commercial implementations for many more systems.

As the system developed and more people started using it, the amount of software contributed by third parties has increased so much that the release has had to be divided into two:

- The **core** distribution — the software supported by the MIT **X**-Consortium.

- The **contrib** distribution — software contributed by users and other third-parties.

The **core** and **contrib** software are distributed on separate tapes, for convenience.

This book describes almost exclusively the system as provided in the MIT **core** release. Nonetheless, we occasionally refer to the **contrib** software, where it illustrates something not available in the **core** or where it offers something which is likely to be of universal interest.

1.5.1 What the MIT Release Contains

The release contains the documentation, source code, configuration files and utilities, and everything else needed to build a complete working system. (No object or binary files are supplied; the system must be built from the sources). Here we are concentrating on how a user sees the system, and so describe only the window-system programs themselves and the tools which a normal user requires, omitting installation utilities, configuration tools, and the like. A full description of the release, including all documentation, build tools, release notes, etc., is given in the Appendices.

The programs in the **core** release fall naturally into a number of classes:

1. Programs which comprise the **X** Window System itself.

2. The tools and other facilities you need because you are using a window system:

   - Tools for routine window-related functions (e.g. dumping the contents of a window to a printer).
   - convenience programs which you often keep on your "desktop", a clock for instance. (These programs are analogous to *desk accessories* on Apple's Macintosh system).

3. General applications which benefit from the windowed environment.

4. Demos and games.

5. Information and status programs.

6. Tools for customising your environment.

We'll cover these in turn in the following sections.

1.5.2 The System Programs

The following programs comprise the basic system on which everything else depends.

X - the display *server* - the software which controls your workstation's keyboard, mouse, and screen. This is the heart of **X**; it is this program which creates and destroys windows, and actually writes and draws in them at the request of other "client" programs. The server program is different for each type of hardware display supported, and the release contains the following versions:

   - Xapollo – for Apollo displays
   - Xhp – for HP's 9000/300's with Topcat displays
   - Xibm – for IBM's APA16 and Megapel displays

- Xmacll – for Apple's Macintosh II
- Xplx – for the Parallax graphics controller
- Xqdss – for DEC's GPX display (VAXstation II/GPX)
- Xqvss – for DEC's QVSS displays (e.g. VS2)
- Xsun – for Sun/2, Sun/3, Sun/4 and Sun/386i Workstations.

Many sites will have only one type of hardware and won't bother to build or install all possible servers. Nonetheless, it is conventional to refer always to the server as **X**, and equate it by some means to the one you actually run on your machine. (E.g. on BSD and derived Unix systems you would use a symbolic link).

xinit - the initialisation program, which starts the system and sets the server running.

xdm - the **X** display manager, a program which provides a convenient and flexible way of starting the system and tailoring the startup to individual requirements. This is an alternative to xinit.

uwm - the *window manager*, the program which determines how you manage your desktop, move windows, resize them etc. With this, you perform window operations via menus or with a combination of mouse buttons and keyboard keys.

Of these, only the server program is essential. You can run applications on an **X** system which has none of the other programs, or with different programs which provide similar sorts of functions. (However, the system would be much more awkward to use).

These programs comprise the window system, but with these alone you can do nothing useful (except move the cursor around on the screen). To do real work, you need some additional utilities (described in the next section) and application programs (described in the section after that).

1.5.3 Window-System Utilities

These are tools which are not part of the window-system proper, but which are almost essential for you to make the most of the system, and use it conveniently. They fall into two broad classes - tools for routine window operations, and small convenience-tool programs which you make use of even when you are working primarily in another application.

Tools for Routine Window Operations

These programs perform day-to-day functions which you require just because you are using a window system instead of a normal computer terminal.

xterm - the **X** *terminal emulator*. Most of the programs on your system were not written specifically to be used with a window system, let alone for **X** in particular. E.g. the normal system programs for listing file directories, editing, compiling programs and so on work on almost any terminal. But how are they to operate with **X**, when they don't even know what a window is? xterm is a program which creates an **X** window, and allows you to run any normal "dumb terminal" program in that window: for all intents and purposes, the program sees xterm's window just like a real terminal. You use xterm to start other **X** programs as well as for ordinary non-window work.

xhost lets you control which other *hosts* (machines on your network) are allowed to access your display screen.

xkill a utility for killing unwanted applications.

xwd dumps to a file the image contained in a window, so you can recreate it later, or print it, or do whatever you want with it.

xpr translates a window image previously captured with xwd into a format suitable for printing on a hardcopy printer.

xdpr combines xwd and xpr with the normal system program to print a file, allowing you to print a window's contents in a single step.

xmag lets you magnify a selected portion of the image on the screen.

xwud "undumps" a window image previously dumped by xwd, i.e. displays the image on the screen again.

x10tox11 is an aid to migration from Version 10 to Version 11, allowing V10 programs to run on a V11 system.

xrefresh is a little program which refreshes your display - you can cause some or all your windows to be re-drawn in full.

Convenience Programs

These are analogous to the small convenience tools you often keep on your office desk - items like a calculator, a clock and so on.

xclock an analog or digital clock.

xcalc a calculator which can imitate a couple of popular modes of scientific calculator. You can run it in analog mode too - as a slide rule!

xload displays the current load average on a machine, in the form of a histogram.

xbiff is the **X** version of biff, the program which **barfs if** mail arrives. xbiff displays an icon of a garden mailbox, and raises the flag on it if there is mail for you.

1.5.4 General Applications and Tools

These are tools for functions not specifically related to the Window System, but which benefit from the windowed environment provided.

xedit - a text editor. You select commands via menus or from the keyboard, and indicate positions and selections in the text with the pointer.

xman - a browser for easy accessing of manual pages / system documentation.

xmh - a mail handling program. In fact this is an **X** front end to the mh mail handler.

1.5.5 Demos and Games

These programs illustrate the graphics and colour capabilities of **X**, and are a good starting point for when you are getting used to the system.

ico draws an icosahedron (or other polyhedron) and animates it, setting it bouncing around in a window.

maze creates a random maze and finds its way through it.

muncher draws lots of animated patterns in a window.

plaid draws continuously changing plaid-like patterns in a window.

xeyes creates a pair of eyes which watch the cursor wherever it goes on the screen.

xlogo prints the **X** logo in a window.

puzzle is a game in which 15 jumbled tiles, numbered 1 to 15, are enclosed in a 4x4 frame, and you have to arrange them in order again.

1.5.6 Information and Status Programs

These programs give you information about your window system, the windows on it, and the various resources like text fonts and so on which are available to you. You often use them in conjunction with the customisation tools.

xfd displays a specified **X** text font in a window, optionally giving some extra information about the elements of the font.

xlsfonts is a directory program for **X** text fonts, i.e. it tells you which fonts are available on a particular display.

showsnf shows details of a font which is in *Server Natural Format* – the native format for your server.

xwininfo displays window-system information about a specific window, e.g. size, position and other characteristics.

xlswins lists all the windows on the system, optionally with some detail about each.

xprop displays *properties* of windows and fonts. Initially you will find this useful mainly for seeing the point sizes and other details of fonts.

xdpyinfo gives details of your display and the server controlling it.

xev is a diagnostic or experimental tool: it prints details of all the **X** "events" relating to its windows.

1.5.7 Tools to Customise the System to Suit You

You won't use these programs much at first, but after a short while you'll find there are some things about the system you'd like to change. Maybe you'd like a bigger default text font, or prefer window borders in a different colour from the normal, or one of a host of other things. Using these programs, you can change your working environment to what suits you best.

xset lets you set your preferences for many characteristics of your display. You can enable or disable key-click, set the volume of the bell, specify where fonts are to be retrieved from, etc.

xsetroot lets you choose the appearance of the background on your display screen. You can change its colour, or pattern, or the cursor to be used when the pointer (mouse) isn't inside any application window.

xmodmap displays the *mapping* of the keyboard, i.e. which character is generated when a given key is pressed, and lets you change it so you can personalise your keyboard. Mostly the program is used to change the action of the special keys (META, SHIFT-LOCK, etc) and the function keys, but you can change any key(s) you want.

bitmap is a program which lets you create and edit *bitmaps*, i.e. little pictures which are used for cursors, icons, background patterns, and lots of other things.

xrdb lets you display or alter entries in a database which holds your preferences about which colour, fonts etc., are to be used by application programs. In effect, you are setting up defaults for these characteristics. You can set defaults to apply to all applications, or only to particular programs.

bdftosnf converts a font from the portable standard *BDF* ("bitmap distribution format") to your server's native SNF format.

1.6   Summary

This chapter has introduced you to **X**, and outlined the facilities you get with it (in the MIT release).

The next two chapters take some of the topics touched on here and describe them in greater depth, especially those which are unique to **X** and give it its power: Chapter 2 covers the network aspects of **X**, and Chapter 3 describes some of its other special features.

Chapter 2   A Conceptual Overview of X — The Basic System Model

In this chapter and the next we describe the basic mechanisms of **X**, and introduce many of its fundamental concepts. The intention is to give you an understanding of the system that you can relate to when you come to use it later on. You will gain an insight into what the system facilities are doing and how they do it: this will enable you to use the system quickly and more effectively. We also point out the benefits of the system's features, and indicate how they affect you as someone actually using the system.

This chapter describes the fundamental components of the system, and how they interact with each other. The next chapter describes some other features of the system, in particular those relating to the user interface and how it is provided. These chapters contain many new concepts. None are very complex, but until you have used the system for a while, they may not mean very much to you, and even if they do, you may not see the motivation for them. Probably the best approach is to read through the overview quickly, and then move on to the practical use of the system. Then, when you have a feel for how the system works, come back and read this overview again, and you will gain a better understanding of what is happening.

2.1   The Fundamental Components of X

Unlike older window systems, **X** is not one homogeneous piece of software. Instead, it consists of three inter-related parts:

1. A "server" which controls the physical display and input devices.

2. "Client" programs which request the server to perform particular operations on specified windows.

3. A "communications channel" which the client programs and the server use to talk to each other.

The basic relationship of server, client, and communications link is shown in Figure 2.1, and the three are described in the following sections.

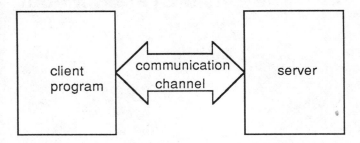

Figure 2.1 The fundamental components of X

2.1.1 The Server

The first basic component of **X** is the server — the software which controls the physical display and its input devices (keyboard and mouse or other pointer device). It is the server which actually creates windows, and draws images and text in them, in response to requests from client programs. It doesn't initiate actions itself — it only performs actions that have been requested by client processes.

Each display has one, and only one, server.

The server is supplied by the vendor of the **X** system, and normally isn't altered by the user. However, as far as the operating system is concerned, the server is just another user program[1] so it is very easy to replace one implementation of a server with another, perhaps from a third-party source.

2.1.2 The Client

The second basic component of **X** consists of the clients — the application programs which make use of the system's window facilities. Application programs in **X** are called "clients" because they are in effect customers of the server: they ask the server to perform particular actions on their behalf. They can't affect any window or display directly: they can only send a request to a server to do what they require. Typical requests might be "write the string 'Hello, World' in window XYZ", or "draw a line of this colour from A to B in window CDE".

Of course, requesting window operations is only one part of a client program: the other part is the code relating to the task the user is trying to perform, e.g. edit text, or draw an engineering diagram of a system or component, or perform calculations in a spreadsheet. In general, this part of the client program is insulated from the window

---

[1] This is the case for existing Unix implementations. However, some vendors may choose to implement some or all of the server within the operating system kernel.

system and knows very little about it. Often (especially in the case of large standard packages for graphics, statistics, etc.) application programs are capable of outputting to many devices; displaying in an **X** window is only one of the many output formats supported by these clients, so the **X**-related part of the program will be only a very small part of the total.

Users will generally use client programs from a variety of sources: some basic ones are supplied with the system (e.g. desk-clock), some will be bought from third parties, and some users will write their own client programs for particular applications.

2.1.3 The Communications Channel

The third basic component of **X** is the communications channel. Clients use it to send requests to the server and the server uses it to send back status and other information to the client programs.

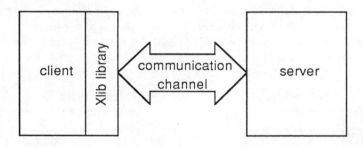

Figure 2.2 Function of the Xlib library

The precise nature of the channel is not very important, as long as both server and client know how to use it. Support for the communication types required on a given system or network is built into the basic **X**-Window library for that system. All dependence on the types of communication is isolated to this library, and all communication between client and server is *via* this library (known as "Xlib" in the standard **X** implementation) as shown in Figure 2.2. As a result, all client programs using the library automatically have the ability to use any of the available communication methods.

Client/server communication falls into two broad classes which reflect the two basic modes of operating the **X** system:

1. The server and client are running on the same computer. Here they can communicate using any method of inter-process communication ("IPC") available on the machine, as shown in Figure 2.3. When running in this mode, **X** is effectively operating like many conventional window systems.

2. The client is running on one machine, but the display (and its server) is on another. Now client and server must communicate across a network

single machine

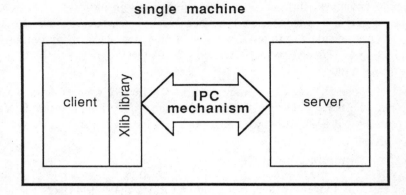

Figure 2.3 Client and server on the same machine

using a mutually agreed protocol. Currently, the most commonly supported protocols are TCP/IP and DECnet, but any other which provides reliable stream transmission could be used. Figure 2.4 shows a typical case where communication is across an Ethernet network.

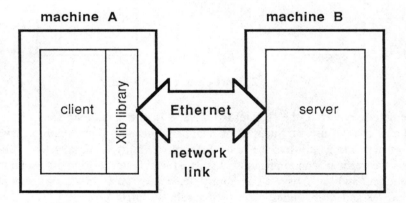

Figure 2.4 Client and server on separate machines

This ability for an application to operate just as easily across a network as on the local machine is called network transparency and is what makes **X** almost unique[2]. It is this feature which makes it suitable for building flexible multi-purpose networks of cooperating machines.

Because the server and client are completely separated, a new type of display station called an *X-terminal* has evolved. Briefly, an **X**-terminal is like a stripped-down

---

[2]There are several window systems in academic use, and **NeWS** from Sun Microsystems, which use network architectures. However none are in widespread use by more than one major vendor.

workstation which is dedicated to running the **X** server and nothing else[3]. It has a keyboard, mouse, and screen, and some way of communicating across the network (so clients on other hosts can display to it). But it doesn't have a file-system of its own, and can't support general purpose programs. Consequently, these programs have to be run elsewhere in the network.

2.2   How Server and Clients Interact

So far we have just stated that server and client communicate across some available channel, but we haven't said how, or what they need to send to each other, or why.

This section describes what is transmitted across the communications link, in both directions. Essentially, a client performs output by asking the server to do it, and input is handled by the server sending notification of events such as pressing of keyboard keys and mouse buttons to the client.

2.2.1   What Clients Send to the Server; Output Handling

A client asks a server to perform an action, say create a window with particular characteristics on a specified screen, or write a text string in some window. The client does this by sending what are called *requests* to the server. A request is packaged in a simple block; the block contains an "opcode" indicating what operation is to be performed, followed by some number of arguments giving more detail of what is required. E.g. to clear a rectangular area of a window, a client sends a 16-byte request block specifying the window in question, the coordinates of the top-left corner of the area to be cleared, and its width and height.

There are several important features of this format:

- The contents of the request block are completely independent of the type of machine(s) on which the server and the client are running. A single client can output to (i.e. send requests for operations on) any **X**-window server on any type of display. Requests (and therefore the network operation of the whole system) are independent of language, machine, and operating system.

- As each request contains details of the window or other resource to be used, all requests from a client to a specific server can be sent over a single connection, so the number of windows which can be supported is not limited by the network mechanism.

- Request blocks are relatively small, typically consisting of twenty or so bytes, because the request is specified at a fairly high level. E.g. a line

---

[3]Strictly, it also needs to run some other program which lets you login remotely to other hosts on your network, to start your client applications.

to be drawn is specified by its end points — not as a list of screen pixels to be marked. Typically the number of pixels affected on a display is ten to a hundred times more than the number of bits in the request block which caused the action. The result is that requests don't load the network too heavily, and performance over a network connection is good — often close to the performance limits of the display device. (So the common misconception, that **X** operates exclusively by transmitting bitmaps between client and server, is wrong).

All output functions are handled with requests to the server. **X** supports a rich selection of facilities for graphic output, including support for multiple text fonts and colour, but at a user-level you are insulated from most of the complexity involved in this area.

2.2.2   What the Server Sends to Clients; Input Handling

The server also uses the communications channel, to send information back to clients about whether their requests were actioned successfully, and to tell the client about particular *events* which the client is interested in, which have occurred on the display. These events include information like "the left mouse button was clicked in window XYZ", or that "key 123 was pressed", or "Window ABC has been re-sized".

Like requests from clients, these server responses are packaged in simple blocks, which are independent of language, machine and operating system.

Events are fundamental to how **X** functions. All keyboard input, and mouse button and motion inputs are handled using the events mechanism. In addition, the client relies completely on events for information about certain occurrences on the system which it needs to know about. We'll look at a few of these, starting with some normal input functions and moving on to some **X**-specific features, to give you a general idea of how events work in practice.

Keyboard Input

When you press a key on your keyboard, this is detected by the server. The server then notifies any applications which have registered an interest in this type of happening, by sending them a <KeyPress> event. There are ways of restricting notification, either to the window that the mouse pointer is currently positioned in, or to a nominated window which for the time being is to receive all keyboard input. This restriction mechanism is called setting the keyboard *focus*.

When the key is subsequently released (usually almost immediately), another event (<KeyRelease>) is generated. However, except for modifier keys such as SHIFT or CONTROL, this is not supported by all types of hardware, and few applications are interested in key-releases anyway.

The message blocks sent to clients to inform them about keyboard events (whether of type <KeyPress> or <KeyRelease>) merely say "key number ... has been pressed (or released)". They do *not* associate any ASCII or EBCDIC character with the key, nor suggest how it is to be interpreted — all that is left to the client program. This may seem to make things very complicated for the client, but the standard Xlib library has routines to handle interpretation of key events quite simply, and by default it is set up so that all the keys behave as you would expect. On the other hand, this "soft" association of keys with characters allows a lot of flexibility: at the server level, the keyboard can be completely remapped to provide a different keyboard layout, and at the client level, individual keys can be "programmed" to insert user-specified strings of text, or perform other functions.

Later on we'll look at these facilities in more detail. Until then, these features will not affect your use of the system, and you need not be too concerned with how **X** actually transforms your pressing the "A" key into an ASCII "A" sent to your application program.

Events Relating to Pointer Position

Clients can ask to be informed whenever the pointer on the screen enters or leaves a window controlled by them. The events sent to clients to inform them about this specify whether the pointer has entered or left the window (event types "<EnterWindow>" and "<LeaveWindow>") and which window was concerned.

This is often used to somehow highlight the window the pointer is currently in. Some applications change the shading of their window border (e.g. from grey to black) when the pointer enters them, to emphasise that this is the application you are currently dealing with. Another common use is where a menu is made up of several windows, one for each selection: as you move the pointer into a selection's window, the window changes colour to indicate this is the current selection, and if you move the pointer out of the window again without selecting, the window reverts to its original colour. You will see many examples of this in later chapters.

What Happens When a Window is Uncovered — Exposure Events

A big difference between **X** and most other window systems is that it is the *client's* responsibility to keep the contents of its windows up to date. The server keeps track of which windows are visible at any time on the screen, but it doesn't keep track of the contents of the windows.

When a window (or part of a window) which was covered by another becomes visible, the server doesn't know what ought to be displayed in that window. Instead, it sends an *exposure event* to the client which owns that window, telling it which parts of the window have just been made visible. It is then up to the client to decide what to do. In many cases, typically in simple applications or for small windows, the client just re-draws the whole window, because the extra computation necessary to re-draw only the uncovered part would not be worth while. In more sophisticated applications, the client will often re-draw only the necessary portions of the window. Which to do is a decision for the programmer who writes the application: it is a tradeoff between performance (how fast the window is updated) and the complexity of the program code necessary for selective re-drawing.

Relying on the client to re-compute the contents of the window can have serious performance effects, especially where pop-up menus are used — once the menu has been used and has vanished you don't want a long and costly update of the window the menu had obscured. To get over this, some implementations of X include a facility called *save-under*: you tell the server that if possible it should save the contents of the windows which this window obscures. Then, when this window is removed, the original display can be instantly replaced, and there is no need to send an exposure event to the client.

A similar, more general, feature called *backing store* may also be implemented. You can tell the server that if possible it should store the contents of this window whenever they are obscured. Again, the idea is to improve performance by reducing the re-draw load on clients. The difference between the two facilities is that backing store saves the contents of this window, whereas save-under saves the contents of windows obscured by this one.

Even in implementations which support save-unders and backing store, the mechanism is not guaranteed. When a client requests these facilities, it is really no more than a hint to the server to say that they would be beneficial; the client must always be prepared to handle exposure events. Even if the server does maintain a window's contents for a time, it can stop doing so whenever it wants (e.g. because it no longer has sufficient memory) and start generating exposure events again.

2.3   Network Aspects of X

We have mentioned that the server and client don't have to execute on the same machine, but can run on separate machines connected by a network. In the following sections we look at how you use this facility in practice, why it is so useful, and how it enhances the growth of a network as an integrated computing resource.

2.3.1   How You Use X Networking in Practice

When the server is running on one machine to which a display is connected, and the client on another, the keyboard and mouse inputs are generated on the machine running the server, but the client which uses those inputs is somewhere else. How do you actually work? To explain this, we'll take an example.

You are using a workstation which is running an X server controlling the display. If it's an isolated workstation, obviously all clients must run on it too. Even if it's connected to a network, most of the time you will probably run clients on your own

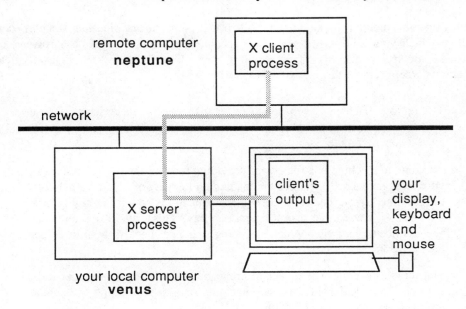

Figure 2.5 Typical use of **X**'s network feature

machine anyway. But let's say you want to use another machine on the network because it has some special facilities which yours does not have, and you want the program's output to appear on your own display. Using the ordinary network facilities provided by your operating system, you set the *client* program running on the *remote* machine, specifying that the output is to appear on the display on your own workstation, as shown in Figure 2.5. With the machine names shown in the figure, and assuming the client program is called xgraph, say, on a Unix system you would initiate this with a command like:

```
rsh neptune xgraph -display venus:0
```

i.e. run the xgraph program on remote machine neptune and tell xgraph to output to display number zero on your own machine, venus. From now on, we will refer to this mode of operating — where the client runs on one machine and the server on a different one — as *remote display*.

To summarise: you normally use the remote display facility by setting the client program running on a remote machine and telling it to display on your own machine which is running the **X** server.

2.3.2   Why X's Network Facilities Are Useful

Why is it useful to be able to run a client program on one machine, but actually display the output on another? There are many every-day situations where remote display is useful or convenient. In general, you will use it where a machine has some special feature which your own hasn't got. That special "something" could be hardware, or software, or special file access or anything else. The following are a few typical situations where remote display would be useful.

- The remote machine is very much faster than your own; perhaps because it contains a floating-point accelerator or a vector processor, or maybe it's even a supercomputer.

- The remote machine is a file server providing most of the disk resources to your local network. To reduce the loading on the network, you may choose to run remotely on the server particular applications which are highly disk intensive — some large search operations, say. This way, only the results, and not all the data files which are being searched, have to be sent across the network.

- The remote machine has a special architecture suited to a particular task. It might be a dedicated database machine, or a special-purpose machine designed for a single application.

- The remote machine has special software facilities available on it alone. With the growth of workstations, it is increasingly common to have some software licenced for only a few machines on the network, because a licence fee has to be paid for each workstation CPU. In cases like these, execution (of the licenced software) on the remote machine is essential, and remote display back to your own machine makes this style of working relatively convenient.

- You need access to several machines simultaneously. This is often necessary for the system administrator.

- You want simultaneous output to several displays. (An example of how this can be used is given in the next section).

In most of these cases, a specialised and/or expensive resource is being made available right across the network, allowing it to be used to the full.

A Special Example – One Application using Several Displays

Most of the time, several client applications share a single display, e.g. on your own screen you have a clock client, an editor client, etc. But a client can open connections to several servers, and output to their screens simultaneously.

This feature can be used effectively in education. If the students in a class have X-Window workstations connected to the network, the teacher can output to them all simultaneously, using the display screens as "dynamic blackboards". This can be extended by having the client programs on the students' terminals displaying to the teacher's, giving full two-way communication. As the only requirement is the network connection, the whole process does not have to be confined to a single room containing all the workstations: it can be carried out with students and teacher in widely scattered locations.

2.3.3 X's Network Architecture Simplifies Growth

As mentioned above, all requests from clients to servers are device-independent because of their format and content. All device dependence is concentrated in the server. For any hardware display, only the server for that display needs to know anything about it. Once the server has been provided, all the other machines which can run **X** client programs can immediately use that display, without re-compilation or re-linking, even without knowing what type of display it is.

This isolation of device dependence in the server makes the use of multi-vendor workstation networks possible and easy. This flexibility is useful in two ways:

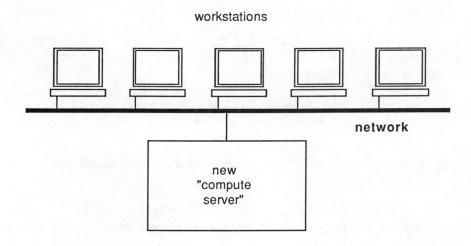

Figure 2.6 Existing displays can use clients on new CPU

- When a new machine is added which runs **X** clients, it can be immediately used by any display running **X**. Figure 2.6 is a view of a network showing how a powerful CPU to be used as a "compute server" is made widely available across a network.

- The converse is where a new display is added. It can immediately make use of all the existing **X** client applications on any machine, as shown in Figure 2.7. Two extreme cases of this would be:

- Adding a very high-performance display: its high-quality and/or speed can be used to enhance any existing **X** applications.

- Adding a very "low-end" display, such as an **X**-terminal. This is a cheap way of providing a graphic and windowed front end onto all the existing facilities.

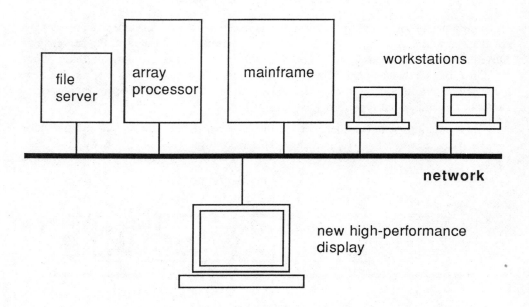

Figure 2.7 New display can be used by existing client applications

2.3.4   Using non-X Applications Over the Network: Terminal Emulators

You can have the advantages of remote display even with applications which were not written as **X** clients and know nothing at all about **X**. To do this you use an X-Window "terminal emulator", i.e. a program which pretends to be a terminal. This enables you to use any application which normally runs on a dumb terminal. The emulator uses **X** to display the output (and get keyboard input), and of course this output can be sent to a local or a remote display. An example of this style of operation, using the xterm terminal emulator to run a mail program, is shown in Figure 2.8 (xterm is supplied as part of the standard MIT distribution of **X**). This can extend your network use considerably, but of course a non-**X** application can't of itself use the **X** features, i.e. a terminal emulator isn't a magic way of transforming a dumb-terminal application into a window based one which uses mouse inputs, graphics operations and so on.

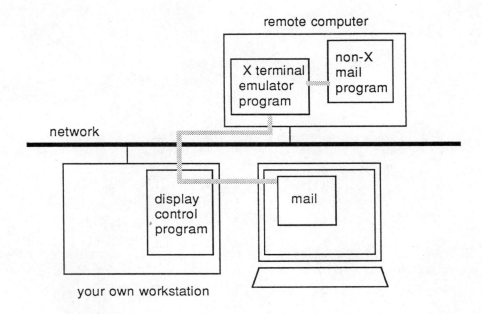

Figure 2.8 Running a non-X mail program remotely

2.4 Summary

In this chapter you have seen the fundamental components which comprise the **X** system: the server which controls the display, the client applications which request the server to perform input and output functions for them, and the communications channel between them. You have seen how they interact with each other to provide the basic functions — input, output and window handling — which are required for any window system, how these features are used in real life, and what advantages they give you as a user or system-builder.

In the next chapter we continue our overview of the system, but at a slightly higher level, concentrating on the aspects relating to the user interface.

Chapter 3 A Conceptual Overview of X — User Interface Features

So far, we have looked at the basic operation of the system. In this chapter we move on to look at the aspects of the system which control the user interface, i.e. how the system appears to somebody using it, and some of the mechanisms involved.

One of the design goals of X was that it should be able to support many different styles of user interface. Instead of providing particular methods of interaction as other window systems do, X provides general mechanisms which the system builder uses to construct the desired style of interaction. E.g. you configure windows in one X system by selecting an action from a menu, but in others you operate on the window directly with the mouse. This flexibility allows system developers to produce different, new, interfaces all based on X. But also, because the interface is not built into the window system, at any time users can choose from the interfaces available on their system, according to their own particular requirements. E.g. novices typically prefer a simpler systems than experts, even if they both have to perform essentially the same tasks — creating, moving, and resizing windows on the screen; with X, each can operate with the user interface that suits them best.

The *user interface* has two parts:

The management interface dictates how top-level windows are configured and re-configured on the screen, i.e. how you manage your "desktop".

The application interface determines the "style" of your interaction with the application program: how you use the window-system facilities to control the application and input to it.

X addresses these two issues separately, and we'll look at them in turn in the following sections.

3.1   The Management Interface: Window Managers

The *management interface* is the part of the system which determines how you control top-level windows on your screen, i.e. how you re-configure your desktop. This part of the system is called the *window manager*. The type of functions it provides are changing the size or position of windows, stacking them, changing them into icons, and so on.

In **X** the window manager is just another client program. It, and the management interface it implements, are completely separated from the server, so you can change them at will. This is analogous to the shell command-line interpreter in a Unix system: the shell is just another user process, and if you change it, you change the user interface to the system too. It is quite feasible to start a session with one manager, and change to another half way through. An extreme case of this flexibility is that it is possible to do without any window manager at all. This isn't usual, but provided that the initial layout of the windows on the screen is satisfactory, the system can be operated quite usefully, and when we get on to using the system, that is how we'll be operating initially.

3.1.1   Manual versus Automatic Window Managers

There are two broad classes of window manager, *manual* and *automatic*. With a manual one, the position, size, etc. of the windows on the screen are completely controlled by the user, and the manager is merely the tool employed by the user to perform the job. Most manual managers allow application windows to overlap.

In contrast, an automatic manager takes upon itself as much control of the desktop as possible, and it manages the layout of the screen with as little user intervention as possible. It decides the size and position of newly created windows, and how to rearrange the remaining windows when windows are removed. Typically, automatic managers "tile" the screen, i.e. arrange the application windows so they don't overlap, and perhaps fill as much of the screen area as possible.

How a Manual Window Manager Works: "Grabbing"

Typically, you tell a manual window manager what action you want performed, either by using a menu or with a combination of pressing buttons on the mouse and moving the pointer. E.g. to re-position a window, you might move the pointer into the window, press the left button, move the pointer and release the button in the new position required. How does the window manager know which mouse events are intended for it, or looking at it another way, how does the server know whether the events are for an application window or the manager?

The answer is that the manager informs the server that there are particular events (button clicks, etc.,) which are to be sent to it, irrespective of which window they actually occur in. This process is called *grabbing*. The manager can specify which mouse button it wishes to grab, and that the grab is to occur when this button is pressed, but only if particular keyboard modifiers are depressed. (E.g. "grab the Middle mouse button when it is pressed and CONTROL and SHIFT are already down"). Once the button is pressed and the grab becomes active, the server sends all mouse events (including mouse motion events) to the manager until the button is released again. The manager interprets data from these events as instructions from the user about what is to be done. Take a "move-window" operation as an example; the manager is notified of the pointer position when the mouse button is pressed, and again when it is released. Simple calculation gives the displacement of the pointer, and the specified window can be translated accordingly.

This has an important effect on the user. Mouse/modifier combinations grabbed by the manager are never seen by any application program, so it's necessary to ensure the manager doesn't grab a combination which the application requires. Most managers can be customised easily to specify what set of modifiers and mouse buttons they reserve for their own use.

3.1.2 Extra Facilities Provided by Window Managers

Window managers may go beyond providing the basic functions for re-configuring windows, and add extra features which improve the quality of the interface. Often, extra functions are added which reduce the amount of typing necessary, by making more use of the pointer.

A common facility provided is a general pop-up menu feature which you can configure yourself. With it you can start window applications just by selecting a menu item; the command then executed will usually include specifications indicating where the application window is to appear, what size it is, which colours are to be used for the text, etc., so the application can start up without further user input. A common use of a menu is when you are working on a network, you define a menu listing all the hosts you use, so you can set up a connection to any machine just by selecting on its name.

3.1.3 Window Managers and Icons

When a window is changed into an icon, where does the icon come from, and what happens to the window?

The icon mechanism is very simple. Icons are just windows in their own right. To *iconify* an application window, the window manager just *unmaps* the window (i.e. tells the server that it's not to be shown on the screen any more) and maps the associated icon window. *De-iconifying* is the same process in reverse. The window manager is able to do this because there is no "access control" or permission restriction which prevents one client (e.g. the window manager) unmapping another client's window: all clients of the same server can do more or less anything with any window.

The window manager usually provides the icon, but the client can provide its own icon and suggest that it be used instead. Some window managers do as requested, others ignore the application's icon and use their own regardless, so the application's request is really only a hint to the window manager. (The application communicates its request to the manager by means of the **X** *property* mechanism, described later in this chapter).

When an application is iconified, its main window has been unmapped. If the window manager aborts for any reason, the window would remain permanently unmapped and would effectively be lost. To avoid this, as the manager iconifies windows, it adds them to a special list called a *save set*. This is a list maintained for each client by the server; entries in it are windows which are to be re-mapped when this client terminates.

3.1.4 Applications Pass Configuration Information to the Window Manager

As well as asking that a particular icon be used, the application can also pass other hints or configuration information to the window manager. This includes:

- names for the application and icon windows.

- information about where the application and icon windows are to be positioned on the screen when they are created.

- restrictions on window size, e.g. the client might say "I can't sensibly make use of a window smaller than *width* x *height*".

- preferences on how the window is to be resized, e.g. an application displaying text in a window might say that if the window is resized, it should be in specific increments, to ensure that the window size is always a whole multiple of the character size so only whole characters are displayed.

Again, the client passes this information to the window manager using the property mechanism.

As an aside, we should note that while it is normal that applications rely on the window manager for resizing, iconifying, and so on, this is only a convention — the window manager is *not* a specially privileged client. Any client can resize itself as it wants, but if all clients did this, there would be chaos. Effectively, the rule for applications which expect to co-exist with others is: don't resize yourself — rely on the window manager, which in turn relies on the user to determine how big each application window is to be.

That concludes our look at the management interface. Later on we'll see how to use one particular manager, uwm, in Chapter 6, and in greater detail in Chapter 19.

3.2 The Application Interface and Toolkits

The application interface determines the style of the interaction between the user and the application program, e.g. how items are selected with the pointer, or text is scrolled up and down in a window, etc. **X** does not provide a standard application interface; instead it provides the basic mechanisms from which these elements can be constructed.

When a consistent set of these elements is put together, it forms a *toolkit*, effectively a higher level of software layered on top of the basic window system. Low-level details of the underlying system are hidden, simplifying programming, and a consistent style of interface can be enforced, resulting in a "visual grammar" for how the user can control application functions. It is important to note that the toolkit is specified in the compilation of the program, so it is at compile-time that the application interface of a client program is determined, and it can't be changed afterwards (without recompiling the program).

Many of the application programs in the MIT release of **X** are written using the standard **X** Toolkit and a set of toolkit software components from MIT. The effect of this is that you get a certain uniformity in the interface (e.g. all the scrollbars work in the same way). Additionally, certain mechanisms are provided for customising the operation of the applications, and setting defaults for them. The **X** Toolkit is described in more detail in Chapter 15, and customisation in Chapter 16 and Chapter 17.

3.3 Other System Features

In the remaining sections in this chapter we look at further aspects of the system, in particular the property mechanism used to communicate information between applications, how windows are organised in a tree-shaped hierarchy, and the advantages of not having **X** embedded in the operating system.

3.3.1 Communication Between Clients — Properties

Clients communicate with the server by sending requests and receiving events. But sometimes clients need to pass information to other clients, e.g. normal applications need to pass indications to the window manager about positioning or sizing. This is achieved using **X**'s property mechanism.

A *property* is a named piece of data, associated with a particular window, and stored in the server. Any client can interrogate the server for the value of a given property on a particular window.

Let's look at an example of how this is used to pass a client's preferred name for its icon to the window manager. The client stores the icon name (as an ASCII string, say) in a property called WM_ICON_NAME associated with its window. Then, when the window manager wants to iconify the application, it looks at the WM_ICON_NAME property for the application's window, and uses the name stored there if there is one, or else uses a name which it chooses itself.

Applications may want to communicate with other applications apart from a window manager. A common example of this is where *cut-and-paste* operations are allowed between windows belonging to different applications. The text which has been "cut" from one application has to be stored in a place which is accessible to the other application so that it can later be "pasted". Properties are used for this too: the display's root window has a number of properties named CUT_BUFFER0, CUT_BUFFER1, etc., which all applications use to interchange data they have "cut".

A final example of the use of properties is the mechanism called *resources*, which is used to define default settings for applications. A list of settings is stored in a property called RESOURCE_MANAGER on the root window. This is accessed by all applications, to see if there are any settings which apply to them so they can act accordingly.

3.3.2 In X, Windows are Hierarchical

This section describes how windows are organised within the system, how they are created, and how this affects applications.

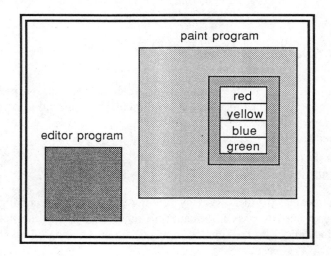

Figure 3.1 Overlapping Windows on a Screen

All windows in **X** are part of a hierarchy which can be viewed as a tree. At the root of this tree is the "root window" which covers the entire screen. Application windows are children of the root window. These top-level windows can have subwindows of their own, and so on. A screen with two application windows is shown in Figure 3.1. In it, the "paint" program window contains a subwindow used for a menu, which in turn has subwindows for each of its selections. The corresponding tree of windows is shown in Figure 3.2.

X has been designed to make windows a fairly inexpensive resource. As a result

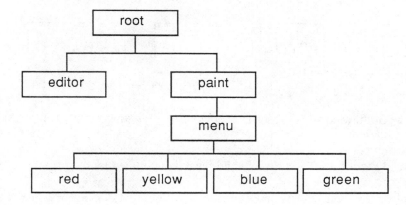

Figure 3.2 Tree-structured hierarchy of windows

you can afford to use them for control items, like menus, scrollbars, control buttons, etc., or in situations where they are needed in large numbers, e.g. for individual cells in a spreadsheet. This is an aspect which is seen more by the programmer than the user, but it does affect the user when customising certain programs; we'll touch on this again when we deal with *resources* in Chapter 15.

By allowing applications to have sub-windows, **X** makes most of the window-system's facilities available to client programs for their own use. This gives a consistency in approach, and avoids the duplication of work which would otherwise be necessary. E.g. a pop-up menu (as in Figure 3.1) can be implemented in an application as a child window, with subwindows of its own for each menu-selection "pane", and the standard mechanisms are used to detect on which selection the user clicks the mouse. Without subwindows, complex programming and input processing would be necessary to achieve the same result.

The position of a window within the hierarchy limits the extent to which it is visible on the display screen. This is described in the next section.

Sub-Windows are "Clipped" by Their Parents

The size and position of a child window are not affected by the parent window. The child can be bigger or smaller, partially or wholly contained in the parent, or completely outside it. However, all output to the child is "clipped" by the parent, i.e. all parts of the child which are outside the parent's boundary are invisible, as shown in Figure 3.3.

A useful practical consequence of this is that you can move top level windows almost completely off the screen, when you want to keep a portion of a window visible without using much screen space.

Another consequence is that a pop-up menu is usually created as a child of the root window. If it were a child of the application window, then in the case where the menu

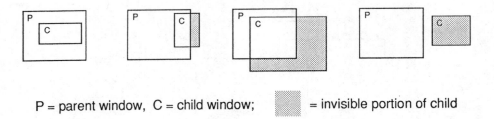

P = parent window, C = child window;　　　　 = invisible portion of child

Figure 3.3 Visibility of child window is limited by the parent

is larger than the application window (as shown in Figure 3.4), the menu would be clipped by the application window and not all of it would be seen.

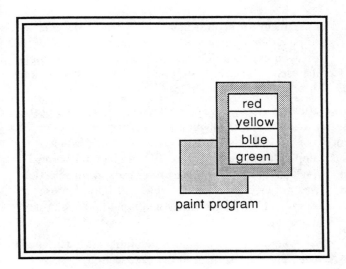

Figure 3.4 Menu larger than window of application using it

3.3.3　X isn't embedded in the Operating System

Unlike most other window systems, **X** isn't embedded in the operating system on which it is running but is a user-level layer on top of it. More precisely, **X** doesn't *have to* be embedded — some vendors may combine the server with the operating system for reasons of their own, perhaps to achieve better performance. This non-embedded architecture has several benefits:

- It is easy to install or upgrade **X**, or even remove it. This work can be done without re-booting the system, and without interfering with other applications.

- Third-parties can easily supply enhancements, or additions or replacements for elements of the system. E.g. if the server supplied by your system vendor isn't good enough, you might buy a better or faster implementation from someone else.

- X is not specific to one operating system, and has become a standard. This in turn encourages developments by third-party sources.

- *For developers:* When carrying out development work on a server, program failures may bring down the window system, but they won't crash the machine as they almost certainly would if they were part of the operating system kernel. Also, non-kernel code is much easier to debug and profile.

3.4 Conclusion

In this chapter we have described the features which enable X to support many different user interfaces. We introduced the concept of the window manager — the program you use to manage your desktop — and described the facilities it uses to interact with the user and with client applications. We then moved on to some other features of the system, in particular the property mechanism used to communicate between clients and how X's hierarchical window structure influences the system, finishing off with a summary of the benefits of not embedding the window system in the operating system.

The purpose of this overview has been to give you a broad overview of X-Window, emphasising those aspects which affect your day-to-day use of the system. As you progress through the rest of the book, we will see how these features come into play; understanding them helps you learn the system more quickly, and make better use of it.

That concludes the first part of the book — the overview of the system. The next part tells you how to use the system in practice.

Part 2

Using the System

Chapter 4   **Terminology and Notation**

We have to employ a few special terms to describe **X** and how to use it. Some of these terms are common to all systems, and a few are specific to **X**. We will defer the explanations of most of them until we meet them in the text, but some are better explained before we use them. Also described in this chapter are the typesetting conventions and other notation used throughout the book, and the hypothetical network which we use as a scenario for all our examples.

4.1   Terminology

4.1.1   Window-Related Terms

In **X**, a *window* is a rectangular area on the screen, the sides of which are parallel to the sides of the screen. Most windows have one colour for the *background* and another one (or more) for the *foreground*. E.g. in a typical text window, the background is white, and the foreground — the text itself — is black. A window may have a *border*, usually in a different colour to the background. Some windows may have a *title-bar* or *control-bar* at the top; in some cases the system uses this to display information about the window, in others you can manipulate the window by performing certain actions on the bar. The system displays a *pointer* (also called a *cursor*) on the screen, which moves as you move the mouse; there is only one pointer for the whole screen. By contrast, many text windows have their own *cursor* specific to themselves, typically indicating where the text you type will be inserted. These features are illustrated in Figure 4.1.

Geometry — Size and Position

X uses the term *geometry* to indicate the size and position of a window. Most **X** programs accept a *geometry specification* in the command line used to start them, to say how big the program's window is to be, and where it should be positioned on the

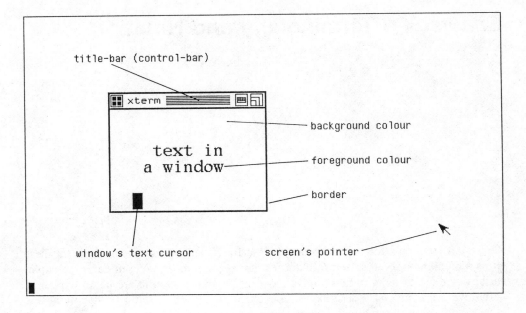

Figure 4.1 Window components

screen. The usual format of a geometry specification is:

width x *height* + *Xoffset* + *Yoffset*

where the multiplication sign is a lower-case x. The units for *width* and *height* are either pixels or characters, depending on the application; the program description usually tells you which units to use. The units for the offsets are pixels. The above spec says that a window of size *width* x *height* is to be created, and that it is to be positioned with its left edge *Xoffset* pixels from the left of the screen, and its top edge *Yoffset* pixels from the top of the screen. Assuming a program which specifies size in characters, the specification:

80x24+600+400

says "create a window 80 characters wide and 24 characters high; place its left edge 600 pixels from the left of the screen, and its top 400 pixels from the top edge of the screen".

If you want, you can specify just the size, or just the position: depending on the context, the program or the system may use default values for the part you didn't specify, or prompt you for it in some way. (You'll see how this works in practice when you start running the system).

Caution: If you specify the size, specify both width and height: omitting one can cause some programs to fail with an error on startup.

4.1.2 Mouse and Pointer Terms

Displays running **X** have some type of input device that you use to indicate items or areas of interest on your screen. Usually this is a *mouse* with several *buttons* (typically three, called *Left*, *Middle*, and *Right*), and as you move the mouse the system correspondingly moves the screen's graphic *pointer* on the screen.

There are several types of mouse operation, and so to describe to you how to do things we need to define precise terms:

> **Clicking a mouse button** : is pushing the button down and then releasing it immediately — the button is down only for an instant.

> **Pressing a button** : means pushing the button down, and keeping it down.

> **Releasing a button** : means letting go a button you previously pressed.

You could say that a click consists of two operations — a press and a release with no time-gap in between them. Usually clicks are used just to point to things, whereas a press followed by a release (typically with some movement of the mouse in between) indicates some form of motion, or describes an area. In particular,

> **Dragging an object** : means positioning the pointer on the object, pressing a button, and with the button still pressed moving the pointer to somewhere else and releasing it there. With this type of operation, when you press the button, the system indicates the object to be moved in some way — perhaps by outlining it with a thin-line rectangular *grid* which moves with the pointer as you drag it.

You often use dragging to change the size of an object. Usually the system displays a grid for this, and as you drag, the grid changes size accordingly; this is called *rubber-banding* — as though the grid were made of rubber bands. In our diagrams, to indicate dragging, we show a down-arrow where you press the mouse button, then a line indicating the moving of the mouse/pointer, and an up-arrow where you release the button. An example is shown in Figure 4.2.

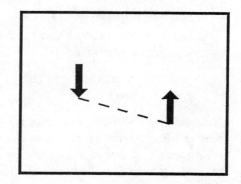

Figure 4.2 Notation for mouse dragging

4.1.3 Keyboard Terms

We often have to specify particular keys on the keyboard. We use the following names for keys, and print them in the style shown:

Standard terminal keys : SHIFT, DELETE, BACKSPACE, ESC or ESCAPE, RETURN, CAPSLOCK.

Cursor control keys : sometimes marked with arrows on the keys. UP, DOWN, LEFT and RIGHT.

Special keys : Holding down the CTRL or CONTROL key when typing another character (usually an alphabetic) gives you a control-character, which we denote as e.g. ctl-A. Some terminals have a META key, which is used rather like the CONTROL key. On some terminals there may be two of these, marked "Left" and "Right". We denote META'ed characters as e.g. meta-A.

4.2   Notation

4.2.1 Typesetting Conventions

To make things clearer, in the body of the text we use the following type-style conventions:

Items of this type ...	*... Are printed in this style*
filenames and directories	*/usr/local/lib/maps*, *mysettings*
program names	grep, /usr/nmm/.Xsession
command lines	ps aux | grep term
keyboard keys	A, b, Linefeed, ctl-C, meta-H
window "buttons" or command boxes	Include File , Quit

If a file is executable, i.e. is a program, it is shown in the style of a program name, for example /usr/nmm/.Xsession above.

Larger examples of input commands and text, and output, are shown in indented sections in a typewriter-like font:

```
cat file1 file2 > file3
grep -i term file*
```

although some very wide examples are shown in a narrower font. In most examples, command-lines are shown exactly as you type them. Sometimes however, if the example is illustrating a dialogue or a whole interaction, the command lines are prefixed with the shell's prompt (usually venus%, or a dollar-sign):

```
venus% wc
the quick brown
fox jumped
```
<end-of-file>
```
2   5   27
venus%
```

In illustrations of windows, where possible we have used exactly the same fonts as you will see, but in a few cases it has been necessary to use non-standard fonts to make the text clearer.

Continuation Lines

In some examples, the commands you enter, or the system's output text, is too long to fit on one line, and has to be split. If it is a shell command, or a piece of C code, we continue it onto a second line by ending the first with a backslash, as in:

```
mkfontdir /usr/lib/X11/fonts/misc \
/usr/lib/X11/fonts/75dpi \
/usr/lib/X11/fonts/100dpi
```

so you could enter the text exactly as it is shown, backslash and all, and it would work on your system. However, there are a few cases where there are long lines input to programs which don't support this backslash mechanism; with these, and with long output lines, we insert the annotation "*(contd.)*" where we break the line. E.g.

```
PID TT STAT TIME COMMAND
1901 co S 0:01 X :0
1902 co S 0:01 xterm -geometry +1+1 (contd).
-n login -display unix:0 -C
1903 p1 S 0:00 -sh (csh)
```

4.2.2 Some Special Directory Names

When **X** is being installed, the release tapes are read into a directory tree somewhere on your system. We refer to the top of this tree as $TOP. On our system, $TOP is the directory */usr/local/src/X11*.

Similarly, we refer to your home directory as $HOME.

4.3 Scenario for Our Examples

The emphasis of this book is practical, and there are lots of examples throughout. To make these more helpful, we have assumed we are working on a network containing the following machines:

venus   *colour screen, normal resolution*
saturn   *mono screen, normal resolution, file server*
mars   *colour screen, high resolution*
neptune   *no graphics screen, own disk storage, computer server*

Our own workstation is venus, which we sit at almost all the time. Sometimes we also sit at mars or saturn and use them instead, when we need high resolution, or want to check out something on the mono screen. And of course, we make constant use of *all* these machines, running remotely from our own.

saturn is the file server for venus and mars, and all three share common file systems. (E.g. accessing the file *$HOME/.login* on any of these always gives us the same physical file). neptune has its own filesystems, and doesn't share with any of the others.

4.4 Configuration of Our Workstation

Just in case some of the examples or program names or pieces of code don't quite agree with your system, here for your information is the system most of our work was done on:

- Hardware: Sun 3/50 workstation, 3-button mouse, screen size 1152x900 pixels, monochrome.

- Operating system: SunOS 3.4, based on BSD 4.2 Unix.

- Window software: MIT-standard distribution of **X** Version 11, Release 3.

Chapter 5 **Starting X and Closing it Down**

So far, we've described what the **X** system is, the software that comprises it, and the basic internal mechanisms it uses. In this chapter, you will see:

- How to start **X** running on your own machine.

- How to perform some elementary operations on windows.

- How to close down **X**.

At this point we are assuming that **X** has already been installed on your system by a system manager or even by yourself. (It *is* quite possible to install MIT's release of **X** without ever having used it, or without knowing too much about it). If you have to install the system, some hints to help you and guide you through the instructions that come with the release are included in an Appendix to this book.

So, you have a system with **X** installed. Before doing anything else, you need to find out (from whoever did the installation) where the **X** executable programs were installed. The default for the MIT release is */usr/bin/X11*, but many sites use */usr/local/bin* or */usr/local/bin/X11*. Whatever the location is, add it to your searchpath: set the PATH environment variable in your *.login* file (or maybe *.cshrc*) if you use the C-Shell, in *.profile* if you use the Bourne shell. E.g. our own *.login* file contains the C-shell command line

```
set path = (. /usr/local/bin/X11 /usr/ucb /usr/bin /bin)
```

If you don't set this, **X** won't start properly. When you have set it, to be absolutely sure, logout and login again and check that your value of PATH is correct (with the command "echo $PATH").

5.1   Starting X

To start **X** on your display, enter the command

    xinit

and the following sequence occurs:

1. Your entire screen is set to a grey colour.

2. A large "X" cursor (shown in Figure 5.1) appears. You can move it around
   the screen with the mouse, but pressing the mouse buttons and keyboard
   keys has no effect on the display at this point.

Figure 5.1 Background window's "big X" cursor

3. An xterm *terminal emulator* window appears in the top-left corner of your
   screen, and it gives your usual shell prompt. Whenever the cursor is in the
   window, xterm is ready to accept commands from you and to indicate this,
   the cursor changes to a *text cursor* (as shown in Figure 5.2).

Figure 5.2 xterm's "text" cursor

A picture of the screen in this initial state is shown in Figure 5.3. **X** has now started,
and you can use the xterm window just as you would use a normal terminal. You
can obviously use this window to run ordinary commands, but its real value is that
it provides a mechanism for you to start other **X** programs with. In just a moment
we'll tell you how to do that, but first we will look a bit more closely at what the **X**
initialisation involves, so you can understand what is happening.

5.1.1   What xinit **Does: Internal Operation**

First, xinit starts the **X** server program running on your display. The server creates its
root window which covers the entire screen. It sets the background window to the gray
pattern which you have seen, and sets the cursor to the big "X" (items 1 and 2 in the
list above).

At this point, only the server is running. As explained in Chapter 2, it is the server
which controls the keyboard and the mouse, and this is why you can move the cursor

Figure 5.3 The screen just after startup

on the screen. But so far there are no client programs which have asked to be informed of keyboard and mouse events. So, the server tracks the mouse movement with the cursor; all other keyboard and mouse input is processed by the server which discards it because no process is interested in it, so it has no effect.

Next, xinit starts the xterm program running (item 3 in the list above) as a client of the server. xterm requests the server to create a window for it, and to keep it informed of mouse and keyboard events in its window. xterm sets a shell running in the window, and is ready to accept input whenever the pointer is in the window. Keyboard input is sent to the shell just as though it had been typed at a real terminal, and output from the shell (and its subprograms) is displayed by xterm in the window. Additionally, xterm accepts mouse input to allow you to set various parameters of the program's operation, and to cut and paste text.

You can see these steps reflected in the status of the processes on the system. E.g. on our system just after startup, executing the command ps a in the xterm window gave:

```
PID TT STAT TIME COMMAND
1900 co S 0:00 xinit
1901 co S 0:01 X :0
1902 co S 0:01 xterm -geometry +1+1 -n login -display unix:0 -C
1903 p1 S 0:00 -sh (csh)
1904 p1 R 0:00 ps
```

This shows that xinit was started on the console display, it initiated the server, X for display zero, and xterm running on a pseudo-terminal. Then xterm started a shell running, to process the commands you type in the xterm window, and finally we ran ps to produce the listing. (We included the a option to ps because xterm needs to run setuid'ed to user root).

xterm is described in more detail in Chapter 8. For the present, we'll just assume that the xterm window behaves like a DEC VT102 terminal, and move on to what you can do with the system now that it has been initialised.

5.2   How to Run Some X Programs

You now have a display controlled by an X server, and a client program, xterm, which you can use to enter commands. This section tells you how to start running other X programs on your system.

Because X client programs are completely separate from the X server, they need no special mechanism to start them — you can just run them as you would any other program. But they *do* need to know which display they are to use. In fact the initial xterm sets the DISPLAY environment variable to the name of the display it is using, and other client programs use this as the default display, so you don't have to do anything explicitly yourself.

5.2.1   How to Run the X Clock, xclock

To start, we'll use the X clock program as a simple example. Make sure the pointer is in the xterm window, and enter the command:

```
xclock
```

A small image of a clock appears in the top left corner of the screen, overlapping the first window, as shown in Figure 5.4. There are three problems to be overcome now. First, — there is a program (xclock) running on the xterm "terminal" so it doesn't accept

Figure 5.4 The screen after xclock has started

any more commands from you: what do you do? The only thing you *can* do is stop xclock by pressing `ctrl-C` or `DEL`, or whatever your interrupt character is; as soon as you do this, the clock vanishes. To overcome this bogey, run xclock asynchronously ("in the background"), like:

xclock &

Now at least xterm accepts other commands you type.

Stopping X *Programs –* xkill

The second problem is: how do you stop xclock — it pays no attention to any keys or mouse buttons you press? **X** itself, i.e. the server, provides no direct interface for stopping applications, but there is a client program xkill which lets you kill **X** applications. Start the program by entering the command xkill in the xterm window. When it runs, xkill displays the *draped box cursor* shown in Figure 5.5. Move the cursor into the window of the application you want to kill, and click the `LEFT` button. The window vanishes and both its application program and xkill exit; you may also get the

Figure 5.5 xkill's draped box cursor

message:

```
xkill: killing creator of resource 0x40004d
XIO: fatal IO error 32 (Broken pipe) on X server "unix:0.0"
after 207 requests (178 known processed) with 0 events remain-
ing.
The connection was probably broken by a server shutdown or Kill-
Client.
```

which is normal. If for some reason you can't get at an application's window to stop it with xkill, you can always use the normal Unix method: find out the ID of the process and kill it. E.g.

```
$ ps a | grep xclock
1907 p2 I 0:00 xclock
1909 p2 S 0:00 grep xclock
$ kill 1907
[1] Terminated xclock
$
```

Positioning X Application Windows: "Geometry"

The third problem is: how can you avoid the clock overlapping your xterm window? Or more generally, how can you specify where an application window is to be situated? You do this with a *geometry* specification, as explained in Chapter 4. As a practical example, enter the command

```
xclock -geometry 200x300+400+500 &
```

This tells xclock to start with a window size of width 200 pixels and height 300 pixels, with its top left corner 400 pixels to the right and 500 pixels down from the top left corner of the screen, as shown in Figure 5.6. Those are the three problems solved. Later on, in Chapter 6, we'll see how to get over them somewhat more elegantly.

Using Colour

If you have a colour display, it is worthwhile experimenting with xclock to get an idea of how you can specify and use colours. xclock has a number of options which take colour specs:

-bg *colour* sets the background to *colour*

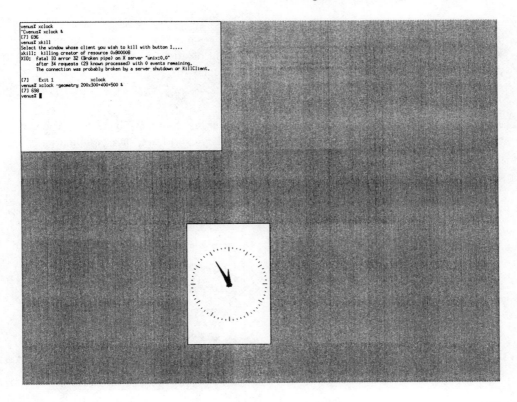

Figure 5.6 Specifying a window's initial position and size with a geometry specification

-fg *colour* sets the foreground to *colour*

-hd *colour* uses *colour* for the clock hands

-hl *colour* highlights the edges of the hands in *colour*

Try the command:

```
xclock -bg turquoise -fg red -hd magenta
```

for a rare visual experience. Try some other colour combinations too. Not all colour names are valid, but if you stick to the common ones you should be OK. (Later on, we'll tell you where to to find a list of valid names).

xclock requires no interaction with the user once it has started. In the next section we look at another small program which uses input from both mouse and keyboard.

5.2.2 Running the xcalc Desk Calculator

xcalc is an **X** calculator. To start it (in a convenient position on the screen) move the pointer into the xterm window, and enter the command

```
xcalc -geometry +700+500 &
```

A window looking like a TI-30 calculator will appear, as shown in Figure 5.7. You can operate the calculator with the mouse, or with the keyboard keys, or a combination.

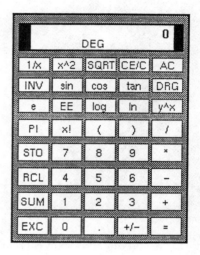

Figure 5.7 The xcalc desk calculator

With the mouse, move the pointer to the calculator button you want: press it by pressing the left mouse button. To operate xcalc with the keyboard keys, move the pointer into the xcalc window; then, press the keys which correspond obviously to the calculator buttons, e.g. to sum 1, 2, and 3, press the keyboard keys 1, +, 2, +, 3 and = in sequence. There are also some less obvious correspondences, but we'll ignore them here, because for now you can use the pointer to access any calculator function you want.

xcalc has one advantage over xclock — it's easy to stop it. Click on the **AC** button with the right mouse button and xcalc exits. (In fact many **X** applications have inbuilt facilities like this for exiting).

5.3 Closing Down X

To close **X** down, move the pointer into the original xterm window, and logout. The window disappears, the server terminates, and **X** is closed down.

In slightly more detail, xterm detects when the shell running in its window terminates, and terminates itself. In turn, xinit detects that xterm has finished; then xinit kills the server, and exits itself.

5.4 Moving On — Getting More Information

You are now able to start the system, run programs, and close down the system, so you can begin to experiment on your own. Run xclock a few times, with different values for the geometry spec. Try some extreme values: you can have enormous clocks or tiny ones, positioned anywhere on the screen (or off it!).

There are Unix man(1) pages included in the MIT release for all the client programs, and these should have been installed with the system. Look at the description of xcalc in particular to see how to use the calculator properly, and if you want, how to specify reverse polish notation (like on an HP-10C calculator). For fun, try the -analog option, which makes xcalc operate like a slide rule.

A word of warning: in the manpages you will see a lot of information about "**X** DEFAULTS", "**X** Environment", Resource Manager and property settings, amongst other things. Ignore these for now — we'll explain them in Chapter 6.

5.5 Conclusion; Limitations We Have Met

In this chapter we have seen how to start **X**, how to run some window applications, and how to shut the window system down. On the way, you have been able to use the system.

However, so far the system has given you very little that you don't get on a dumb terminal (apart from colour, perhaps). And, there are a number of functions you would like — and need — to perform, for which no mechanisms have been provided. For instance

- Resizing a window, making it wider/narrower, and/or longer/shorter.

- Moving a window to somewhere else on the screen.

- Moving a window from underneath other windows to the top of what is on your "desktop" (or sending it to the bottom of the pile).

- Starting window applications in a convenient way.

All these functions and more are provided not by the basic **X** system, but by a *window manager*, described in the next chapter.

Chapter 6 Window Manager Basics – uwm

In the previous chapter we saw that the basic **X** system provides only essential windowing features, and that something more is needed to make the system convenient and easy to use. In **X**, those facilities are provided by a window manager. This chapter outlines what a window manager is, and goes on to tell you how to use uwm – the only window manager supplied as part of the MIT **core** release.

6.1 What Is A Window Manager?

Here we'll quickly summarise what we covered in the overview, to remind you of the window manager's function. The basic system, i.e. the server, provides only elementary window functions, i.e. creating windows, writing and drawing in them, handling keyboard and mouse input, and destroying windows. It does not specify the user interface - it merely provides mechanisms with which an interface can be built.

We divided the user interface into two parts - management and application interfaces. This chapter deals with the management interface – the part with which you manage your desktop – and the window manager which controls this interface. It provides facilities for creating application windows, moving them on the screen, resizing them, and so on.

You also need to be able to:

- Uncover a window which is obscured by others.

- Start and stop applications easily.

- Refresh the screen.

- Iconify and de-iconify.

Now we'll describe uwm, and see how it allows you to do all these things.

6.2 Starting uwm

Once **X** has started, you can start uwm from any shell window you have on your screen, because a window manager is just an ordinary program. You *can* start it at any time during your **X** session, just not at the beginning, but except when you are experimenting with the system that's not of much interest. Later on, in Chapter 19, we'll see how you can have the window manager started automatically when **X** comes up.

So, if you haven't done that already, start **X** (with xinit as described in Chapter 3), and from within xterm start uwm with the command:

```
uwm &
```

uwm runs and rings the terminal bell to signal that it has initialised itself and is ready to work for you. But you see no change on the screen. Do a ps a, and you see there is now a uwm process, but otherwise nothing has altered since we started **X**:

```
PID TT STAT TIME COMMAND
1900 co S 0:00 xinit
1901 co S 0:01 X :0
1902 co S 0:01 xterm -geometry +1+1 -n login -display unix:0 -C
1903 p1 S 0:00 -sh (csh)
1904 p1 I 0:00 uwm
1905 p1 R 0:00 ps
```

Now we have a window manager, so we'll go on and see how to use it to perform some basic management operations.

6.3 Basic Window Operations – uwm's Menu

uwm has a menu facility you can use to manipulate your windows. To access the menu:

1. Position the pointer anywhere on the grey screen background.

2. Press the middle mouse button and keep it pressed: uwm *pops-up* a menu headed *WindowOps*, so your screen now looks like Figure 6.1.

3. Still keeping the button pressed, move the pointer up and down the menu: the option under the pointer is highlighted and when you release the button, this highlighted option is the one selected.

Figure 6.2 shows the menu more clearly, with the *Refresh Screen* option highlighted.

Figure 6.1 Screen showing uwm's **WindowOps** menu

If you decide you don't want to select anything after all, press any other mouse button, or just move the pointer sideways out of the menu altogether, and the menu vanishes.

Now try it yourself - select Refresh Screen, and release the button: the screen flashes - and is completely re-drawn.

In the rest of this chapter we'll see how to use the other menu selections to perform most of the facilities which in the last chapter we found we needed.

6.4 Moving a Window

To move a window on the screen:

1. Position the cursor on the background, and pop-up uwm's menu by pressing the middle mouse button.

Figure 6.2 uwm's **WindowOps** menu

2. Select the *Move* option, and release the button. The cursor changes to the "pointing hand" shown in Figure 6.3.

3. Move the hand into the window you want to move, press any button, and keep it pressed. A nine-square grid appears, superimposed on the window, and the cursor changes to an "arrow cross", shown in Figure 6.4.

4. Still keeping the button pressed, move the cursor, and with it *drag* the grid to wherever you want to reposition the window.

5. Release the button: the window jumps to the new position, and the grid vanishes.

Figure 6.3 The "pointing hand" cursor

Figure 6.4 The "arrow cross" cursor

This is shown graphically in Figure 6.5. Now try it yourself: move the xterm window to the bottom right corner of the screen.

   Caution: you can move the window so that it is partially off the screen. If you do this by accident, just select *Move* again, and bring the window back to where you want.

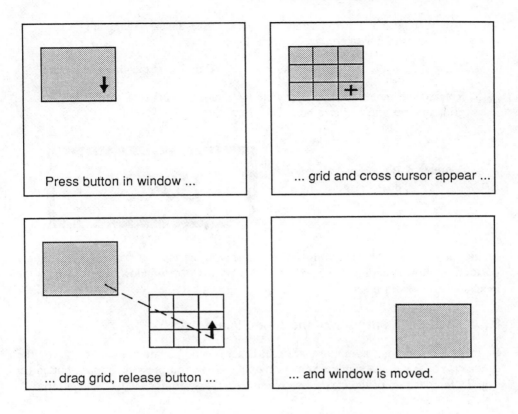

Press button in window ...

... grid and cross cursor appear ...

... drag grid, release button ...

... and window is moved.

Figure 6.5 Moving a window with uwm

6.5 Resizing a Window

You can resize a window in one dimension or two, e.g. you might make it just wider, or make it both taller and narrower at the same time. To resize a window:

1. Pop up uwm's menu, and select the *Resize* option. As with *Move*, you get the "hand" cursor.

2. Move the cursor into the bottom right hand corner of the window you want to resize.

3. Press any mouse button, and keep it pressed. Three changes occur:

   - The cursor changes to an "arrow cross", as before.

   - A nine-square grid appears, but this time it doesn't cover the whole window. It is smaller than the window, with its diagonal between the cursor and the window's top left corner.

- A box showing the window's current size appears diagonally opposite the cursor, as shown in Figure 6.6.

4. Move the cursor, and stretch or squash the grid until it is the size you want.

5. Release the mouse button: the window changes dimension to match the grid, and the grid and size-box disappear.

Figure 6.6 Box showing window's size, during a **Resize** operation

Making a window taller and narrower, while leaving its top left corner in its original position is shown in Figure 6.7. Now resize your xterm window, and see how the mechanism works in practice.

6.5.1 Resizing: Purpose of the Nine-Square Grid

In a *Resize* operation, the nine-square grid has a function apart from showing you the future size or shape of a window you're changing. When you press the mouse button (in step 3), the position of the cursor relative to the grid determines what you can do:

- If you press the mouse button in one of the four **corner** rectangles of the grid (as we did in steps 2 and 3 above) or in the **middle** rectangle, you can change both vertical and horizontal dimensions of the window, to make a rectangle of any shape or size you want.

- If you press in one of the four **mid-side** rectangles of the grid, then you can only alter one dimension of the window: you can only move that side of the window which is nearest to the rectangle you pressed the button in.

The obvious flaw in this scheme is that the grid doesn't appear until you press the button, by which time the type of change is already determined.

Resize a window, and see for yourself how the grid works.

6.5.2 Size Constraints, and Dimensions

You use the above technique to resize any window, not just xterm. But two aspects of the resize may differ slightly.

First, the dimensions shown in the "current size" box can mean different things for different windows. For character (i.e. text) windows, the size is given as "number of

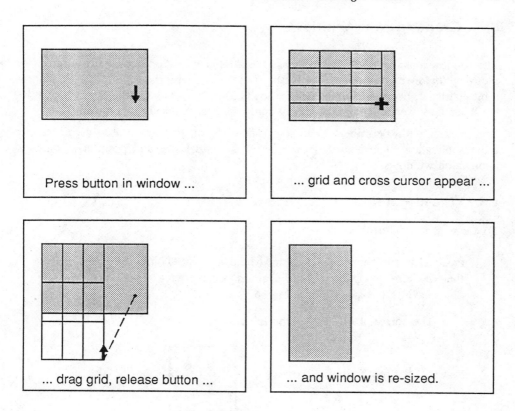

Figure 6.7 Resizing a window

columns times number of rows of characters". E.g. a normal xterm size would be 80x24. With graphics windows, the size will generally be in number of pixels, e.g. the default size of xclock is 150x150.

The second feature you may notice is that some windows have restrictions on the shapes and sizes they will take up. E.g. xcalc has a minimum size: it won't let you make it so small that not all its buttons are visible. And xterm, even though it appears to take on any size you want is constrained only to resize in whole character increments - you just don't get half-lines of text at the bottom. By contrast, xclock is unconstrained and will take on almost any shape or size.

6.6   Creating New Windows

The window manager uwm makes it easy to start an application in a new window, using the *NewWindow* menu option. The facility as it comes with the default system setup is a bit restricted, because the new application is always xterm. Later on, in Chapter 19, we'll see how we can generalise this to start whatever application you want.

For now, we'll describe how to start a new xterm, how uwm assists you starting other applications, and how you can control the initial size and position of the new application windows.

6.6.1   Creating a New xterm Window

To create a new (xterm) window:

1. Position the cursor on the background window, pop up UWM's menu and select the *NewWindow* option. Three changes occur after a short pause – you don't have to press any mouse button:

    - The cursor changes to a "top left corner" (Figure 6.8).

    Figure 6.8 "Top left corner" cursor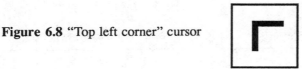

    - A flashing outline of the new window appears, with the cursor as the top left corner.
    - A box, like the one we saw with resizing, but containing the name of the application as well as the size, appears in the top left of the screen. (Figure 6.9).

2. Move the cursor to wherever you want the top left corner of the new window to be.

3. Click the left mouse button: after a pause a new window the same size as the flashing outline appears, and both the size box and the outline disappear.

You can use this xterm window just like the original one, both for ordinary work and to start X applications.

Caution 1: if you click another mouse button instead of the left one, the sizing of the window works differently. In particular, if you click the middle button, your new window is so tiny you can hardly see it. If this happens, you can try and resize it via the menu, to make it bigger. Alternately, just leave it for now and create another new

```
xterm:    80x24
```

Figure 6.9 Box with window's name and size, as a new window is created

window, but make sure you click on the left button this time. (We'll explain this effect later in this chapter).

Caution 2: as explained in the overview, you can position a window so that it is partially off the screen. So it *is* possible to click the button somewhere which results in only part of the window being on the screen. If you do this by mistake, use the **Move** menu selection to pull the window back to where you want it.

6.6.2 Creating a New Window for Any Application

To start an application other than xterm, for the time being we still have to use the same method as before – type the command to a shell in an xterm window. But now you have a window manager running: it can interact with you to control the initial position of the window if you don't want to give a full geometry specification in the command line. (In fact, uwm lets you control the initial size too – we'll deal with that in the next section).

As an example, let's start an xclock and position it in the top right corner of the screen:

1. In an xterm window, enter the command

   xclock &

   Just like you saw with the **NewWindow** menu selection, you get a size box, a "top left corner" cursor, and a flashing outline the same size as the clock will be.

2. Don't press any button - just drag the outline with the cursor to the position you want.

3. Click the left mouse button: the clock appears in place of the flashing outline.

Caution: If you click another button instead of the left one, the sizing works differently (but at least the effect isn't as nasty as with xterm).

6.6.3 Specifying a New Window's Size

In the instructions above you have been told to press the left mouse button, to indicate where the new window is to be created; and that something strange might happen if you press a different button. In fact all three buttons have specific functions, and you can choose whichever suits best at the time:

left button : Clicking this button configures the window as follows:

> **position** : top left corner under the cursor.
>
> **size** : the default size as specified within the application.

middle button : You don't click this button – instead press it to fix one corner of the new window, then drag the flashing outline with the cursor to where you want the diagonally opposite corner, and release the button, giving the configuration:

> **position** : one corner where you pressed the button, and the opposite corner where you released the button. Which corner is fixed by the initial press depends on which way you subsequently drag. When you do it in practice, the rubber-band outline will show you clearly what is happening.
>
> **size** : determined by the positioning of the corners.

If the application has specified a minimum size, you won't be allowed to create a window smaller than this: the rubber-band outline will never show smaller than the minimum, so it makes it clear what is happening.

Caution: A strange effect can happen if you specify a window of zero area, e.g. if you start xclock, and press and release the middle button without any intervening movement. What happens is the window is created of default size, in the top left corner of the screen!

right button : Pressing this gives the configuration:

> **position** : top left corner under the cursor.
>
> **size** : the width is the default as specified by the application. The height is from the cursor to the bottom of the screen; if this is less than the minimum specified by the application, the specified minimum is used instead and this will mean the bottom of the window will be off the lower edge of the screen.

6.6.4 More About Geometry Specifications

The geometry specs we have used so far have specified window positions by locating the top-left corner of the window relative to the top-left corner of the screen. In fact, the mechanism is more general than this — you can locate a window relative to any corner. A geometry specification has the general form:

width x *height*<**xpos**><**ypos**>

The meaning of the position components is:

<**xpos**> determines the horizontal location of the window, and can be expressed in two ways:

> **+offset** : position the *left* edge of the window *offset* pixels from the *left* edge of the screen.

> **-offset** : position the *right* edge of the window *offset* pixels from the *right* edge of the screen.

<**ypos**> determines the vertical positioning in a similar way:

> **+offset** : position the *top* edge of the window *offset* pixels from the *top* edge of the screen.

> **-offset** : position the *bottom* edge of the window *offset* pixels from the *bottom* edge of the screen.

Here are several examples (all using the same size, for clarity):

100x100+50+60 : the type of spec we have seen before — top left corner 50 pixels away from the left edge, and 60 from the top edge of the screen.

100x100-0-0 : bottom right corner exactly at bottom-right corner of the screen, i.e. the window is tucked exactly into the corner.

100x100-80+160 : window positioned near the top right corner, 80 pixels from the right edge, and 160 pixels down from the top.

100x100+20-40 : window positioned near bottom left corner, 20 pixels from the left edge, 40 pixels above the bottom edge.

In all these specs, the plus and minus signs indicate which edge of the screen you are positioning relative to — they are not specifying positive or negative offsets. In fact you *can* use negative offsets in any of the position specs, to indicate the window edge should be positioned *offset* pixels off the screen. E.g.:

100x100+600+-50 : the window is positioned in the middle of the top edge of the screen, with the top half of the window off the screen.

100x100--50-+20 : the window is positioned near the bottom right corner of the screen, 20 pixels from the bottom edge, with its right-hand side half off the screen.

6.7 Managing Your Screen Space

Now that you can start lots of applications easily, there will often be times when the window you want to work on is covered by another one, or you'll just have too many windows on the screen for comfort. There are three ways of making sure you have convenient access to the windows you currently want to use − enough "elbow room" on your screen:

- Make some of the windows smaller, using **Resize**, as we've described already.

- "Stack" your windows so that the ones you want now are at the top and are visible, and the other ones are stacked lower down. You use the menu selections **Raise, Lower, CircUp**, and **CircDown** for this.

- Change windows into special very small windows called **icons**, so they take up very little space on the screen, but can be transformed back into the full window anytime you want. You use the menu selections **NewIconify** and **AutoIconify** for this.

We've already described the **Resize** function, and in the next sections we'll describe **Raise, Lower, NewIconify** etc.

6.7.1 Shuffling Windows in a Stack

Windows on your screen can overlap, just like pieces of paper on your desk, forming one or more stacks, as shown in Figure 6.10. To make it easy to get at the window you want, uwm lets you:

- Bring a window to the top of the stack, irrespective of its present place in the stack.

- Send a window to the bottom of the stack, irrespective of its present place in the stack.

- *Circulate* the stack, shuffling all windows along one position, and sending the last one to the other end of the stack. You can circulate upwards or downwards.

Bringing a Window to the Top − Raise

The **Raise** selection brings a window to the top of the stack, so that all of the window is visible. You can **Raise** any window, irrespective of its original position in the stack. This is shown schematically in Figure 6.11. To raise a window:

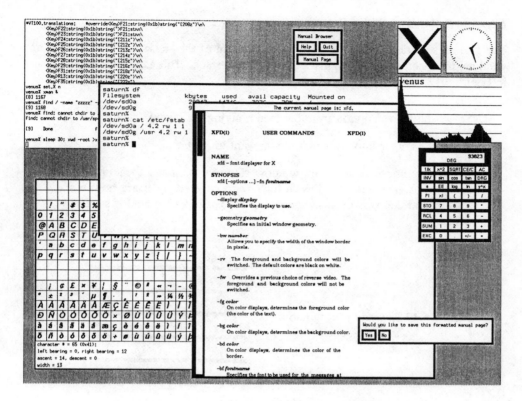

Figure 6.10 Screen showing stacked, overlapping windows

1. Select the **Raise** option from the menu, giving the "hand" cursor.

2. Move the cursor into the window you want to raise.

3. Click any mouse button: the window stays in the same location on the screen, but any portions of it which were obscured by other windows become visible, and those windows are now covered by this one.

Figure 6.11 Raising a window to
the top of a stack

Sending a Window to the Bottom – **Lower**

The **Lower** selection sends a window to the bottom of the stack. You can **Lower** any window, irrespective of its original position in the stack. This is shown schematically in Figure 6.12. To lower a window:

1. Select the **Lower** option from the menu, giving the "hand" cursor.

2. Move the cursor into the window you want to lower.

3. Click any mouse button: the window stays in the same location on the screen, but any other windows which were covered by it are now made visible, and the parts of this window overlapped by other windows are now obscured.

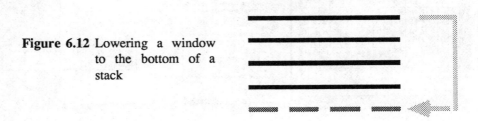

Figure 6.12 Lowering a window to the bottom of a stack

Circulating the Stack – **CircUp** *and* **CircDown**

The **CircUp** and **CircDown** menu selections rotate the stack of windows on the screen. They differ from each other only in the "direction" in which the circulation is done. The action of these functions is shown schematically in Figure 6.13. To circulate down a stack of windows:

- Select the **CircDown** option from the menu: all the locations of the windows on the screen remain unchanged, but the topmost window which was obscuring any other window is sent to the bottom, so it is now obscured by the windows it was previously covering.

Circulating up is exactly analogous - you select **CircUp**, and the bottom-most window which was obscured comes to the top.

Raising/lowering are very similar to circulating up/down. Raising the bottom-most window is exactly equivalent to circulating up, and lowering the topmost window is the same as circulating down. Which functions you use are a matter of personal preference.

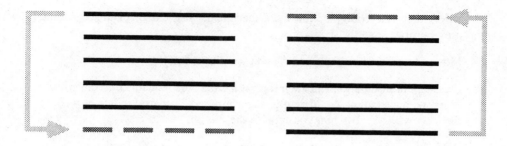

Figure 6.13 Circulating windows up and down

What do the circulate functions do if you have more than one stack of windows on the screen, so there aren't unique top and bottom windows? In fact what happens is that each time you select a menu function, only one stack is changed, but if you select the function several times in a row, it is applied in turn to each of the stacks on a round-robin basis.

6.7.2 Iconifying a Window

You can now make sure that no matter how many windows you have on your screen you can always get at the one you want, by using the raise and lower mechanisms. Even so, there will be a time when there are just too many windows on the screen for comfort. To give yourself more space on the screen, you can *iconify* some of the ones that you don't need right now: change them into very small windows, and put them to one side until you need them again. Some applications have their own special icons, but most leave it to the window manager to create one. uwm's default icon is a grey rectangle with the application name inside it. The normal icon for xterm is shown in Figure 6.14. There are two ways of iconifying a window; the first is particularly

Figure 6.14 The normal icon for xterm

suitable for windows which have never been iconified since they were created, and the second for windows which have been.

Iconifying a NewWindow – NewIconify

1. Select the **NewIconify** option from the menu. The cursor changes to the now-familiar "hand".

2. Move the cursor into the window you want to iconify.

3. Press any mouse button and keep it pressed: the cursor changed to the arrow cross, with a small nine-square grid superimposed. The grid indicates where the icon will be left when you release the button.

4. With the button still depressed, drag the grid to the position you want.

5. Release the button: the grid is replaced by the icon, and the original window vanishes.

While this method is particularly good for new windows – because it lets you specify where you want the icon to be placed – you can use it on any application window, especially if you know you want the icon in a different place this time.

Iconifying a "Not New" Window – AutoIconify

This operation differs from **NewIconify** in that it will position the icon where it was previously, or at the cursor position if the window was never iconified before.

1. Select the **AutoIconify** option from the menu, giving the "hand" cursor.

2. Move the cursor into the window you want to iconify.

3. Click any mouse button: the original window vanishes, and the icon appears where is was last positioned, or at the current cursor position if this is the first time the window was iconified.

Moving an Icon

An icon is just a window, and you can move it like an ordinary window, using the **Move** menu selection.

6.7.3   De-Iconifying – Changing an Icon back into a Window

To change an icon back into a normal window, you go through exactly the same process as you did when iconifying. You even use the same menu items. So what the iconify menu items really do is:

If the item you are operating on is a window, turn it into an icon. If the item is an icon, turn it back into a window.

The same positioning mechanisms apply too. **AutoIconify** causes the window to reappear in the position it was in last as soon as you click on the icon. With **NewIconify** on the other hand, when you press the mouse button you get a nine-square grid showing you the size the window will be, and you can drag this around with the cursor to position it where you want; the de-iconify doesn't occur until you release the button.

6.8   Terminating Application Windows

The uwm menu has a selection which lets you kill an application, when you decide you don't need it any more and want to remove it. To kill an application:

1. Select the **KillWindow** option from the menu. You get the "hand" cursor.

2. Position the cursor on the window you want to remove.

3. Click any mouse button: the window vanishes, and the application which owned it terminates.

After the window has gone, you get a message in the original xterm window just as you did when you used xkill in Chapter 5.

   Caution: if you kill the original xterm window, xinit will detect this and close down the server, just like we described in Chapter 5.

   Caution: if you kill an icon window, this terminates the window manager, and *all* the icons change back into their full windows. This is reasonable behaviour, because it is the window manager who owns icon windows.

6.9   Another Way of Calling Up uwm's Menu

Up to now, the way we have called up uwm's menu is by positioning the cursor on the screen background and pressing the middle mouse button. What happens if there is an application window covering the whole of the screen? Because there is no background showing, you can't call up the menu, so you can't lower the window, or resize it, or anything else?

   The solution is simple: there is an alternative way of calling up the menu, which works whether the cursor is in an application window or on the background:

1. Press the META and SHIFT keyboard keys simultaneously and keep them pressed.

2. Press the middle mouse button, and keep it pressed: the uwm menu appears as before. (You can release META and SHIFT now, or later).

3. Select a menu item, exactly as described before.

The menu operates as before, with one difference: if you move the cursor sideways out of the menu, the menu doesn't just vanish – it is replaced by a new menu headed **Preferences** which you can use to set some parameters like keyclick, volume of the bell, and so on. If you don't want any of these selections either, move the cursor out of the menu. Alternatively, click any other mouse button to get rid of the menu, no matter which one you are in.

6.10 Summary

In this chapter you have seen how to start and use the uwm window manager. With uwm's menu, you have been able to create new application windows, to move and resize windows, to change them into icons and back, and finally, to kill off client applications. These facilities cover most of your needs.

uwm is one of many window managers: it can be replaced with any other one that is available. No other window manager is included in the **core** MIT release, but several have been contributed by third parties, and are included in the **contrib** section of the release, along with some semi-obsolete MIT window managers. So, you can choose from lots of different styles of interface, or even have none, which is just what we had in the previous chapter.

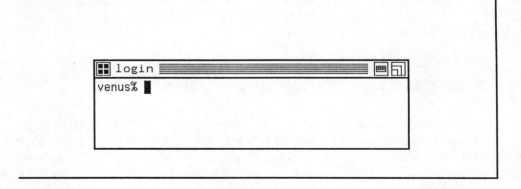

Figure 6.15 A window with a control bar provided by the twm window manager

Two window managers are worth particular mention:

twm is a manager which attaches a *title bar* to the top of each application window, and you manipulate the window by clicking or dragging on particular
parts of the bar. This interface is similar to the one on Apple's Macintosh.
A twm control bar is detailed in Figure 6.15.

rtl is a *tiling* window manager – it arranges the application windows so they never overlap. Optionally, it can also arrange that the windows fill as much of the screen area as possible (then later, if you want one window to be expanded, rtl will contract the neighbouring windows to make room for it). Figure 6.16 shows a screen controlled by rtl.

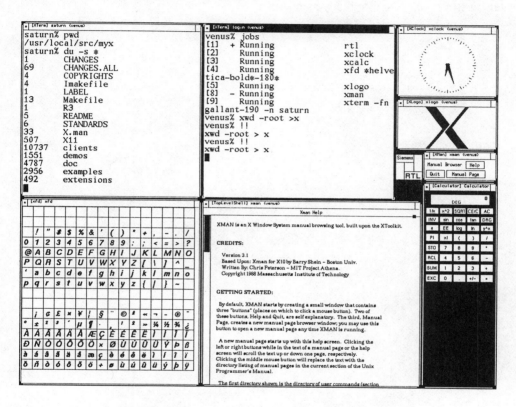

Figure 6.16 A screen controlled by the rtl window manager

You can switch from one window manager to another in mid-session if you want – kill off one, and start the other. As an exercise, set up several windows and iconify some of them. Then kill off uwm, with ps and kill as described in Chapter 5, or by selecting the **Exit** option from the menu: all icons vanish and are replaced by their corresponding application windows, and you are unable to configure your windows. If you now start uwm, you have full control again, but you have to re-iconify any windows you want to be still iconified. If you had another window manager on your system, the procedure to start it on mid-session would be just the same.

In a later chapter we look at uwm in more depth, and see the rest of the facilities it offers in its menu. We also show how uwm lets you manage your windows directly – without using a menu – which is quicker and more convenient.

Window managers determine only the management interface. The other half of the user interface is the *application interface* – how you interact with an application and use the mouse and keyboard to control it. In Chapter 8 we use xterm as an example, and look at many features of its application interface. Before that though, we'll digress a little and tell you how to use X's network capabilities, so you can be using most of the system's facilities as quickly as possible.

Chapter 7   Using X's Network Facilities

X's network features let you run applications on machines anywhere in your network, with the output from the applications appearing on your own machine's display. This is one of X's most important and powerful facilities, but it is still very simple to use.

The following sections describe how you specify a remote display, and how you use the facility in practice. (For completeness, some of Chapter 2's discussion of *remote display* has to repeated but this chapter includes a lot more practical detail). Finally, we describe how to control or limit access to your display from other machines on the network.

7.1   Specifying a Remote Display — The -display Option

Almost every X program accepts a command-line option specifying which display to use (or looking at it another way, which X server to connect to). The format of this option is:

>   **-display** *displayname*

Let's look more closely at the format of the *displayname*.

You are telling the program which display it is to output to, out of all the possible choices on your network . Obviously the specification you give it must include the name of the particular machine on the network. But more information is required: some (large) machines have several i/o stations, each with its own keyboard, mouse, etc. And further, one station may control several monitors. (There are also monitors which have only one physical CRT-tube, but with a number of logical screens which you switch between by moving the mouse-pointer in a special way. E.g. some colour models of the Sun-3/110). So in all, the display name needs to contain three elements, *hostname, display number* and *screen number*. We'll now explain each element in detail, and then give several examples.

7.1.1   The Hostname

The *hostname* is the name of the network machine that the display is physically connected to.

This part of the display spec also determines how the application communicates with the server, in a very simple way:

Server on your own, local, machine : You have two options.

1. Omit the hostname altogether. The system will choose the most efficient way of talking to the server.

2. Specify the hostname as "unix". The system will use *Unix domain sockets* for communication. ("Unix domain" means that the sockets are named according to the normal conventions for Unix filenames like */dev/urgent*. Sockets in the "Internet domain" are named differently).

Follow the name by a single colon (:). Even if you omit the name, you still need the colon.

Server on a remote machine : Again there are two options, depending on the communications systems available on your network:

1. TCP/IP, available on most Unix systems: the easiest way is to specify the host by the normal name as it's known on your local network, (e.g. "venus" or "saturn"). You can also use its full Internet name (e.g. "expo.lcs.mit.edu", or its Internet address ("129.89.12.73").

   Follow the name by a single colon (:).

2. DECnet: the name is the DECnet nodename of the machine you are connecting to.

   Follow the name by two colons (::).

7.1.2   The Displaynumber

A *display* is a set of monitors, screens and logical screens attached to one keyboard and mouse, i.e. it is a work position for one user. On a given CPU, displays are numbered, starting from zero, and the *display number* part of the full display-spec says which one to use.

The display number must be included in the display-spec even if it is zero.

7.1.3   The Screennumber

Multiple screens on a given display are also numbered, starting from zero, and the *screen number* specifies which one you want to use. Separate it from the displaynumber with a period (.).

The screen number is optional: it defaults to 0. If you omit the screen number, omit the period too.

7.1.4 Putting it All Together – Some Examples

The following examples illustrate all the usual sorts of display specs you are likely to use.

- To specify your own local machine, defaulting to screen zero, use either of:

  ```
  unix:0
  :0
  ```

- If you want to specify your own machine (venus as usual), but you want to check out the TCP/IP network operation, and to specify the screen explicitly:

  ```
  venus:0.0
  ```

- To specify screen no. 1 on remote machine pluto's only display, on a TCP/IP network connection:

  ```
  pluto:0.1
  ```

- To specify display no. 1 on remote machine vomvx2, communicating via DECnet, defaulting to screen 0:

  ```
  vomvx2::1
  ```

7.2 Using a Remote Display in Practice

Now that you have seen how to specify a remote display, how do you use it in real life? Let's assume you are working on venus and want to run an application, xterm say, on saturn. You must execute xterm on saturn specifying venus's display. So the command will be something like the following. (For clarity in the examples, in this section we will include the machine name as the shell's prompt).

```
venus% xterm -display venus:0.0    N.B. incomplete!!
```

but on its own that doesn't start xterm on the remote machine. (In fact it starts it on your local machine, venus, also displaying to venus).

If your operating system didn't support remote execution, you could walk over to a terminal connected to saturn and type in exactly the same command there:

```
saturn% xterm -display venus:0.0    N.B. incomplete!!
```

xterm would start executing on saturn, creating its window on venus, as you specified, and that window would take input from venus's mouse and keyboard, which is what you want. Then you would walk back to venus, and work away, using the window onto saturn.

But your operating system does support remote functions, so you can do exactly the same thing without moving from your own machine: you just specify that the command entered is to be executed on the *remote* machine, viz:

```
venus% rsh saturn xterm -display venus:0.0
```

using the normal (BSD Unix) remote shell facility, rsh.

Caution-1: The command may fail because saturn has not been granted access to venus's display. To get over this, enter the command:

```
venus% xhost +
```

and try again. (xhost's function is explained later in this chapter).

Caution-2: You will probably want to run the rsh asynchronously, i.e. with an & at the end of the command line, to run it in the background. The interaction of your shell and rsh may cause rsh to "block", waiting for input which will never arrive. To get over this, amend the command to read:

```
venus% rsh saturn xterm \
-display venus:0.0 < /dev/null &
```

Note: The remote machine (saturn in this case) does *not* need to have an **X** server running – it need not even have a bitmapped display. The only requirement is that it be able to execute application programs and support communication over the network.

In summary, your mode of working is to set applications running on other, remote, machines, with all of them connecting back to the display on your own machine. This is shown schematically in Figure 7.1.

7.2.1 An Easy Mistake to Make

If you get confused and initially use a command like:

```
venus% xterm -display saturn:0.0     N.B. incorrect !!
```

what happens? xterm starts executing on your local machine, and creates its window remotely on saturn (if it is allowed – more on this later). All you see on your screen is that the shell has read the command line, but otherwise nothing. So the system is behaving correctly, but what you told it to do isn't what you really wanted.

If you are lucky, you may not be able to connect to a server on saturn (either because you are not allowed or saturn doesn't have a server running) and xterm will give an error message like

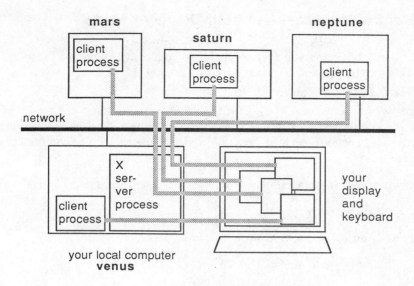

Figure 7.1 Remote client displays to local server

X Toolkit Error: Can't Open display

and exit. Then, at least, you know something is wrong.

7.2.2 Setting a Default Display

If you don't specify a display name explicitly, by default programs look at the Unix environment variable DISPLAY to see which display to use. The initial xterm sets this variable when it starts up, so most of the time you don't have to worry about it at all.

However, if you remote-login to another machine, and in that remote session you want to run **X** applications displaying back to your own machine, you would set the DISPLAY variable explicitly. So the start of a session might look like:

```
venus% rlogin saturn
Last login: Mon Nov 28 20:01:02 on console
...              login banner on remote machine
saturn%          shell prompt from remote machine
saturn% setenv DISPLAY venus:0.0
saturn% xcalc &
```

The alternative, if you don't set DISPLAY, is to include the option -display venus:0.0 for every **X** program run on saturn.

7.3   Controlling Access to Your Display – xhost

We mentioned above that you may be unable to connect to a particular display sometimes. This usually happens because **X** has denied you access, because you don't have
the necessary permission.

X uses a very simple mechanism for controlling access: you specify a list of hosts
that are allowed to access your display. Applications running on these hosts can do anything
on your display, those on other hosts aren't allowed to connect at all. You control acces using
the program xhost:

To grant access to a machine, or machines : enter the command

> **xhost** +*host1* [+*host2* . . .]

To remove access from machines : use the command

> **xhost** –*host1* [–*host2* . . .]

To let any machine have access : enter

> **xhost** +

This disables access control completely.

To re-enable access control : (typically after a previous xhost +). Enter the
command

> **xhost** –

This re-enables access control, so only machines that were explicitly granted
access previously are allowed.

Caution: Access control applies to *all* processes — not just those started by other
users. So if *you* run an application on a remote machine displaying back to your own,
that machine must have been granted access or the connection will fail.

7.4   Conclusion

In this chapter you have seen how to tell an **X** program which display, local or remote,
it is to connect to, and how you use the network facilities in practice. Finally, you saw
how to permit or forbid other machines on the network to access your display.

Now that you can use the network, and have a window manager to control your
display, we'll move on to describe xterm, and look in detail at the application interface
it offers.

Chapter 8 **The Terminal Emulator:** xterm **in Detail**

xterm is the **X** *terminal emulator* – the program which makes an **X** application window look like an ordinary terminal to programs which know nothing about the window system. We have already used xterm quite a bit, but in this chapter we look at it in more depth, and see some of the extra facilities it has to offer. This will also illustrate several features of the application interface common to many **X** programs.

xterm emulates a dumb terminal, as we've seen. But it also offers several features that you don't get on a normal terminal:

- pop-up menus to set terminal modes and other characteristics.

- a *scrollbar* that you can use to move the screen image up and down – when text lines have scrolled off the top of the screen, you can bring them back again.

- emulation of a Tektronix 4014 terminal.

- optional recording of the screen lines in a *log file*.

- cut and paste of chunks of text.

- your choice of colours for the text, window background, etc.

- choice of fonts for VT100 and Tek windows.

- settable ("programmable") keys.

To start we'll describe the menu mechanism which lets you select other features, and then move on to using the features themselves.

8.1 Selecting xterm Features – Menus and Command-Line Options

xterm has its own in-built menu mechanism which lets you change settings in mid-session. There are three menus available, as shown in Figure 8.1:

xterm X11 : Most of the entries here are for program control functions, e.g. **Continue program** or **Kill program**. To pop-up this menu, press CONTROL and the LEFT mouse button simultaneously.

modes : mostly sets terminal characteristics and selects Tektronix emulation. To pop-up this menu, press CONTROL and the MIDDLE button (while in the VT102 window).

Tektronix : controls the appearance of the Tektronix window. To pop it up, press CONTROL and the MIDDLE button while in the Tektronix window.

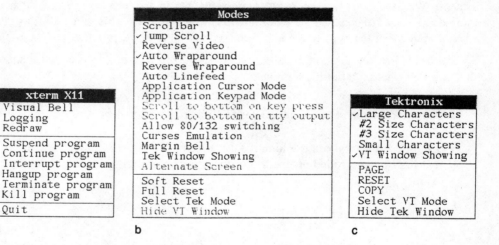

a   b   c

Figure 8.1 xterm's three menus

The menus operate just like uwm's. You pop up the menu by pressing a mouse button, and with the button still depressed move the pointer to the option you want to select; releasing the button causes that option to be selected. (And you can abandon the menu just by moving the pointer outside the menu before releasing the button). However, one point of difference is that menu items which cannot currently be selected (because it doesn't make any sense to at the time) are shown in light type, e.g. the **Hide VT Window** item is shown light if you haven't opened a Tektronix window yet.

Many of the features in the menus can also be selected when you issue the command to start xterm, by specifying command-line options. (And there are other features which can be selected *only* with command-line options). As we go through the following sections, we'll tell you both the menu selections and the command-line options you can use to set the various features.

8.2 Scrolling xterm's Screen

Pop-up the **xterm X11** menu (by pressing CONTROL and the LEFT mouse button together), and select the **Scrollbar** option. A *scrollbar* appears on the left of the xterm window, as shown in Figure 8.2. The highlighted region tells you two things:

1. The ratio of the number of lines on the screen to the number of lines saved in the scrollbar's buffer.

2. What section of the buffer is currently displayed on the screen.

```
rotprt
sendmail
sendmail.cf
sendmail.hf
sendmail.main.cf
sendmail.subsidiary.cf
spell
suntools
tabset
term
textswrc
tmac
units
vfontedpr
vgrindefs
yaccpar
venus% ▮
```

Figure 8.2 xterm window with a scrollbar

E.g. in Figure 8.2: there are about 20 lines on the screen; the highlighted section is about a fifth of the total, so the buffer contains about 100 lines, and it is the bottom-most section of the buffer that is currently shown (because the highlighted area is at the bottom of the scroll region).

You can move the highlighted section within the scroll region, and correspondingly alter which section of the text is displayed on the screen, using the mouse buttons. This is explained in the following sections; to simplify the description we'll assume that the scroll buffer contains 100 lines.

Caution: xterm's scrollbar usage differs considerably from many other window systems, notably Apple's Macintosh.

8.2.1 To Move the Scrollbar to a Specific Point

If you want to move to a specific place in the text, e.g. you want to see lines 50 onwards:

1. Move the pointer into the scroll region. The cursor becomes a double-headed vertical arrow (Figure 8.3a).

2. Press the MIDDLE button: the cursor becomes a horizontal arrow (Figure 8.3b) and the highlighted area jumps so that its top is at the cursor. (E.g. if you wanted to see from line 50 on, you would have positioned the pointer half-way up the scroll region).

3. You can release the button now if the window is displaying what you want, or ...

4. ... Still keeping the button depressed, move the pointer: the highlighted area will track the pointer (and the text in the window will track the highlighted area) until you release the button.

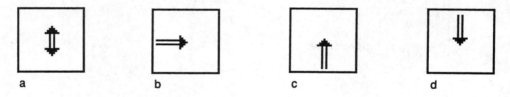

a   b   c   d

Figure 8.3 Cursors employed in the scrollbar

8.2.2 To Scroll Text Forward

Scrolling the window text forward moves lines off the top of the screen: the highlighted area moves towards the bottom of the scroll region, and you see the more recent text. To scroll up:

1. Move the pointer into the scroll region, giving the double arrow as before.

2. Press the LEFT button: the cursor becomes an up arrow (Figure 8.3c).

3. Release the button: the line which was alongside the arrow head jumps to the top of the screen, and the highlighted area is adjusted accordingly.

This is shown schematically in Figure 8.4. Note that the extent of the scroll movement depends on where in the scroll region you release the button: if you release it near the top, you get a small movement, but near the bottom of course you get a larger jump.

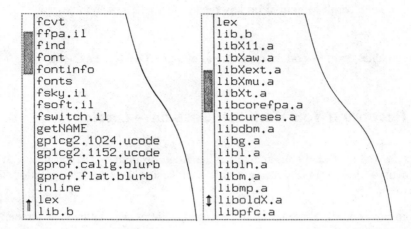

Figure 8.4 Scrolling the text in a window

8.2.3   To Scroll Text Backwards

Scrolling the window text backwards moves lines off the bottom of the screen, so you see the older text. The procedure is like scrolling forward, but in reverse, and you use the RIGHT button this time, giving a down arrow cursor (Figure 8.3d).

8.2.4   Other Scrolling Options

Once you have enabled scrolling, two **Mode**-menu options (which until now were shown grey) become available.

Scroll to bottom on tty output : if you are not at the bottom of the scroll region, as soon as some terminal output arrives the window is automatically repositioned to the end of the scroll region. This is enabled by default. If this option is off, you must explicitly scroll the window when you want to see the new output.

Scroll to bottom on key press : if you are not at the bottom of the scroll region, as soon as you press a key the window is automatically repositioned to the end of the scroll region. By default, this is *not* enabled, but usually your terminal is set so that characters are echoed as you type: these echoed characters are tty output, and will cause the window to be repositioned.

8.2.5   Controlling Scrolling with Command-Line Options

-sb : enable the scrollbar. (Default: not enabled).

-sl *num* : save *num* lines which have scrolled off the screen. (Default 64).

-sk : enable scroll to bottom on key press. (Default: not enabled).

-si : enable scroll to bottom on terminal output. (Default: enabled).

8.3   Recording Your Terminal Session – *Logging*

Pop-up the **xterm X11** menu, and select the **Logging** option. (If you now call up the same menu a second time, you see a tick-mark beside the **Logging** selection showing it is active).

From now on, all terminal output is sent to a file as well as to your screen, so you get a permanent record of your session. By default, the output is written to the file *XtermLog.pid*, where *pid* is xterm's process id. The file is created in the directory that xterm was started in. (You can change the log-file name via a command-line option, below).

You can disable the logging by popping up the **xterm X11** menu and selecting **Logging** again (and if you look again, you will see the option is no longer ticked). You can repeatedly enable and disable the logging, selectively recording parts of your session; the output is always appended to the file — it does *not* overwrite the log file each time.

8.3.1   Controlling Logging with Command-Line Options

-l : enable logging.

-lf *file* : write the logging output to *file* instead of to the default-named file. (Specifying this option only sets the log-file name and doesn't of itself enable logging; if that's what you want, you have to specify **-l** in addition).

Using a Pipeline as a Logging "File"

The **-lf** option has a special feature: if the *file* argument given to it begins with the pipe symbol (|), the rest of the argument is taken as a pipeline into which the logging output is to be piped. E.g. assuming your shell prompt is venus%, use the following command to start an xterm and record in the file *cmdlog* only the commands you typed:

```
xterm -l -lf '| grep "^venus% " > cmdlog'
```

8.4 Cutting and Pasting Text

You can *cut* portions of text from the xterm window, i.e. copy the text to a *cut buffer*, from which it can later be *pasted*, i.e. retrieved. You can paste the text into the same window, or another xterm window, or any window that supports the same mechanism. You can paste it now or later, but you have only one buffer, and subsequent **cuts** overwrite earlier ones. The current selection is highlighted in inverse video; an xterm window with about two lines selected is shown in Figure 8.5.

```
X is a network transparent window system
developed at MIT which runs on a wide
range of computing and graphics
machines.  The core distribution from
MIT has both client and server support
for the following operating systems:
venus% █
```

Figure 8.5 Text is highlighted in a "cut" operation

8.4.1 Cutting

To cut a section of text:

1. Move the cursor to one end of the text you want to **cut**.

2. Press the `LEFT` mouse button, and keeping it pressed ...

3. ... Drag the cursor to the other end of the text you want to cut: the text between the cursor and the start point is highlighted as you move.

4. Release the button: the selected text remains highlighted, and any previously highlighted selection – even in another window – is un-highlighted.

8.4.2 Pasting

To paste a section of text:

1. Move the cursor to where you want the text inserted.

2. Click the `MIDDLE` button: the last selected text is inserted. (The current selection, if any, remains highlighted).

When you past text into a window, it is exactly as if you had typed it at the keyboard – you can use the normal line-editing keys to delete characters, words, or the whole line. (Of course, if you paste multiple lines in one operation, you can only edit the last one, just as you can only edit the last line you have typed).

Caution: if you try to paste too much text into an xterm window, xterm may hang forever. (We have pasted chunks of about 4000 characters with no problem, but there doesn't seem to be a rigid threshold at which the trouble occurs).

8.4.3   Cutting a Word or a Line

If you want to cut a word or a line, you can select it directly instead of dragging over it.

> **To cut a word** : Position the pointer anywhere in the word, and double-click the LEFT button: the word is selected.

> **To cut a line** : Position the pointer anywhere in the line, and triple-click the LEFT button: the whole line is selected.

Double- and triple-clicking are commonly used on mouse-based systems, but in this instance there is a special feature: what determines if successive clicks are separate or part of a multiple click is the time between the button-up and button-down movements – nothing else matters. So, the following counts as a triple-click:

```
DOWN ... pause for a few seconds ... UP DOWN .. another
pause ... UP DOWN ... pause
```

This is useful because: as long as you keep the button down after a click, you can change the selection mode (from "by character" to "by word" to "by line") just by doing further UP/DOWN sequences.

8.4.4   Extending a Selection or "Cut"

Once you have a selection, you can extend it (or contract it), as follows:

1. Move the pointer to where you want the new end of the selection to be, whether that is inside the existing one (when you want to contract it) or outside (when you want to extend it).

2a Click the RIGHT button: the selection is adjusted to end at the current pointer position. *Or, ...*

2b ... Instead of clicking, you can press, drag and release, in which case the end of the selection follows the cursor, and the selection is highlighted just as it was in Section 1.4.1.

A handy trick for selecting is to "mark" one end of text you want to select by clicking LEFT, and the other end by clicking RIGHT: the intervening text is selected. (This is a degenerate case of extending a selection. The initial selection is empty — i.e. you have clicked the LEFT button but haven't dragged it over any text — and you then extend this empty selection by clicking RIGHT).

8.4.5 Selecting on Word or Line Boundaries

If you want to select a number of whole words or lines, you can obviously do it by carefully positioning the pointer before clicking. But there is a short-cut — using multiple clicking again. To select on word or line boundaries:

1. Move the cursor to one end of the text you want to **cut**.

2. Press the LEFT mouse button, and keeping it pressed ...

3. ... Drag the cursor to the other end of the text you want to cut: the text between the cursor and the start point is highlighted. (Figure 8.6, top).

4. Release and press the button again in rapid succession: the highlighted region extends to the nearest word boundaries. (Figure 8.6, middle).

5. Release and press the button again in rapid succession: the highlighted region extends to the ends of the lines already selected. (Figure 8.6, bottom).

6. Release and press the button again in rapid succession: the highlighted region reverts to its original size, i.e. the selection is back on character boundaries. (Figure 8.6 top, again).

This same technique applies when extending an existing selection with the RIGHT button.

8.5 Using the Tektronix Emulation

xterm can emulate a Tektronix 4014 terminal as well as a VT102, so you can use it to display graphics. This is particularly useful when you are running a non-**X** application on a remote machine, and want to see the graphics on your own display.

xterm uses a separate window for each of the "terminals", so you can keep all the text in one window and the graphics in the other, as shown in Figure 8.7. Only one window is active at a time, i.e. all the keyboard input – and pasted text – goes to that window even if the pointer is in the other. You select the window you require with terminal escape sequences or explicitly using the **modes** menu. You can manipulate the two windows completely separately using your window manager. E.g. you can iconify

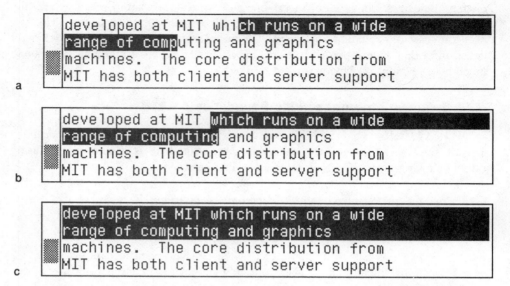

Figure 8.6 Cutting text by character, by word, and by line

the VT window while leaving the Tek one open, etc. You can also hide or show one or other window by using the appropriate xterm menu selections (**Tek Window Showing**, **Hide VT Window**, etc).

   Caution: Hiding is not the same as sending to the bottom of the stack, or iconifying. If you "hide" a window using the menu, when next you ask for the window to appear again you will have to position it (via the window manager) just as if you had created a new application window.

8.5.1 Tektronix-Specific Functions

The **Tektronix** menu (which you get by pressing CONTROL and the MIDDLE button) gives you more or less the same facilities for controlling xterm's windows as the **Modes** menu. But it also includes several items which are applicable only to the Tektronix window:

   Changing the character size : you can select from four different sizes of character, ranging from **Large Characters** (which is the default) down to **Small Characters**. You can change size at any time, even in mid-line. Characters which were on the "screen" before the change are unaffected.

   Clearing the screen : a feature of the Tektronix is that its screen doesn't scroll. There are two columns (left and right) for text on the screen, and when the end of one is reached, output switches over to the other. However, the characters already displayed are *not* erased, so the screen can soon

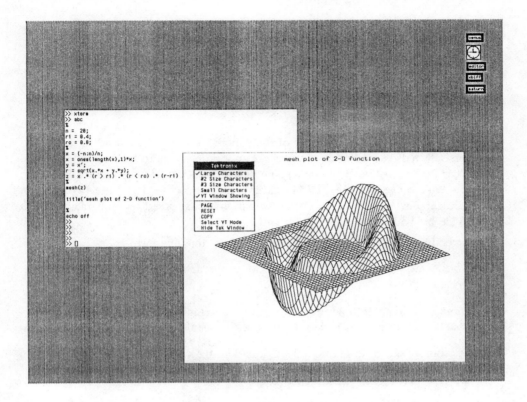

Figure 8.7 Screen showing xterm's normal and Tektronix windows

become a mess unless you clear it explicitly. To do this, select **PAGE** in the **Tektronix** menu: the screen is cleared, and the cursor moves to the top left.

To reset the "terminal" : select **RESET** in the **Tektronix** menu. The character size and the line style (which may have been changed by a program outputting to the window) are set back to the default, and a **PAGE** screen-clear is performed.

To copy the window contents to a file : select **COPY** in the **Tektronix** menu. Everything written to the screen since the last **PAGE** function is copied to the file *COPYyy-MM-dd.hh.mm:ss*, where *yy-MM- ...* is the current time. The file is created in the directory that xterm was started in.

Redrawing the Tek window can take quite a while: while this is happening, the cursor in the Tek window changes to an alarm clock (Figure 8.8).

Figure 8.8 "Alarm clock" cursor emplyed in xterm's Tektronix window

8.6 Using Different Fonts

xterm lets you choose from a variety of fonts, both for normal text, and for bold text. The fonts selected must be of fixed width (i.e. not proportionally spaced) and the same size as each other. As yet you don't know how to find which fonts are available, but there is a wide range available, and in the example below we'll just use two of them which are supplied as part of the **core** distribution 8x13 (based on a character grid 8 pixels wide by 13 high) and 8x13b (a bold variant).

To specify particular fonts you use the command-line options:

-fn *font* : use *font* for normal text, instead of the default-named font (which is called "fixed").

-fb *font* : use *font* for bold text, instead of the default-named font (which is also called "fixed"; by default xterm doesn't distinguish emboldened text).

E.g. the window shown in Figure 8.9 was run with the command

```
xterm -fn 8x13 -fb 8x13b
```

explicitly specifying normal and bold fonts. We'll deal with fonts in more depth in the chapter *"Using X-Window Fonts and Colours"*.

```
at MIT which runs on a wide range of computing and
graphics machines.  The core distribution from MIT
has both client and server support for the
following operating systems:
sapphire% []
```

Figure 8.9 xterm window with bold and normal type

8.7 Using Colour

If you have a colour display, you can set a number of elements of the window to specific colours with command-line options:

-fg *colour* : print the foreground, i.e. the text, in *colour*

-bg *colour* : use *colour* for the window background

-bd *colour* : use *colour* for the window border

-ms *colour* : use *colour* for the mouse pointer

-cr *colour* : use *colour* for the cursor

You may find it useful to "colour-code" windows depending on which machine on your network they are connected to. Also helpful is to set the cursor and mouse to striking colours so you can easily see them in a cluttered window.

8.8   Other xterm Options

There are many more options accepted by xterm. Some of them set terminal characteristics, e.g. -mb enables the margin bell, -rv causes a window to be displayed in reverse video. Others set parameters relating to the window system, e.g. -display and -geometry which we have seen before. All are described in the xterm manpage, but here are a few useful miscellaneous ones:

-iconic : xterm should start as an icon instead of as a normal "open" window. (When using uwm as your window manager, the icon's initial location will be where the cursor happens to be when the icon is created. We'll see how to specify an explicit icon position in the chapter *"Resources — Setting Defaults for Your Applications"*.

-title *string* : Use *string* as the window title. This title is what appears in the startup size-box we saw in Figure 6.8, and some window managers may include it in a window's title-bar.

-C : this window should receive output sent to the system console (e.g. disk full messages, device errors, etc). If you don't have one window with this option specified, console messages may appear directly on your screen (i.e. not in a window) and disturb the display; if this happens, just use uwm's menu selection **RefreshScreen** to restore the display to normal.

-e *prog* [*args*] : run *prog* with optional arguments *args* in the window, instead of starting a normal shell. (This option must be the last on the command line, as everything after it is taken as part of the *args*). You often use -e to rlogin to a remote system which doesn't support X, e.g.

```
xterm -title saturn -e rlogin saturn -l root
```

8.9   Setting Terminal Keys

X itself lets you change the mapping of your keyboard, so you can for instance change it to suit a particular national convention. But this mapping only determines which "character code" is associated with a given key.

Client programs, like xterm can go further than this, and assign arbitrary strings of characters to any key or keys. Using this mechanism you can set up an xterm which is particularly suited to the way you use a mail program, say, or a debugger, by assigning common commands to function keys, or control characters, or whatever.

The details of this mechanism are complex, so we'll defer them until the chapter *"Customising Your Keyboard — Translations"*.

8.10   Conclusion

xterm is a complex program with a large number of options and features. Fortunately you tend not to use them most of the time, and when you do it's usually when you are setting up your preferred configuration when you are starting xterm. The xterm manpage is a lengthy reference document on the program's features. Before reading it in detail, you are probably better off getting used to the general operation of the program, and only then delving into specifics.

Caution: the manpage refers to the document *Xterm Control Sequences*. This document is currently only in preparation, and has not been distributed as part of the release.

Many of the interface features, for instance scrollbars and how you select sections of text with the pointer, are implemented within the program by means of standard pieces of software called *widgets*. (There is more about widgets in the Section The Toolkit, in the Chapter on *"Resources"*). You will find the same interface offered by other **X** applications, e.g. in xman and xedit described in Chapter 10. Before moving on to those, however, we'll look at some small but useful programs in the next chapter.

Chapter 9   Convenience Programs and Window-Related Tools

So far we have covered the basic elements of using the system, and with xterm's facilities you are starting to gain real advantages from the window system. In this chapter we describe several small programs which start to make fuller use of the system and make your work more convenient.

The first part of the chapter is devoted to "desk accessory" convenience programs, and the second part to a set of tools for capturing, restoring and printing screen images.

9.1   Convenience Programs

This section describes a number of programs whose function is minor but which nonetheless make life easier and more convenient. We've seen a couple of these already — xclock and xcalc — which we'll describe more methodically, and we'll look at some new ones which display the current machine load, and tell you when mail has arrived.

9.1.1   An Analog or Digital Clock — xclock

In Chapter 5 we used xclock as an example program, with the following command-line options:

To specify the window's initial size and/or position : use -geometry *geomspec*.

To set the background colour : use -bg *colour*

To set the foreground colour : use -fg *colour*

To set the colour of the hands : use -hd *colour*

To highlight the edges of the hands : -hl *colour* highlights the edges of the hands in *colour*

Figure 9.1 Digital
        xclock.

> Fri Dec 23 21:33:12 1988

Some other useful ones are:

To use a digital clock : -digital tells xclock to use a 24-hour digital format, shown in Figure 9.1, instead of the default analog style.

To specify "clock-tick" frequency : -update *num* says update the clock display every *num* seconds. On the analog clock, if *num* is less than 30 secs, a diamond-shaped seconds "hand" is shown (as in Figure 9.2) and it moves every *num* seconds. (Default: 60 secs).

Set a half-hourly bell : -chime rings the terminal bell once on the half-hour and twice on the hour.

Figure 9.2 xclock with a seconds "hand".

9.1.2   A Desk Calculator – xcalc

This is another program we've used before. The command-line options we used were:

To specify the window's initial size and position : use -geometry *geom-spec*.

To set the background colour : -bg *colour*

To set the foreground colour : -fg *colour*

Other options are:

To specify slide-rule mode : -analog runs the program as a slide-rule (Figure 9.3) instead of as an electronic calculator. This is really a curiosity, but some further instructions are included below because they are not included in the manpage.

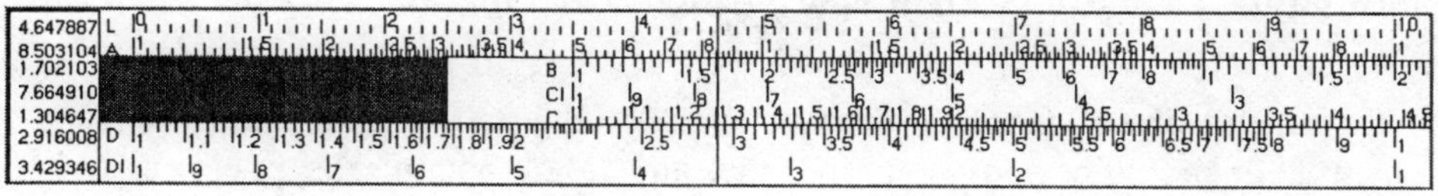

Figure 9.3 Analog xcalc is a slide rule

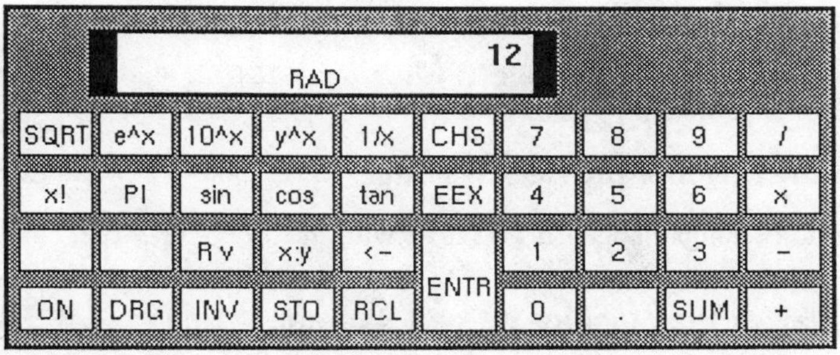

Figure 9.4 Reverse-Polish xcalc calculator

Specify HP-10C calculator type : -rpn (for Reverse Polish Notation) tells xcalc to emulate the HP-10C calculator, as shown in Figure 9.4.

Further instructions on running either of the calculator modes are included in the man-pages. (When you iconify xcalc, no matter which mode you run it in, you get the rather nice icon shown in Figure 9.5).

Figure 9.5 xcalc's special icon

Using the Slide Rule

You operate the slide rule with the mouse buttons. When the mouse pointer is in the window, it changes to the hand cursor.

To position the slide – left end : Move the pointer into the slide area, position it where you want, and click the LEFT button: the left end of the slide jumps to the pointer position.

To position the slide – right end : As for the left edge, but click the RIGHT button.

To position the slide-rule's cursor : Position the pointer on the body of the rule at the point you want, and click the LEFT button: the rule's cursor jumps to the pointer position.

To slide the slide-bar : Position the cursor on the slide, press the MIDDLE button, and keeping it pressed ... drag the slide to the position you want. Then release the button.

To double the length of the rule : Click the MIDDLE button on the rule body.

To halve the length of the rule : Click the RIGHT button on the rule body.

Caution: curious things happen if you drag with the LEFT or RIGHT buttons.

9.1.3 Display of the Machine's Load Average – xload

xload displays a histogram of the system load average (the average number of jobs in the run queue) which it updates on a regular basis. Typical output is shown in Figure 9.6a; xload's special icon is shown in Figure 9.6b.

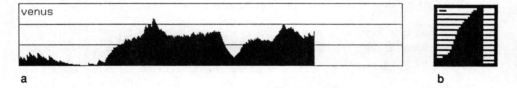

a   b

Figure 9.6 xload's normal and icon windows

9.1.4 Mail Notification Program – xbiff

xbiff is a small program which monitors your mail file and lets you know when new mail arrives. It displays a picture of a mailbox; the flag on the box is down when there is no new mail (Figure 9.7a). When new mail arrives, xbiff rings the bell, raises the flag, and shows the picture in inverse video (Figure 9.7b).

You can force the flag down by clicking on the xbiff window with any mouse button.

xbiff accepts the usual command-line options for colours (-bg, -fg, -bd) and for window characteristics (-display, -geometry, -bw). Others include

Specify frequency of checking for mail : -update *num* tells xbiff to check the mailbox every *num* seconds to see if new mail has arrived. (Default: 60 seconds).

a   b

Figure 9.7 The two forms of xbiff mail-monitor window

To specify a particular mail file : -file *filename* makes xbiff check for mail
in the file called *filename* instead of the default-named file. (Default:
/usr/spool/mail/username where *username* is your login name).

xbiff, particularly with the **-file** option, is very useful where the mail on your network
is handled centrally and your mailbox is handled on another machine. You run xbiff on
the mail machine (mars, say), looking at your mailbox, and displaying back to your
own machine venus:

```
rsh mars xbiff -file /var/spool/mail/smith\
-display venus:0 &
```

9.2 Saving, Displaying and Printing Screen Images

X is a graphical system, and you will be using it to display text and graphics in windows.
Often you will want to capture some of the images on the screen, so you can re-display
them later, or print them on a hard-copy device. The following sections describe the
facilities for doing this.

9.2.1 Saving an Image of a Window – xwd

xwd dumps the image of an **X** window to a file. This file can later be processed by
other programs (to print a hard copy, etc).

There are a few ways of using xwd. You can explicitly specify an output file (using
the command-line option **-out** *name*), or you can make use of the fact that xwd dumps
the image to the standard output. And you can explicitly specify the window you want
dumped, or you can let xwd "prompt" you.

Let's take the simplest example: start the program with the command

```
xwd > outfile
```

Figure 9.8 The "cross-hairs" cursor

in an xterm window. Once xwd starts, the cursor changes to the *cross-hairs* shown in Figure 9.8. Move the pointer into the window you want to dump, and click any button: xwd rings the bell once to indicate that it has started recording the window image, and rings it twice when it has finished. Then the cursor reverts to normal.

Caution-1: If you try do dump a window which is not completely on the screen, the program may fail and give you a long error message in your console xterm window (if you have one).

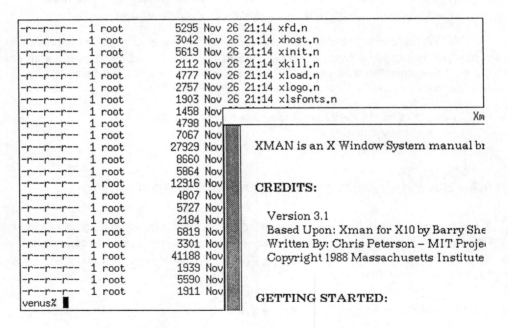

Figure 9.9 Window-dumps show any overlapping windows

Caution-2: The image that is captured is what you *actually see* on the screen, within the window's boundaries. In particular, if the window is partially covered by another, the dumped image also will show the visible part of the window covered and include the overlapping portion of the obscuring window. (E.g. Figure 9.9 shows an xwd dump of an xterm window which was overlapped by an xman). This may seem an inconvenient feature, but it has advantages: to get a dump of your complete screen, you just xwd the root (background) window; as everything you see on the screen overlaps the root window, the image you get this way is a complete picture of the screen.

How to Specify Explicitly the Window to be Dumped

Using command-line options there are two ways of telling xwd which window is to be dumped.

-root : dump the root window. E.g., to get a complete picture of the screen you could use the command:

xwd −root > screenpic

-id *win-id* : dump the window whose *window identifier* is *win-id*. (Every window created by the **X** server has a unique *window identifier*: it is just a number which identifies the window. We'll tell you how to find a particular window's id in the chapter on *"Information and Status Programs"*).

(These options are not described in the xwd manpage).

The benefits of using these options are that you don't have to use the mouse to specify the window you are interested in. This is important where you have to use the mouse for some other purpose when the dump is to be done, e.g. to call up a pop-up menu, or to make a command-button appear in the state you want. E.g. to save the screen image shown in Figure 6.1, the mouse had to be used to pop-up the uwm menu – so there was no way to use the mouse simultaneously to specify the target for xwd. Here is how you capture an image like that:

1. In an xterm window, enter the command

   sleep 10; xwd −root > uwmfig

   giving yourself time to get the screen into the state you want before the "snapshot" is taken.

2. Move the pointer onto the background window.

3. Press the MIDDLE button, giving the **WindowOps** menu, and keeping the button pressed ...

4. ... Wait, until xwd beeps once to say it has started, and twice more to say it has finished. Then release the button.

The same technique was used to snapshot the xterm menus illustrated in Chapter 8, although there we had to use explicit window identifiers. (We'll come back to this again in *"Information and Status Programs"*).

9.2.2 Magnifying a Portion of the Screen Image – xmag

xmag lets you snapshot arbitrary rectangular portions of the screen, and magnify them up by an arbitrary (integral) factor.

In its simplest form you interactively specify the area you are interested in:

1. Start the program (e.g. with the command xmag): xmag displays a flashing rectangular outline.

2. Position the rectangle over the area you want.

3. Click any button: xmag snapshots the outlined area, and displays a flashing outline of a window in which it is going to display the enlarged image of the snapshot.

4. Position the outline with pointer and mouse buttons in exactly the same way as you did when starting xclock in Chapter 6. (E.g. click LEFT to position the window where the pointer is currently).

5. xmag draws the enlarged image in the window you have just positioned.

You now have a choice of actions:

- You can exit, by pressing Q or q or CTRL-C with the pointer positioned in the xmag window.

- You can press the MIDDLE or RIGHT button to remove the current magnified window, and xmag gives its flashing rectangle again, so you can magnify another area of the screen.

- Press the LEFT button: xmag displays the coordinates of the pixel under the pointer, the *pixel number* of the pixel (which is an internal representation of the colour of the pixel), and the pixel's *RGB value*, i.e. values of the Red, Green and Blue components of the pixel's colour. As you move the pointer, this display is continuously updated, until you release the button.

Note that the program records the snapshotted image only for immediate re-display – there isn't any way to get it to dump the image to a file.

xmag's Command-Line Options

The default operation is limited in several ways – you must interactively specify the area to be magnified, the shape and size of the area is fixed, and the magnification factor is always five. You can change all these with command-line options:

To specify a different magnification : -mag *num* says magnify the image by a factor of *num* (which must be an integer). E.g. -mag 2 will produce an image which is twice as tall and twice as wide as the original. (Default: 5).

To specify the size and location of the area to be magnified : use -source *geomspec* where *geomspec* is complete, e.g.

```
-source 300x100+450+762
```

xmag won't "prompt" at all, but will move straight to the stage where it displays the outline of the enlarged window. If *geomspec* consists of a location-part only, the size-part defaults to 64x64.

To specify only the size of the area to be magnified : use -source *geomspec*, where *geomspec* consists of a size-part only as in

```
-source 300x100
```

xmag will display a flashing rectangular outline of that size for you to position and click on as before.

9.2.3   Saving an Image of a Part of the Screen

xwd operates only on single, entire, windows. If you want to snapshot part of a window, or several windows together, you have to use a two-stage process:

1. Use the program xmag to select the area you want, and display it in a single (i.e. xmag's own) window.

2. Use xwd to dump the xmag window to a file. (If you want the dumped image to be the same size as the original, don't forget to specify -mag 1 to xmag).

9.2.4   Displaying a Previously Dumped Image – xwud

xwud "undumps" an image previously dumped to a file, i.e. it displays the image on the screen again. By default it reads the dump file from the standard input, so to undump from a file you would use something like

```
xwud < screenpic
```

xwud displays the flashing outline of the window ready for you to position with the window manager; when you have positioned it, the image is displayed. Clicking with any button in the window terminates the program. But of course you can move the window, resize it, iconify it, etc., with the window manager just like any other window.

Caution: The -inverse option mentioned in the manpage may not work.

9.2.5   Printing a Previously Dumped Image – xpr

xpr translates a previously-dumped image into the format required for printing on a hardcopy printer. It supports a variety of printers — PostScript, DEC LN03 and LA100, and IBM PP3812. By default it writes to the standard output, so typical usage would be:

```
xpr -device ln03 < screenpic | lpr
```

xpr's Command-Line Options

xpr accepts several options which control positioning, sizing and layout of the image on the paper, as well as specifying which type of printer the output is destined for:

Specifying the printer type : Use -device *type*, where *type* is one of ln03, la100, ps (for PostScript) or pp (for PP3812).

Controlling the image size : By default, xpr prints the image as large as it can. You can specify maximum width or height with -width *num* or -height *num*, where *num* is a dimension (not necessarily integral) in inches.

Scaling the image : You can scale the image with -scale *num*, where *num* is an integer. The operation is similar to xmag's -mag option, but the magnification may be distorted because the screen and printer probably have different resolutions, i.e. differents numbers of dots (pixels) per inch. E.g. -scale 2 says that each pixel on the screen is to be printed as a 2x2 square of dots on the printer, so if your screen is 75dpi and your printer 300dpi, the printed image will only be half the size of the screen image (75*2/300 = 0.5).

Adding headings to the image : use -header *string* and/or -trailer *string* to add a text string above or below the image, respectively.

Dumping and Printing a Window in a Single Operation – xdpr

xdpr is a program which uses xwd to dump a window image, formats the image for printing using xpr and then sends the output to the printer using lpr. It accepts all the command-line options accepted by the programs it uses. (In fact xdpr is a shell script providing a convenient wrapper for the three programs: it checks the command-line options and just passes them on in turn to the appropriate program).

9.3   Conclusion/Summary

In this chapter you have met a number of little programs which help you in your day-to-day work, and some other very specific tools to record and re-create screen images. With these you are beginning to take advantage of the window system and to make use of its graphics capabilities.

In the next chapter we continue in the same direction and see several general utility programs which employ the window system to simplify their operation and enhance their user interface.

Chapter 10 **Application Programs which Use** X

This chapter describes some general utility programs included in the **core** distribution whose main function is not related to the window system per se, but which use it to provide a good user interface:

- xedit – a general-purpose window-based text editor.

- xman – a manpage browser or tool for browsing through system documentation.

- xmh – a windowed front-end to the mh mail handling program.

10.1   A Text Editor – xedit

xedit is a fairly simple text editor with a window interface. You perform some operations by clicking on selection boxes which xedit displays, but you can do a lot more using keyboard keys, particularly the control characters. Most of the keyboard-based functions in this program are provided by a standard piece of software – a "building block" if you like – called a *text widget*. (We'll have more to say about widgets in the chapter on *"Resources"*). Because this is a general mechanism, and you will meet the same editing functions elsewhere, we are going to describe the facilities in some detail in the following sections.

10.1.1   Starting and Stopping the Program

If you want to edit a file, *foobar* say, enter the command

```
xedit foobar &
```

in an xterm window. (If are editing from scratch and don't want to work on an existing file, just use "xedit &"). xedit starts and displays its window, as shown in Figure 10.1.

The window is divided into three parts:

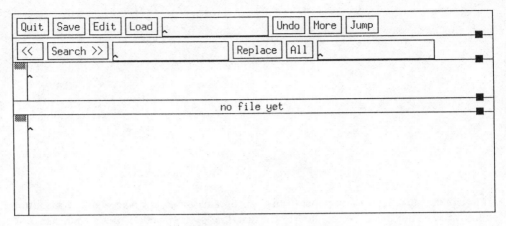

Figure 10.1 The xedit text editor

- The top section is the *Commands Menu*, with command boxes labelled Quit, Save, etc.

- The middle section is the *Message Window*, in which xedit displays error and status messages to you. You can also use this as a *scratch area*, and in it type pieces of text which you want to cut and paste into other places.

- The large section at the bottom is the *Edit Window*, which displays the text you are editing or creating.

When you are finished with the program, click the LEFT button on the Quit box. If you have made any changes which you haven't saved, xedit prints the warning

Unsaved changes. Save them, or press Quit again.

in the messages window; otherwise it quits.

10.1.2 Inserting Text

Ensure the pointer is in the edit window, and just type in the text you want to enter – all printing characters on the keyboard are inserted directly as you type them. As you type, you will notice that the new text is "pushing" a small caret cursor ahead of it: this cursor is the *insertion point*, or just *point* for short. Any text you type or paste-in is inserted at point. Point is always located *between* two characters, never on top of a character (as is the case with a normal terminal's cursor).

Automatic Line-Wrapping – xedit*'s "Paragraphs"*

When inserting text near the end of a line, if the word you are typing is too big to fit on the current line, xedit will move you onto the next line automatically. If you subsequently shorten the word so that it will fit on its original line, it will jump back up again.

This action is closely connected with xedit's definition of a paragraph: a section of text terminated by an explicit newline character. (In practice, it means text typed in continuously *without any newlines* inserted by you). xedit line-wraps only within a paragraph, and handles special cases correctly, e.g. where moving a word onto this line means this line must wrap onto the next etc.

Caution-1: this definition of a paragraph is what virtually every other Unix program considers to be a line. If you use xedit to edit a normal file, xedit will treat every line read in as a paragraph.

Caution-2: there is no obvious indication on the display to show whether a line on the screen has a newline at the end of it or not, i.e. whether xedit thinks it's the end of a line or of a paragraph.

Caution-3: files created using xedit may end up having very long lines when viewed by other programs. This may cause trouble.

Special Insertion Operations

There are a few special commands for inserting newlines in slightly differing ways:

Insert a newline, and position point after it : press RETURN. This inserts a newline in exactly the same way as any printing character, and is the normal way to move onto a new line if you are not relying on xedit's line wrapping.

Insert a newline and indent : press LINEFEED. This inserts a newline and moves point to the next line, but any printing text you type will be indented to align with the text above it. (Useful for typing tables, etc).

Insert a newline but don't move point : press ctl-O. This inserts a newline, but point remains on the same line. (Often used when you want to split a line and add text onto the end of the first of the two resulting lines).

10.1.3 Cutting and Pasting

You can select and cut text just as you did with xterm, but there is one annoying difference: when selecting by words or lines you have to double- or triple-click rapidly – you can't pause between button-down and button-up movements.

To paste in text at point, you can click the MIDDLE button as before, or press meta-Y.

10.1.4 Moving the Insertion Point

The simplest way to move point is to use the mouse: position the window text cursor (the vertical bar we saw in Figure 5.2) wherever you want, and click the LEFT mouse button. Point's caret marker jumps to the new position.

But often it is easier to move point using the keyboard – when you are editing it can break your rhythm to have to pick up the mouse, move it, and reposition your fingers on the keys again. xedit offers a large set of keyboard commands for moving point by character, word, line, or page:

Moving Point by Characters

This is the most basic form of moving:

Forward a character : press ctl-f or RIGHTARROW

Back a character : press ctl-b or LEFTARROW

Up a character, i.e. to previous line : press ctl-p or UPARROW

Down a character, i.e. to next line : press ctl-n or DOWNARROW

If you are near the beginning of a line, press ctl-b a few times: you move back onto the previous line. You can move back to where you were with a few ctl-f's. The same sort of effect occurs if you are on the top (bottom) line of the page: moving to the previous (next) line will cause the text to scroll so that the line you moved to is visible.

Moving by Words, Lines, and Paragraphs

These are the natural motions you need when editing text:

Forward a word : press meta-F or meta-f

Back a word : press meta-B or meta-b

Move to end of this line : press ctl-E

Move to beginning of this line : press ctl-A

Forward a paragraph : press meta-]

Back a paragraph : press meta-[

You can see a convention is starting to emerge: where ctl-*char* operates on units of characters, meta-*char* will usually do the same thing for a word. E.g. ctl-F moves forward a character, meta-F moves foward a word.

Large Motions - by Page and File

If you want to move around in large jumps you can use the scrollbar, just as you did with xterm. However, scrolling the text does *not* move point: as soon as you type or delete anything the text will automatically scroll back to where point was, so you can see what you were doing. If you want to scroll the display and move point too, use:

Forward a page : press `ctl-V`

Back a page : press `meta-V`

Go to beginning of the "file" : press `meta->`

Go to end of the "file" : press `meta-<`

10.1.5 Removing Unwanted Text – Deleting or Killing

There are two styles of text removal – *deleting* which removes the text and nothing more, and *killing* which removes the text but also stores it in a cut buffer so you can get it back again later. There are kill commands only for larger units of text – if you delete a character it's as easy to type it in again as to un-kill it.

In the descriptions below, "next" means "just after point", and "previous" means "just before point".

Deleting Text

Delete previous character : press `DELETE` or `BACKSPACE` or `ctl-H`.

Delete next character : press `ctl-D`

Delete next word : press `meta-d`

Delete previous word : press `meta-h`, or `meta-DELETE` or `meta-BACKSPACE`
without the `SHIFT` key

Caution: `meta-h` is *not* the same as `meta-H`.

If you are at the beginning of a line and press `DELETE`, this removes the newline at the end of the previous line, joining the two lines together.

Killing Text

Kill next word : press `meta-D`

Kill previous word : press `meta-H` or `shift-meta-DELETE` or `shift-meta-BACKSP`

Kill from cursor to end-of-line : press `ctl-K`

Kill from cursor to end-of-paragraph : press meta-K

Kill the current selection : press ctl-W. (The "selection" is the area of text
selected with the mouse buttons, exactly the same as when you are cutting
and pasting).

Un-Killing Text; Copying and Moving Text

Once you have killed some text, you can un-kill it by pressing ctl-Y: the last killed
text is inserted at point. There are a few points to note:

Only the last killed text is available for un-killing – you can't cycle back
through a series of kills.

The un-killed text is inserted at the current value of point – not where the
text was originally taken from.

You can un-kill the same text as many times as you want, i.e. pressing ctl-Y
doesn't affect the contents of the kill buffer.

Because killing works this way, you can use it for moving or copying areas of text.

To move text : kill it, move point to where you want to re-position the text,
and un-kill.

To copy text : kill it, un-kill it immediately so there is no net change, move
point to where you want the copied text, and un-kill.

10.1.6 Undoing Changes

If you discover that you made a change — killed or deleted or entered or pasted text
— which you don't want, you can *undo* it. Click the LEFT button on the Undo box:
the last change is undone. Undo'ing counts as a change itself, so if you click Undo
again, it negates the effect of the first undo; you can toggle like this forever if you
really want.

Undo only undoes the last change. If you want to go further back, you can undo
successively earlier changes by clicking on the More box.

10.1.7 Using Files

We saw that you can specify whether you want to edit an existing file when you start
the program. When it's running, too, you can access files. For this you will make use
of the text box located between Load and Undo which we'll call the "filename box".

To save the text to a file : click LEFT on the Save box; xedit writes the
text in its edit window to the file named in the filename box; if there is no
name, xedit complains with

`Save: no filename specified -- nothing saved`

in its message window, so you have to position the pointer in the filename box and type in a name before clicking on Save again. xedit confirms in its message window when it has saved the file.

To edit a different file : type the name of the file in the filename box, and click LEFT on Load. xedit will complain if it can't access the file.

To insert a file into the current text : press meta-I: xedit pops up a little window (Figure 10.2). In the text box at the top, type in the name of the file you want to insert, and then click on DoIt with the LEFT button. The contents of the file are inserted at point.

Figure 10.2 xedit's insert-file menu window.

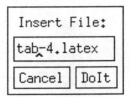

Note: when typing text in the filename box, and the text box in the "insert file" window, you can use all the keyboard-based editing commands that we've described. In fact, you are not limited to typing: you can cut from them and paste into them too.

Caution: when typing filenames, *don't* terminate them with a RETURN – xedit will treate the RETURN as part of the filename and will get confused.

10.1.8 Searching for a Specified Text String

If you want to find where a specific string occurs in the text you are editing:

1. Type the string in the box (which we'll call the "searchstring box") to the right of the Search >>.

2. Click the LEFT button on Search >>: point moves to the next occurrence of the string in the text, and highlights it.

Searching starts at point – by default xedit won't find occurrences of the string earlier in the buffer when searching forward. If you want to search backwards from point, click on the box << instead.

Caution: if you click on Search>> or << when there is no text in the searchstring box, xedit copies into the box the last piece of text selected in any **X** application on your machine and searches for that. This can be very surprising if you are not expecting it.

10.1.9 Replacing one String with Another

If you want to replace multiple occurrences of one string (the "old") with another ("the new"):

1. Search for the first occurrence of the new string, as descibed in the previous section.

2. Type the new string in the "replace-string box" which is to the right of the $\boxed{\text{All}}$ box.

3. Click the LEFT button on $\boxed{\text{Replace}}$: the old string is replaced by the new, and point moves to the next occurrence of the old string.

4. If you want to replace this one too, click $\boxed{\text{Replace}}$ again, otherwise ...

5. ... If you don't want to replace this one, but will want some later occurrences changed, click on $\boxed{\text{Search>>}}$ until you get to where you want, and then you can replace again.

You can't replace while moving backwards through the file, so e.g. you can't replace occurrences located before point in a simple way.

   Caution: if you try to replace and you are not currently positioned at an occurrence of the old string due to an earlier search, xedit complains with the message:

   ReplaceOne: nothing replaced

But the $\boxed{\text{Replace}}$ itself caused a search to be done, so you can continue just by clicking $\boxed{\text{Replace}}$ again.

Replacing Every Occurrence of a String

If you want to replace *every* occurrence of the old string with the new, click on $\boxed{\text{All}}$.

   Caution: $\boxed{\text{All}}$ replaces every occurrence, everywhere in the text, *not* just those occurrences after point.

10.1.10 Miscellaneous Functions

To redraw the text display : e.g. if the window has got garbled for some reason, press ctl-L

To scroll one line forward : press ctl-Z

To scroll one line backwards : press meta-Z

To jump to a specific-numbered line : in the message window, type in the number of the line you want to jump to, with the mouse select the text you've just typed, and click on ⬚Jump with the LEFT button: point jumps to the beginning of the line specified. (If there is a piece of text *in any application* on your screen which contains the number you want, you can select that instead — you don't have to use xedit's message window).

That finishes our description of xedit. In the next section we move onto another application program, and we will see some similarities in the way the user interface operates.

10.2   Reading Manual Pages – xman

xman lets you browse through the Unix manpages on the system, selecting the items you want from a series of menus.

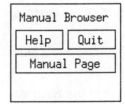

Figure 10.3 xman's main options window

To start the program, in an xterm window enter the command "xterm &": xman starts and displays its main options window, shown in Figure 10.3. The next sections describe these options in detail.

10.2.1   On-Line Help for xman Itself

xman has its own in-built help option. To use it, click ⬚Help in the options window. xman creates its "Xman Help" window, shown in Figure 10.4. You can scroll through the help text using the scrollbar and the mouse. Alternately, in the text window itself:

To move forward through the text : press f, or click the LEFT button, and you move forward by a pageful.

To move back : press b or click the RIGHT button, and you move back a pageful of text.

Caution: moving back through the text by clicking RIGHT or pressing b may not work reliably.

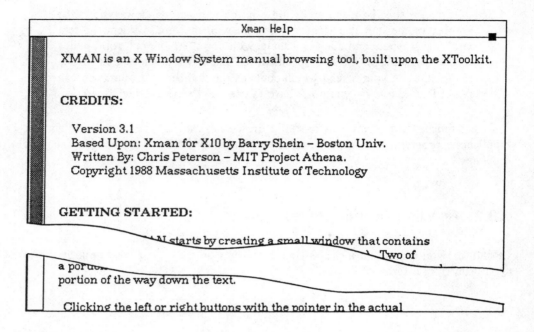

Figure 10.4 xman's Help window

Other Options in the Help Window

Move the pointer into the Help window's top border. The menu shown in Figure 10.5 pops down. The available options are:

Remove Help : remove this window, but leave any other xman windows as they are. (In our case, we've still got the main options window at this point).

Open New Manpage : is equivalent to the Manual Page box in the main options window, and is described below.

Quit : causes the whole program to exit.

To select an option, move the pointer into its menu area and click with the LEFT button; if you don't want to select anything, just move the pointer out of the menu.

Caution: xman pops up its menu *any* time the pointer enters the top border. This can be irritating if you cross over the border by accident when you are moving the pointer for another purpose.

```
┌─────────────────────────┐
│ Xman Options            │
├─────────────────────────┤
│ Change Section          │
├─────────────────────────┤
│ Display Directory        │
├─────────────────────────┤
│ Display Manual Page      │
├─────────────────────────┤
│ Help                    │
├─────────────────────────┤
│ Search                  │
├─────────────────────────┤
│ Show Both Screens        │
├─────────────────────────┤
│ Remove Help             │
├─────────────────────────┤
│ Open New Manpage         │
├─────────────────────────┤
│ Quit                    │
└─────────────────────────┘
```

Figure 10.5 xman's Help- and Manpage-window
options menu

10.2.2 How to Read a Manpage

Click on │Manual Page│ in the main options window: xman creates a manpage window, which initially contains the same text as the help window we saw above.

From this point, to read a manpage you follow a three-step process:

1. Choose which section of the manual you want to look at. ("Section" refers to the standard division of the Unix manpages, viz. section no. 1 contains the user commands, no. 2 contains system calls, etc.)

2. Display the directory for the section you chose, and then choose an entry from the directory.

3. Read the displayed manpage.

Choosing a Section of the Manual

When it starts, xman by default has selected Section 1 of the manual. If that's the section you want, you can omit this step in the procedure. Otherwise, to specify a section:

```
┌──────────────────────────┐
│ Manual Sections          │
├──────────────────────────┤
│ User Commands (1)        │
├──────────────────────────┤
│ System Calls (2)         │
├──────────────────────────┤
│ Subroutines (3)          │
├──────────────────────────┤
│ Devices (4)              │
├──────────────────────────┤
│ File Formats (5)         │
├──────────────────────────┤
│ Games (6)                │
├──────────────────────────┤
│ Miscellaneous (7)        │
├──────────────────────────┤
│ Sys. Administration (8)  │
├──────────────────────────┤
│ Local (1)                │
├──────────────────────────┤
│ New (n)                  │
└──────────────────────────┘
```

Figure 10.6 xman's Manual Sections menu

1. In the manpage window, move the pointer into the top border. The same menu pops up as we got in the help window. Now, however, all the selections are available.

2. Click on the ⌐Change Section⌐ item: the menu is replaced by the one listing the available manual sections (Figure 10.6).

3. Click on the section you want: xman displays a directory of the manpage entries in the manpage window (Figure 10.7).

```
                          Directory of: New (n)                         ■
X            Xserver     bdftosnf    bitmap      ico          maze      mkfontdir
muncher      plaid       puzzle      resize      showsnf      uwm       x10tox11
xbiff        xcalc       xclipboard  xclock      xcutsel      xdm       xdpr
xdpyinfo     xedit       xev         xeyes       xfd          xhost     xinit
xkill        xload       xlogo       xlsfonts    xlswins      xmag      xman
xmh          xmodmap     xpr         xprop       xpseudoroot  xrdb      xrefresh
xset         xsetroot    xterm       xwd         xwininfo     xwud
```

Figure 10.7 xman's directory of Manpage entries

Display the Directory; Choose the Manpage

If you have explicitly chosen a manual section as described above, xman has already displayed a directory of manpages. Otherwise, pop-down the menu from the top border, and click on ⌐Display Directory⌐ and you get the manpage directory as above.

To choose a manpage from the directory: just click on the name you want in the directory, and xman displays the manpage in the window (Figure 10.8). (If the directory listing is too big for all of it to fit in the window, it will have a scrollbar on one side. So if the name you want isn't visible, you can scroll the directory to the required position and then click).

Looking at a Manpage

Once the manpage is in the window, you have several options:

Scrolling the manpage text : you scroll the manpage exactly as you did with the help text, i.e. press f or click LEFT to move forward, b or RIGHT to move back.

Switching to/from the directory : click the MIDDLE button in the manpage window, and the text is replaced with the directory listing. (And clicking in the directory switches you back to the last manpage text displayed).

Searching for a specific manpage :

The current manual page is: bitmap.

BITMAP(1)   **USER COMMANDS**   BITMAP(1)

NAME
  bitmap, bmtoa, atobm – bitmap editor and converter utilities
  for X

SYNOPSIS
  bitmap [–options ...] *filename* *WIDTH*x*HEIGHT*

  bmtoa [–chars ...] [*filename*]

  atobm [–chars *cc*] [–name *variable*] [–xhot *number*] [–yhot
  number] [*filename*]

DESCRIPTION
  The *bitmap* program is a rudimentary tool for creating or
  editing rectangular images made up of 1's and 0's. Bitmaps
  are used in X for defining clipping regions, cursor shapes,
  icon shapes, and tile and stipple patterns.

  The *bmtoa* and *atobm* filters convert *bitmap* files (FILE FOR–
  MAT) to and from ASCII strings. They are most commonly used
  to quickly print out bitmaps and to generate versions for
  including in text.

USAGE
  Bitmap displays grid in which each square represents a single bit in the picture being edited. Squares can be set,
  cleared, or inverted directly with the buttons on the
  pointer and a menu of higher level operations such as draw
  line and fill circle is provided to the side of the grid.
  Actual size versions of the bitmap as it would appear normally and inverted appear below the menu.

  If the bitmap is to be used for defining a cursor, one of
  the squares in the images may be designated as the *hotspot*.
  This determines where the cursor is actually pointing. For
  cursors with sharp tips (such as arrows or fingers), this is

Figure 10.8 xman window displaying a Manpage

Figure 10.9 xman's search window

```
┌─────────────────────────────┐
│ Type string to search for   │
│ ┌─────────────────────────┐ │
│ │bitmap↲                  │ │
│ └─────────────────────────┘ │
│ ┌─────────────┐ ┌─────────┐ │
│ │ Manual Page │ │ Apropos │ │
│ └─────────────┘ └─────────┘ │
│ ┌─────────────────────────┐ │
│ │         Cancel          │ │
│ └─────────────────────────┘ │
└─────────────────────────────┘
```

1. Pop down the menu from the top border and select Search .
   xman pops up a search window (Figure 10.9).

2. In the text box at the top, type in the name of the manpage you
   want (without any section suffix, e.g. you type diff, not diff(1)
   or diff.1

3. Click on Manual Page : xman displays the manpage you've
   asked for. (If it can't find it, it prints a message in the manpage
   window's top border).

   Caution: the name you enter must be complete (di won't match
   diff), and must match the manpage name exactly for case (xaddhost won't match XAddHost).

Displaying Several Items Together

You can create extra xman windows any time you want. Pop down the menu from the
top border, and select Open New Manpage to create a manpage window, or Help to
create an xman help window.

   You can create as many different windows as you like, and all can be managed
independently as far as the window manager is concerned, e.g. you can resize some,
iconify others, etc. For clarity, the icons for the main options window, the help window
and the manpage window are different (Figure 10.10a, Figure 10.10b and Figure 10.10c).
(The "U.P.M." in the icons stands for "Unix Programmer's Manual").

a   b   c

Figure 10.10 xman's various icons

   Within any one xman window, you can display both the directory and the manpage
by selecting Show Both Screens : the window splits showing the directory in the top
portion, and the manpage in the bottom (Figure 10.11). (When you have done this, the
top-border menu will change slightly: the Display Directory and Display Manual Page

```
┌──────────────────────────────────────────────────────────────────┐
│                   Directory of: New (n)                           ■│
│ X          Xserver     bdftosnf    ▣bitmap▣    ico       maze       mkfontdir │
│ muncher    plaid       puzzle      resize      showsnf   uwm        x10tox11  │
│ xbiff      xcalc       xclipboard  xclock      xcutsel   xdm        xdpr      │
│ xdpyinfo   xedit       xev         xeyes       xfd       xhost      xinit     │
│ xkill      xload       xlogo       xlsfonts    xlswins   xmag       xman     ■│
├──────────────────────────────────────────────────────────────────┤
│                                                                    │
│  BITMAP(1)            USER COMMANDS            BITMAP(1)            │
│                                                                    │
│                                                                    │
│  NAME                                                              │
│    bitmap, bmtoa, atobm – bitmap editor and converter utilities    │
│    for X                                                           │
│                                                                    │
│  SYNOPSIS                                                          │
│    bitmap [–options ...] *filename WIDTHxHEIGHT*                   │
│                                                                    │
│    bmtoa [–chars ...] [*filename*]                                │
│                                                                    │
│    atobm [–chars *cc*] [–name *variable*] [–xhot *number*] [–yhot  │
│    *number*] [*filename*]                                         │
│                                                                    │
│  DESCRIPTION                                                       │
│    The *bitmap* program is a rudimentary tool for creating or      │
│    editing rectangular images made up of 1's and 0's. Bitmaps      │
│    are used in X for defining clipping regions, cursor shapes,     │
│    icon shapes, and tile and stipple patterns.                    │
│                                                                    │
│    The *bmtoa* and *atobm* filters convert *bitmap* files (FILE FOR-│
│    MAT) to and from ASCII strings. They are most commonly used    │
│    to quickly print out bitmaps and to generate versions for      │
│    including in text.                                             │
│                                                                    │
│  USAGE                                                             │
│    *Bitmap* displays grid in which each square represents a sin-   │
│    gle bit in the picture being edited. Squares can be set,        │
│    cleared, or inverted directly with the buttons on the          │
│    pointer and a menu of higher level operations such as draw      │
│    line and fill circle is provided to the side of the grid.       │
│    Actual size versions of the bitmap as it would appear nor-      │
│                                                                    │
└──────────────────────────────────────────────────────────────────┘
```

Figure 10.11 Split xman window showing both directory and manpage

selections are shown in grey — as they are not currently applicable — and the menu item which was [Show Both Screens] now reads [Show One Screen]).

You can change the relative sizes of the two "panes" of the window if you want. Near the right-hand side of the line dividing the window there is a small black square, called a *grip*.

1. Position the pointer on the grip.

2. Press any mouse button, and keeping it pressed ...

3. ... Drag the separating line to where you want it.

4. Release the button: the panes of the window are re-arranged appropriately.

Caution: you will see many of these grips in various **X** applications, but relatively few of them let you pull them about to re-proportion their neighbouring windows. E.g. nothing happens if you try to pull the grip on the line separating xman's top border from the text or directory window.

10.3   Mail/Message Handling System – xmh

xmh is an **X** interface to the mh mail/message handling system. When you start it up, xmh creates a window like that in Figure 10.12.

The window-related aspects of the program – editing text, and managing the window panes – are very much the same as in xedit and xman, and indeed are provided by the same internal mechanisms. Because of this, and because most of the description of the program concerns its mail functionality and has little to do with **X**, we won't discuss it further. If you want to use the program, the manpage contains a simple but comprehensive description.

10.4   Conclusion/Summary

Here you have started to see some consistent features emerge in the user interface offered by **X** application programs, e.g. the operation of scrollbars, and general text-editing facilities. This chapter just about concludes our description of the general user programs included in the **core** release — the next chapter deals with some demonstration programs, and after that we move into Part 3 of the book which deals with customising the system.

But in many ways you have only now started to take real advantage of the system. What you need now is more application programs, to let you do a wider range of work within the **X** framework. This is where the **contrib** portion of the MIT release is

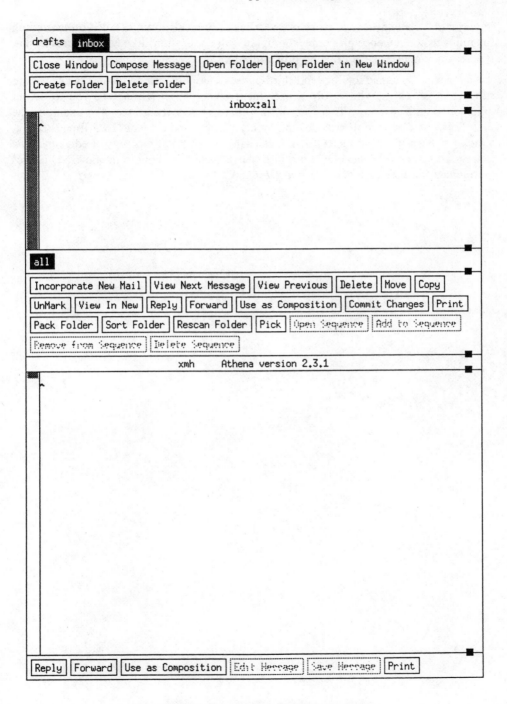

Figure 10.12 The xmh mail-handler window

important. It contains a wide range of programs at all levels, from detailed programming functions to convenience programs, through to full applications like xdvi for previewing typeset documents, or the drawing program xfig.

Increasingly, manufacturers and third-party vendors of programs and packages are supporting **X**, either with a full **X** user interface, or at least enabling you to output graphics to an **X** window. There are other sources of **X** software too. For example, the Free Software Foundation provides the highly flexible and elegant GNU Emacs editor, which has been integrated into **X**. (In fact, many of the xedit bindings of edit functions to keys are exactly the same as those in Emacs). Details of how to obtain GNU Emacs are included in the appendix *"How to Obtain X"*.

Chapter 11 Demos and Games

There are a few demos and only one game provided with the **core** MIT release. They give some indication of the power of the window system, and can give pretty effects — especially on colour screens.

11.1 Find a Path Through a Random Maze – maze

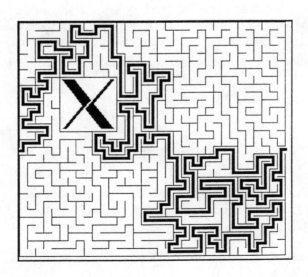

Figure 11.1 The maze program

maze creates a random maze in a window (Figure 11.1). It searches for the path which will lead it through the maze from the entrance to the exit. It traces its tracks as it proceeds, erasing them when it has to backtrack out of a blind alley.

You can start, pause, continue or abort the program with the mouse buttons, as described in the manpage. maze doesn't support colour.

Caution: the action of the MIDDLE button, for pausing and restarting, is unreliable.

11.2 Big Eyes which Stare at the Pointer – xeyes

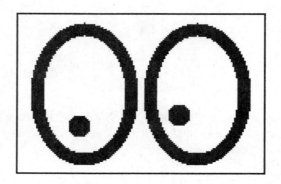

Figure 11.2 The xeyes program

xeyes draws two big eyes in a window, and they keep on looking forever at the pointer (Figure 11.2). As the pointer moves around, the eyes adjust accordingly (and if you position the pointer between the eyes themselves, they go cross-eyed!)

You can explicitly set the colour for each element of the window – pupils, background, outline, etc.

Caution: xeyes can really slow down your system.

11.3 The "Re-Order the Tiles" Game – puzzle

puzzle is the classic game where 15 numbered square tiles are enclosed in a 4x4 frame, and you have to arrange them into order again by sliding the tiles about. (Figure 11.3).

You use the mouse buttons to control the game:

To start the game : Re-scramble the tiles by clicking any button in the top-left box of the control bar.

To move tiles : position the pointer in the same row or column as the empty space. Click on a tile to move that tile and all the others in front of it into the empty space. (So after the move, the empty space is in the location where you clicked).

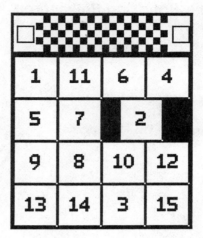

Figure 11.3 The puzzle game

To cheat, and get puzzle to solve itself : click any button on the right-hand box in the control bar.

To exit : click the MIDDLE button in the middle of the control bar.

11.3.1 puzzle's Command-Line Options

To use a size other than 4x4 : use the option -size *width* x *height* where the dimensions are in "tiles".

To alter the rate at which tiles are moved : use -speed *num* where *num* is the number of moves per second. (Default: 5).

11.4 Print a Large X Logo – xlogo

xlogo creates a window and prints the X logo in it (Figure 11.4). If you resize the window, the logo is drawn again, as large as possible.

Figure 11.4 The xlogo program

11.5   The Bouncing Polyhedron – ico

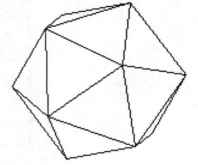

Figure 11.5 The ico program

ico creates a window and in it an icosahedron – a solid body with 12 faces – as shown in Figure 11.5. The figure is animated, and bounces around the window. On mono displays, you can only have a wire-frame figure (use option -i for reverse video), but on colour you can have solid coloured faces. As an example try:

```
ico -noedges -faces -colors red blue yellow green
```

You can have the figure created and set bouncing in the root (background) window instead of a special window of its own using the -r option. Additionally, ico supports a number of polyhedron types, not just the icosahedron: for a full list enter the command:

```
ico -objhelp
```

11.6   Dynamic Geometric Patterns – muncher **and** plaid

muncher and plaid repeatedly draw changing "interesting" geometric patterns (Figure 11.6a and Figure 11.6b).

11.7   Conclusion

There isn't a very wide range of demo programs supplied as part of the **core** distribution. If you have access to the **contrib** tapes, you may find the following programs of interest:

paint : a simple paint program (like a drawing program, but you can texture
or colour areas, not just lines).

xcolors : a nice demo illustrating all the named colours on your system.

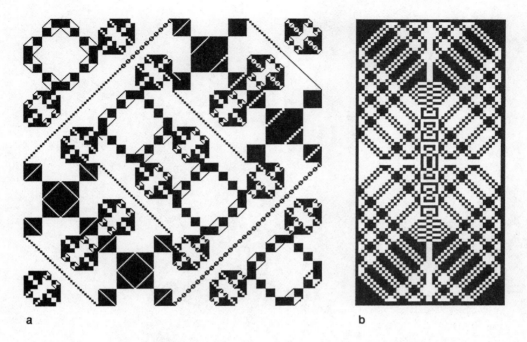

a   b

Figure 11.6 The muncher and plaid programs

xfish : sets fish swimming all over your background window. The zany part is that you can shoot them with the mouse.

qix : a version of the qix arcade game.

xmille : plays the card game Milles Bournes with you.

xsol : plays a solitaire card game with you.

xtrek : an addictive space game.

Part 3

Customising the System

Chapter 12 **Information and Status Programs**

In this chapter we describe a number of programs which give you information about the window system itself, and its current status. These include tools for examining the various properties of the windows on the system, and also a program which gives you an insight into how **X**'s event mechanism works.

These programs are useful in a number of ways:

- When you are getting used to the system, the information they give you on the system's internal organisation and operation can add to your understanding of what is happening.

- They help you identify, and give you information on, components of the system which you want to process in some way. (E.g. you need to find the window-id of a window, so you can dump it with xwd).

- You will often use the information obtained from them as input to the customisation tools described in the later chapters.

12.1 List Your X Server's Characteristics – xdpyinfo

xdpyinfo lists various items of information about your **X** server and the screens it controls. A typical output (from a server running on a Sun 3/50 monochrome workstation) is shown in Figure 12.1.

12.2 Getting Information About Windows

There are three programs which give you information about the windows currently on your display. They each address particular, different, aspects of the system:

```
venus% xdpyinfo
name of display:    unix:0.0
version number:    11.0
vendor string:    MIT X Consortium
vendor release number:    3
maximum request size:  16384 longwords (65536 bytes)
motion buffer size:  0
bitmap unit, bit order, padding:    32, MSBFirst, 32
image byte order:    MSBFirst
keycode range:    minimum 8, maximum 129
default screen number:    0
number of screens:    1

screen #0:
  dimensions:    1152x900 pixels (325x254 millimeters)
  resolution:    90x90 dots per inch
  root window id:    0x8006b
  depth of root window:    1 plane
  number of colormaps:    minimum 1, maximum 1
  default colormap:    0x80065
  default number of colormap cells:    2
  preallocated pixels:    black 1, white 0
  options:    backing-store YES, save-unders YES
  current input event mask:    0x1b8003c
    ButtonPressMask            ButtonReleaseMask        EnterWindowMask
    LeaveWindowMask            SubstructureNotifyMask   SubstructureRedirectMask
    FocusChangeMask            ColormapChangeMask       OwnerGrabButtonMask
  number of visuals:    1
  default visual id:  0x80064
  visual:
    visual id:    0x80064
    class:    StaticGray
    depth:    1 plane
    size of colormap:    2 entries
    red, green, blue masks:    0x0, 0x0, 0x0
    significant bits in color specification:    1 bits
venus% []
```

Figure 12.1 Typical output from the xdpyinfo program

1. Printing the Hierarchy of Windows – xlswins

2. Detailed Information About a Single Window – xwininfo

3. Listing Window Properties – xprop

12.2.1   Printing the Hierarchy of Windows – xlswins

As mentioned in Part 1, all windows on the system are arranged in a hierarchy or tree, with the root window (also called the background window) at the top. Below this are the application windows, and each application may have a whole hierarchy of sub-windows of its own.

xlswins prints out this tree structure, starting either at the root or from a specified window lower down in the tree. For each window, xlswins lists the window's window-id and its name (if it has one) in parentheses; this window's children are listed on subsequent lines, indented two spaces further to the right to show they are lower down in the tree. The following figures show the output for three sub-trees all relating to a single xman application, and show how xlswins can give an insight into the structure of the system.

Figure 12.2a: this is the tree for xman's main options menu. You can see that within the application window (0x600011) there is another window (0x600012) which contains the remaining four windows; without knowing anything about the program sources, you could reasonably guess that this is some sort of container window which somehow manages the layout of its child windows. (In Chapter 15, we describe the "X Toolkit" which many applications are based on. It uses a hierarchy of *widgets* — windows plus associated functions — to provide the user-interface parts of the application. When you are familiar with the ideas in the Toolkit, you will have a better idea of X program structure, and could then guess that the window 0x600011 is something like a Box widget, which is managing the layout of the others. The four lowest level windows are presumably the Label widget for the "Manual Browser" title, plus three widgets for the option buttons).

Figure 12.2b: is the tree for an xman manpage window. This is more complex than the previous example, and it's not clear looking at a manpage where all these windows and sub-windows are. So ...

Figure 12.2c: this is a more detailed form of xlswins output, using the command-line option -l, for the same sub-tree as before. The extra information is the depth of nesting, the geometry of the window relative to its parent, and the location of its top-left corner relative to the root window (i.e. the window's absolute position on the screen). Now you have the location of the windows, you can look and see what's on the screen at that position. (If you are going to do a lot of this sort of thing, you'd probably need to make a ruler calibrated for pixels). If you still can't understand what's there, try running xwd, specifying the window-id given in the xlswins output. In this figure, we can see that window (0x60005d) is tall and very thin, so it is probably the scrollbar. So we tried the command:

```
xwd -id 0x60005d | xwud
```

and indeed a picture of xman's scrollbar appeared. This is essentially the technique we used to print uwm's pop-up menus, as we discussed in Section 9.2.1, (although there we sent the output to a file rather than immediately piping it to another program). You can use this method to analyse any window, printing successively lower levels in the window-tree.

Caution: not all windows are printable. If you try to print one of these, you will get an error like:

```
X Protocol error: BadMatch, invalid parameter
attributes
Major opcode of failed request: 73 (X_GetImage)
...
```

For reasons of space, we have included only three small portions of a complete xlswins output. If you run it yourself on a system which has several applications active, you will see all the sub-trees relating to menus for uwm and xterm, and so on, and the individual windows which are the command buttons in xmh and xedit.

```
0x600011 (xman)
  0x600012 ()
    0x600013 ()
    0x600014 ()
    0x600015 ()
    0x600016 ()
```

a

```
0x600054 (xman)
  0x600055 ()
    0x600059 ()
    0x60005a ()
      0x60005b ()
      0x60005c ()
      0x60005d ()
    0x60005e ()
    0x60005f ()
    0x600060 ()
    0x600061 ()
      0x600062 ()
        0x600063 ()
```

b

```
0:  0x600054 (xman)    576x675+687+291  +687+291
1:    0x600055 ()      576x675+0+0  +688+292
2:      0x600059 ()    576x17+-1+-1  +687+291
2:      0x60005a ()    576x657+-1+17  +687+309
3:        0x60005b ()    558x657+18+0  +706+310
3:        0x60005c ()    574x16+0+-26  +688+284
3:        0x60005d ()    16x655+0+0  +688+310
2:      0x60005e ()    8x8+558+13  +1246+305
2:      0x60005f ()    8x8+558+671  +1246+963
2:      0x600060 ()    8x8+0+0  +688+292
2:      0x600061 ()    20x19+0+0  +688+292
3:        0x600062 ()    20x19+0+0  +689+293
4:          0x600063 ()    20x19+0+0  +689+293
```

c

Figure 12.2 Three outputs for xlswins

12.2.2 Detailed Information About a Single Window – xwininfo

xwininfo gives you a lot of information about one specific window. You can tell xwininfo which part of the information you want with command-line options (which are described in the manpage). The sample output shown in Figure 12.3 contains a full listing (obtained by specifying option -all) for the window from which the figure itself was printed.

You specify which window you are interested in in exactly the same way as with xwd, viz:

- Interactively (the default): xwininfo gives you a cross-hairs cursor when it starts; you click this on the window you want.

- Using command-line options: you can specify the root window using the option -root; specify some other window using -id *window-id*.

You can see that the information given can be divided into a few categories:

This window's *window-id* : the window system's reference which identifies this window uniquely. As you've already seen, several programs (including xwininfo itself) let you specify a number by window-id. E.g. if you want to dump a window, you can first run xwininfo to get its window-id, and then use that as the argument to xwd's -id option.

Hierarchy information : the id's of the root window and this window's parent, the number of children, and their id's. This duplicates the information you get from xlswins, but here the information is limited to the window's immediate children — you are shown only one level lower, not the whole sub-tree.

Geometry details : the size and position of the window, and the location of its corners.

Server-related reconfiguration parameters : such as "gravity" and "backing store" states. These are used by the server when the window changes size, or is covered by another window and then exposed again. You will not use them explicitly yourself, but they can help you understand how the system is behaving.

Event parameters : again, these are used by the server, not the user.

Window manager information : in the overview of the system, you saw that applications communicate with window managers by giving them "hints" about their preferred size, and limitations as to how they are resized. This part of xwininfo's output shows you these data. The Program supplied location is where the application suggests it be placed; if you give a geometry spec, either on the command-line or in a resource file, this will be

```
venus% xwininfo -all

xwininfo ==> Please select the window about which you
         ==> would like information by clicking the
         ==> mouse in that window.

xwininfo ==> Window id: 0x90000f (xterm)

         ==> Root window id: 0x8006b ( X Root Window )
         ==> Parent window id: 0x8006b ( X Root Window )
         ==> Number of children: 1
             ==> Child window id: 0x900012 (has no name)

         ==> Upper left X: 165
         ==> Upper left Y: 9
         ==> Width: 515
         ==> Height: 886
         ==> Depth: 1
         ==> Border width: 1
         ==> Window class: InputOutput
         ==> Colormap: 0x80065
         ==> Window Bit Gravity State: NorthWestGravity
         ==> Window Window Gravity State: NorthWestGravity
         ==> Window Backing Store State: NotUseful
         ==> Window Save Under State: no
         ==> Window Map State: IsViewable
         ==> Window Override Redirect State: no
         ==> Corners:  +165+9  -470+9  -470-3  +165-3

         ==> Bit gravity: NorthWestGravity
         ==> Window gravity: NorthWestGravity
         ==> Backing-store hint: NotUseful
         ==> Backing-planes to be preserved: 0xffffffff
         ==> Backing pixel: 0
         ==> Save-unders: No

         ==> Someone wants these events:
             ==> KeyPress
             ==> EnterWindow
             ==> LeaveWindow
             ==> StructureNotify
             ==> FocusChange
             ==> ColormapChange
         ==> Do not prograte these events:
         ==> Override redirection?: No

         ==> Window manager hints:

             ==> Client accepts input or input focus: Yes
             ==> Initial state is Normal State

         ==> Normal window size hints:

             ==> Program supplied location: 1, 1
             ==> Program supplied size: 564 by 340
             ==> Program supplied minimum size: 4 by 4
             ==> Program supplied x resize increment: 7
             ==> Program supplied y resize increment: 14
             ==> Program supplied size in resize increments:  80 by 24

         ==> No zoom window size hints defined

venus% █
```

Figure 12.3 Typical xwininfo output

shown as User supplied location instead. The same is true for the size. The resize increments explain why some windows (notably xterm and xfd) can't be sized to an arbitrary number of pixels: the application has told the window manager that it is only sensible to resize in multiples of these increments. (For xterm and xfd these are related to the size of the character font being used). You often use these to see the current position of the window, so you can recreate it in the same position later. (E.g. when you enter a spec into a resource database to define a default startup location for an application, or specify -geometry *spec* for the application in a shell script or other list of commands).

12.2.3 Listing Window Properties – xprop

As we mentioned in the overview, a *property* is a named piece of data associated with a window. The program xprop lets you list all the properties for a particular window. You can also print the properties of a font.

You select a window in the usual way — by clicking, or using the -root or -id *wid* options. To specify a font, use the option -font *fontname*.

For a window, the format of the display is: for each property, its name is given, the the property type or format in parentheses, and finally the value of the property. Most of the properties you will meet are of type STRING, and the values are enclosed in double-quotes. Other types are formatted appropriately, and it's clear what the values mean. The format of the font display is slightly different, in particular no type is given, but its meaning is obvious also.

Caution: the manpage for xprop is quite complicated. Until you are quite proficient with **X**, you can forget all about property formats, so the only parts of the manpage you need to bother with are the descriptions of some of the options and the first three or four paragraphs of the DESCRIPTION section.

Let's now look at the different outputs you get for an application window, the root window, and a font.

Application Window Properties

Figure 12.4 shows the xprop output for an application window. You have already seen some of the information, in xwininfo, but here you can see that it is stored in the named properties WM_NORMAL_HINTS and WM_HINTS.

The other items shown here are:

WM_COMMAND : the actual command-line used to start this application, broken into "words", with each word quoted.

WM_CLIENT_MACHINE : the name of the *client* on which this application is running. (In the example here, the application is running on the same

```
venus% xprop
WM_COMMAND(STRING) = { "xterm", "-fn", "sun-screen*", "-name",
"demo", "-title", "demo (status and info)" }
WM_CLIENT_MACHINE(STRING) = "venus"
WM_CLASS(STRING) = "demo", "XTerm"
WM_NORMAL_HINTS(WM_SIZE_HINTS):
                program specified location: 1, 1
                program specified size: 564 by 340
                program specified minimum size: 4 by 4
                program specified resize increment: 7 by 14
WM_HINTS(WM_HINTS):
                Client accepts input or input focus: True
                Initial state is Normal State.
WM_ICON_NAME(STRING) = "demo"
WM_NAME(STRING) = "demo (status and info)"
venus% ▊
```

Figure 12.4 Property listing for an application window

machine — venus — as the server).

WM_CLASS : two strings giving the instance name of the application, and its
class name. The instance name is what is set when you use the command-
line option -name.

WM_ICON_NAME : the name to be displayed in the application's icon.(Only
if your window manager supports it. For this example, we had explicitly
set the icon name using a procedure which is described in Chapter 19).

WM_NAME : confusingly, this is *not* the application name, but the title
defined for the window with the option -title. Some window managers may
display this in a title bar attached to the application window.

Caution: the command-line options -name and -title mentioned above are widely
used, but they are not universal. They are provided as standard options by programs
written using the **X** Toolkit (see Chapter 15).

Properties of the Root Window

Figure 12.5 shows the xprop output for our root window. Sensibly, it doesn't have
any window manager properties itself (because of course a window manager doesn't
reconfigure the root window).

The interesting items here are:

RESOURCE_MANAGER : this root-window property is one of the sources
of input for the resource mechanism described in Chapter 16. We'll describe
it in detail there.

```
venus% xprop -root
CUT_BUFFER6(STRING) = " void report_error()"
CUT_BUFFER5(STRING) = "\tputs(\"ev\")"
CUT_BUFFER4(STRING) = "\tsleep(5);\n\t}"
CUT_BUFFER3(STRING) = "    for (i = 0; i < 5; i++)"
CUT_BUFFER2(STRING) = " "
CUT_BUFFER1(STRING) = "#include <stdio.h>"
CUT_BUFFER0(STRING) = "main()\n{\n    if "
CUT_BUFFER7(STRING) = "~"
WM_NAME(STRING) = " X Root Window "
RESOURCE_MANAGER(STRING) = "*Command*Foreground:\tpink\nXTerm*B
acground:\t\\#242\nXTerm*BorderColour:\tblue\nXTerm*Foreground:
\tyellow\nXTerm*boldFont:\t*-courier-bold-r-*-180-*\nXTerm*font
:\t*-courier-medium-r-*-180-*\ndemo*boldFont:\t*-courier-bold-r
-*-240-*\ndemo*font:\t*-courier-medium-r-*-240-*\nxload*Geometr
y:\t+0+0\nxload*Height:\t80\nxload*Width:\t1152\n"
venus% █
```

Figure 12.5 Property listing for the root window

Several CUT_BUFFERs : when you cut text (as in "cut and paste"), the text
you cut is placed in a cut buffer. These buffers are stored as properties of
the root window. For cutting, the buffers are usually used in a ring, e.g.
if the the last one used was no. 5, the next to be used will be no. 6, then
no. 7, then no. 0, no. 1, etc. (But pasting is of course from the last buffer
used for a cut).

Font Properties

Figure 12.6 lists the properties of a font which we specified as *times*bold*-i-*-180-*.
Initially at least, you won't be concerned with most of this information, but you may
be interested in the FULL_NAME and POINT_SIZE (in tenths of points, i.e. 1/720'ths
of an inch). Chapter 13 gives more information on fonts.

12.3 Looking at X Events – xev

Events more or less drive the whole window system. All input — whether from mouse
or keyboard — is handled through events, and events are also used to inform windows of
reconfiguration and exposure. The xev program lets you see what events are generated
when various actions occur, together with the information associated with that event.

When xev starts, it creates a window like that shown in Figure 12.7, and in the
window it was started from it lists the event details, as shown in Figure 12.8.

xev is a useful program for "experimenting" with the system, as it gives a lot of
detail of the system's internal operation. There are two extra command-line options

```
xprop -font "*times*180*"
FONTNAME_REGISTRY = 0x54
FAMILY_NAME = Times
FOUNDRY = 0x57
WEIGHT_NAME = 0x70
SETWIDTH_NAME = 0x5d
SLANT = 0x74
ADD_STYLE_NAME = 0x54
PIXEL_SIZE = 0x12
POINT_SIZE = 180
RESOLUTION_X = 0x4b
RESOLUTION_Y = 0x4b
SPACING = 0x63
AVERAGE_WIDTH = 0x62
CHARSET_REGISTRY = 0x66
CHARSET_ENCODING = 0x68
DEVICE_FONT_NAME = 0x80
CHARSET_COLLECTIONS = 0x6c
FULL_NAME = Times Bold Italic
COPYRIGHT = Copyright (c) 1984,
 1987 Adobe Systems, Inc., Port
ions Copyright 1988 Digital Equ
ipment Corp.
CAP_HEIGHT = 0xd
X_HEIGHT = 8
FONT: font id # 0x98
WEIGHT = 280
RESOLUTION = 103
QUAD_WIDTH = 11
venus% █
```

Figure 12.6 Property listing for a font

(not listed in the manpage) which let you affect how xev behaves:

   -bs *option* : this changes the xev's hints to the server about whether to use
   backing store or not; using backing store should decrease the number of exposure events, and so the work the application has to do to keep its window
   up to date. Valid *option*s are always, whenmapped, and notuseful.

   -s : enables save-unders, i.e. the server is asked to preserve the contents of
   windows obscured by xev's window.

12.3.1   xev **and The Keyboard**

If you position the pointer in xev's window and press a key on your keyboard, you get
one or more keyboard events generated. The event information includes the corresponding *keycode* and *keysym*. This is the easiest way to find out which keycode relates to

Figure 12.7 The xev window

```
     root 0x8006b, subw 0x0, time 2404170460, (70,136), root:(420,500),
     state 0x0, keycode 84 (keysym 0x61, a), same_screen YES,
     XLookupString gives 1 characters:  "a"

KeyRelease event, serial 14, synthetic NO, window 0xc00001,
     root 0x8006b, subw 0x0, time 2404170580, (70,136), root:(420,500),
     state 0x0, keycode 84 (keysym 0x61, a), same_screen YES,
     XLookupString gives 1 characters:  "a"

MotionNotify event, serial 14, synthetic NO, window 0xc00001,
     root 0x8006b, subw 0x0, time 2404176160, (68,136), root:(418,500),
     state 0x0, is_hint 1, same_screen YES

LeaveNotify event, serial 14, synthetic NO, window 0xc00001,
     root 0x8006b, subw 0x0, time 2404176420, (-72,115), root:(278,479),
     mode NotifyNormal, detail NotifyNonlinear, same_screen YES,
     focus YES, state 0

VisibilityNotify event, serial 14, synthetic NO, window 0xc00001,
     state VisibilityPartiallyObscured

VisibilityNotify event, serial 14, synthetic NO, window 0xc00001,
     state VisibilityUnobscured

Expose event, serial 14, synthetic NO, window 0xc00001,
     (0,0), width 162, height 10, count 3
```

Figure 12.8 Output from xev

which key on your machine: run xev, press the key, and xev gives you the information. This will be useful when you come to customising your keyboard, in Chapter 18.

12.4   Conclusion

These programs let you look into the internals of your system, getting details about its operation, and specific information about windows and other components of it. On their own, they can aid understanding of the system, but they are probably most useful when used in conjunction with programs for customising the system. All the remaining chapters deal with customisation and setting up the system to suit your way of working.

The next chapter deals with fonts and colours, and how to use them.

Chapter 13 **Using X Fonts and Colours**

X supports multiple fonts and almost infinitely variable colours. Most applications let you specify colours of your choice for the various elements of that application's window, and almost all **X** programs which use text let you specify which font you want to use.

Fonts in **X**:

- Can be fixed-width (like the characters on dumb terminals) or proportionally spaced (like the text in most books).

- Can consist of text characters, or symbols or both.

- Come in a variety of point sizes.

- Can be tailored for a specific screen resolution (e.g. for the same point size of a particular font you may have one version for a 75 dots-per-inch (dpi) screen, and another for a 100 dpi screen.

- Have a standard naming convention.

- Can be accessed by their full name, or by a wildcarded specification.

- Are stored in specified configurable directories; fonts can be added or removed while the server is still running.

There is a standard format for interchanging fonts between systems, and there are tools for converting from this format to the one your particular server understands. Tools are included for listing the fonts available, and looking at the contents of a particular font.

This chapter begins with a short "getting started" section about fonts so you can start using them as soon as possible. It then moves on to explain the mechanisms, tools, formats, etc., in more detail. The final sections deal with colours, how to specify them and how to use them.

13.1   Getting Started with Fonts

This section aims to get you using fonts as quickly as possible. It tells you how to find out what fonts are available, specify the names of fonts you want to use, look at a font to see if it's what you want, and how to use fonts with **X** applications.

13.1.1   Listing the Available Fonts

```
-bitstream-charter-medium-i-normal--14-100-100-100-p-76-iso8859-1
-bitstream-charter-medium-i-normal--15-140-75-75-p-82-iso8859-1
-bitstream-charter-medium-i-normal--17-120-100-100-p-92-iso8859-1
-bitstream-charter-medium-i-normal--19-140-100-100-p-103-iso8859-1
-bitstream-charter-medium-i-normal--19-180-75-75-p-103-iso8859-1
-bitstream-charter-medium-i-normal--25-180-100-100-p-136-iso8859-1
-bitstream-charter-medium-i-normal--25-240-75-75-p-136-iso8859-1
-bitstream-charter-medium-i-normal--33-240-100-100-p-179-iso8859-1
-bitstream-charter-medium-i-normal--8-80-75-75-p-44-iso8859-1
-bitstream-charter-medium-r-normal--10-100-75-75-p-56-iso8859-1
-bitstream-charter-medium-r-normal--11-80-100-100-p-61-iso8859-1
-bitstream-charter-medium-r-normal--12-120-75-75-p-67-iso8859-1
-bitstream-charter-medium-r-normal--14-100-100-100-p-78-iso8859-1
-bitstream-charter-medium-r-normal--15-140-75-75-p-84-iso8859-1
-bitstream-charter-medium-r-normal--17-120-100-100-p-95-iso8859-1
-bitstream-charter-medium-r-normal--19-140-100-100-p-106-iso8859-1
-bitstream-charter-medium-r-normal--19-180-75-75-p-106-iso8859-1
-bitstream-charter-medium-r-normal--25-180-100-100-p-139-iso8859-1
-bitstream-charter-medium-r-normal--25-240-75-75-p-139-iso8859-1
-bitstream-charter-medium-r-normal--33-240-100-100-p-183-iso8859-1
-bitstream-charter-medium-r-normal--8-80-75-75-p-45-iso8859-1
6x10
6x12
8x13
8x13
9x15
cursor
dec-adobe-symbol-medium-r-normal--10-100-75-75-p-61-adobe-fontspecific
dec-adobe-symbol-medium-r-normal--12-120-75-75-p-74-adobe-fontspecific
dec-adobe-symbol-medium-r-normal--14-140-75-75-p-85-adobe-fontspecific
dec-adobe-symbol-medium-r-normal--18-180-75-75-p-107-adobe-fontspecific
dec-adobe-symbol-medium-r-normal--24-240-75-75-p-142-adobe-fontspecific
dec-adobe-symbol-medium-r-normal--8-80-75-75-p-51-adobe-fontspecific
fixed
venus% ▊
```

Figure 13.1 Typical font directory listing

The xlsfonts program lists the fonts available on this server, one per line. Figure 13.1 shows part of xlsfonts's output on a system containing only the standard fonts from MIT.

13.1.2 Naming Fonts

Some of the fontnames are almost too long to be usable. Fortunately, most of the name isn't usually of interest, and, **X** supports wildcarding of font names:

? matches any one character

* matches any string of zero or more characters

which is similar to the Unix shell conventions for wildcarding filenames. With wildcards, you can use much-abbreviated font specs.

Caution: If you are specifying a wildcarded font name in a shell command-line, enclose the name in double quotes to prevent the shell expanding the wildcard characters itself.

13.1.3 Looking at a Particular Font

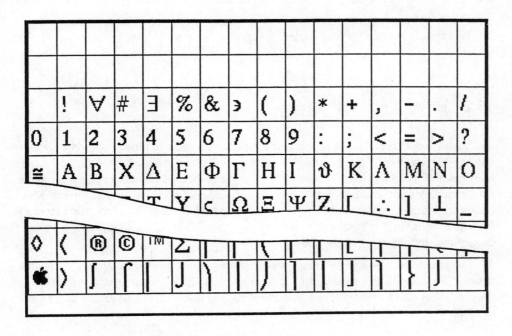

Figure 13.2 Font display, for a symbol font

The program xfd ("**X** **f**ont **d**isplayer") takes as its argument the name of a font, creates a window and displays characters of the font in a grid within the window. E.g.

```
xfd -fn "*symbol*-180-*"
```

displays the window shown in Figure 13.2.

13.1.4 Using Fonts with X Programs

Most **X** programs use text and they usually allow you to choose which font is to be used. The precise details of how to do this may vary with each program – check the manpage if in doubt – but almost always you can specify the font with command-line options -fn *fontname* or -font *fontname*. bitmap, xclock, xterm, xload, xmh and xedit all operate this way. E.g. if you want to run xterm with a very large font for a demo, say, you might use

```
xterm -fn "*courier-bold-r-*-240-*"
```

Caution: if the spec you give to a program matches more than one font, the server is free to choose whichever it wants. E.g. if you omitted the -r- from the spec in the example above, you could just as easily get an italic or reverse oblique font as a roman one.

That concludes the "getting started" overview. Now we'll look at the various points in detail.

13.2 How Fonts Are Named

In **X**, while fonts *may* have any name at all, there is a definite move towards a standard naming scheme where the font name is based on the properties of the font, and almost all fonts now follow the convention. The motivation behind this is to make font names server independent (previously, they tended to be related to the name of the file in which they were stored), and to enable applications to extract reasonable information from the fontname, (e.g. that it is an italic font, or its point size is 12) without having to delve deeply into the internals of the font.

To explain the naming, we'll take a sample font name, and work through its components. Components are separated by dashes (–), and may contain spaces. Font names do not distinguish between upper- and lower-case characters. As an example, let's take the font

-adobe-times-bold-r-normal--12-120-75-75-p-67-iso8859-1

and look at the most interesting fields – a full description of the components is included in the documentation file

$TOP/doc/fontnames/fnames.txt

in the release directories.

adobe : the supplier of the font

times : the type family. Others include courier, helvetica and new century schoolbook.

bold : the weight ("thickness") of type. Others include light and medium.

r : the slant of the type, (r is roman). Others are i(italic), o(oblique).

12 : the height of the characters, in pixels.

120 : the point-size of the font, in tenths of points. (E.g. 120 means 12-point, where a *point* is about 1/72 of an inch).

75-75 : horizontal and vertical resolution (in dots per inch) of the device this font was designed for.

p : the *spacing* of the font. p is proportional, as opposed to m(monospaced, i.e. fixed width).

What you are usually interested in is the type family, the weight, the slant and the pointsize. Often you can specify the font you want using only these, by making use of wildcarding.

13.2.1 Wildcards and Font Names

In the "getting started" section, we explained the rules for wildcarding, viz star (*) matches zero or more characters, and query (?) matches any single character.

An unusual feature of the wildcarding here, though, is that you may use a wildcard spec *anywhere* you can use a full explicit spec. If your spec matches more than one available font, the server is free to choose which one to use (although there are some restrictions on this — see *Font Search Path*, below). If the spec matches no font at all, you will usually get a message, and the server will use its default font.

You should wildcard on the point-size of the font, not the pixel-size, because on displays with different resolutions a font of a given point-size will have different pixel-sizes. So wildcarding on point-size gives you an element of device-independence. E.g. in the example above you would specify:

```
*-times-bold-r-*-120-*
```

i.e. specify the -120- instead of the -12-.

13.2.2 Listing the Available Fonts – xlsfonts

xlsfonts lists the available fonts on your server (or another server if you use the command-line option -display *spec*). By default, it lists all the fonts, but just as with Unix's ls, if you give it a spec it will list only the items matching that spec. E.g.

```
xlsfonts "*-times-*-180-*"
```

lists all 18-point Times fonts.

In principle xlsfonts tries to print as many fontnames as it can on each line of output; in practice, most of the names are so long that only one fits at a time anyway. But be careful: as font names can contain spaces, multiple names per line could be confusing.

Caution: many of the fonts have names that begin with a dash, and xlsfonts may wrongly try to interpret a spec as a command-line option. E.g. the command

```
xlsfonts "-adobe-*"
```

will fail. You can get over this by using either the option -fn before the spec, or just prefix the spec with a star. E.g. use either of

```
xlsfonts "*-adobe-*"
xlsfonts -fn "-adobe-*"
```

13.3 Looking at the Contents of a Particular Font – xfd

xfd is a "font display" program. It creates a window, and in it displays the elements of the font in a rectangular grid. The window may not be big enough to show all the characters in the font at the one time (especially if you have resized it) but you can access them all if you want:

To move forward through the characters : click the RIGHT mouse button in xfd's window — the next window-ful of characters is displayed.

To move back through the characters : click the LEFT button.

To get information about a character : click the MIDDLE button on the character, and xfd gives you the character's number. If you specify the command-line option -verbose when you start the program, at this point you get some extra information about the size of the character and its location within the character "cell".

13.4   How and Where Fonts are Stored

In this section we describe the various formats in which fonts can be represented, and tools for converting between the various formats. Then we go on to describe the way in which the fonts are filed so they can be accessed by the server, and tell you how you can alter your selection of fonts. Finally, we give a complete example of how to add a new font into your system.

13.4.1   The Format of Fonts – Server Natural Format, SNF

Fonts are stored on the server in *Server Natural Format*, or *SNF*. This format is not standard, but is particular to the server. So you can't necessarily move fonts from one type of server to another.

The program showsnf prints out information about a font stored in an SNF file, a lot of which is similar to the information you get by running xprop on the font itself. (showsnf's argument is the name of a file, xprop's is the name of a font; font names are not related to file names).

Bitmap Distribution Format, BDF

To overcome this problem of font distribution, the **X**-Consortium specifies a standard format for font interchange, the *Bitmap Distribution Format*, or *BDF*. BDF is an ASCII representation of the character's bitmap and contains only printing characters, so it is completely portable.

A full description of BDF is contained in the *"Bitmap Distribution Format"* document.

Converting from BDF to SNF – bdftosnf

For BDF to be useful, you must be able to convert BDF font files to SNF files, and this is now a requirement laid down by the **X**-Consortium for implementations of **X**.

In the MIT release, you use the program bdftosnf to perform the conversion.

Converting from Other Formats

Most graphics machines have their own vendor-supplied fonts, which are often particularly suited to their display. It would be nice to be able to use them within **X**, but they aren't in the correct format, so you can't.

The MIT **core** release does not address this problem, but the **contrib** software does. There are many tools for converting from vendor-specific fonts to BDF. And from BDF, you can convert to your own SNF using bdftosnf. We give an example of this later in this chapter.

13.4.2   Where Fonts are Stored – Font Directories

Fonts are stored in one or more *font directories* on the server. A font directory consists of three parts:

1. An ordinary file directory where the SNF files containing the fonts reside.

2. A database mapping the names of the SNF files onto the font names used by **X**.

3. An optional aliases file which allows you refer to one font by more than one name. (You only need one aliases file, no matter how many directories you are using).

You set up and maintain font directories with the program mkfontdir, described in the next section.

Maintaining Font Directories – mkfontdir

The procedures for setting up new font directories, and for altering existing ones, are the same:

1. In the file directories collect the files of all the fonts you want to use. These can be BDF files (whose filename should end in .bdf), SNF files (.snf), or compressed SNF files (.snf.Z) — mkfontdir will automatically convert the non-SNF files to SNF. ("Compressed" files are those that have been run through the BSD compress program to save file space).

2. If you want to alias font names, create (or edit) the file ***fonts.alias*** in one of the fontfile directories. Details of the file's format are given in the mkfontdir manpage, but simply, it consists of lines with two fields separated by white space: the first field is the alias you are defining, and the second the name of an existing font (which may include wildcards). E.g.

    ```
    tbi12 *-times-bold-i*-120*
    ```

    Caution: the first alias you define for a font makes the real fontname unavailable, so after the example above, you could access the font *only* with the name tbi12. This may change in later releases, but for now the fix is to put in a second line which is the reverse of the first (but you can't use wildcards in the alias field). So overall you would have:

    tbi12   *-times-bold-i*-120*(contd.)
    -adobe-times-bold-i-normal--12-120-75-75-p-68-iso8859-1 tbi12

    You must enter the name in full (without wildcards) on the second line, because you are defining an alias now, not referencing an existing name.

3. Run mkfontdir, giving it as arguments the names of the file directories. E.g. for the default **X** configuration you use:

```
mkfontdir /usr/lib/X11/fonts/misc \
/usr/lib/X11/fonts/75dpi \
/usr/lib/X11/fonts/100dpi
```

(If a file directory doesn't contain a font database, mkfontdir ignores it).

Caution: creating a font directory doesn't cause the server to notice it. You must either restart the server (which is drastic) or reset the font search path as described below.

Font Search Path – xset

You can use any number of font directories you want, but if you are using anything other than the default configuration you must explicitly tell the server. The list of directories you use is called your *font search path*, or *font path*, and you specify it as a comma-separated list of file directories.

To see what your current font path is : use the command xset q. This prints a lot of information which includes a line giving your font path which looks like:

> **Font Path:** **/usr/lib/X11/fonts/misc/,** *(contd.)*
> **/usr/lib/X11/fonts/75dpi/,/usr/lib/X11/fonts/100dpi/**

To set up a different font path : use a command of the form xset fp *new-path*. E.g. if you have a lot of local fonts, and don't want most of the standard ones you might use:

```
xset fp /usr/local/Xfonts,/usr/lib/X11/fonts/75dpi
```

Caution: there is no dash in front of the fp: the syntax is *not* -fp. (-fp means something else — see below).

To reset the font path to the server's default value : use the command:

```
xset fp default
```

To tell the server to re-read its font directories : The command

```
xset fp rehash
```

tells the server that you have probably changed the contents of the font directories and that it should re-read the font databases. Any new fonts that have been added can now be accessed.

To add new font directories to the existing path : The command

> **xset +fp** *dirlist*

adds the comma-separated list of new directories *dirlist* to the *front*, i.e. left, of the existing path, and

> **xset fp+** *dirlist*

adds *dirlist* to the *end*, i.e. the right, of the path.

To remove font directories from the path : Either of the two commands

> **xset -fp** *dirlist*
> **xset fp-** *dirlist*

removes the directories in *dirlist* from the current path.

Caution: the font path is held in the server, and applies to all clients using that server. As a rule of thumb it should only be set by whoever is working on that server's display.

The Order of the Font Path is Important

The order of entries in the path spec is significant in one way. We have already said that if a font spec matches more than one font, the server can choose which to use. However, if the matched fonts are in different directories the one the server chooses must be in the directory which occurs earliest in the path.

You can use this rule to arrange that the fonts which best match your display's resolution become the 'preferred' ones. Let's assume your display has a resolution of 100dpi. Set up your path so that the 100dpi fonts occur earlier than the 75dpi ones, e.g.

```
xset fp /usr/lib/X11/fonts/100dpi/,\
/usr/lib/X11/fonts/75dpi/
```

If you now specify a font, e.g.

```
*-times-bold-r-*-120-*
```

which has both 75dpi and a 100dpi versions, you will get the 100dpi one, which is what you want.

13.5   Example: Adding a New Font to Your Server

Now we'll work through a full example of adding a font to your server. To make it realistic, we'll take one of the (Sun) vendor-supplied fonts on our workstation, convert it to BDF, and then install that. The font we are starting from is

```
/usr/lib/fonts/fixedwidthfonts/screen.r.7
```

To convert the Sun font to BDF, we have to make use of a program vtobdf in the **contrib** software which does just this. (There are a number of similar tools for other specific systems, too). vtobdf takes two arguments, the name of the input (Sun) file, and the name of the BDF file to be created. We have previously extracted the program from the **contrib** tape, compiled it, and inserted it in our directory of executables, so we can start. We'll name the new font more or less according to the **X** standard. We'd like to give the output file the suffix *.bdf*, but if we do that vtobdf will include .bdf in the fontname it generates, so we have to omit it, and rename the file afterwards. Thus:

```
venus% cd /tmp
venus% vtobdf /usr/lib/fonts/fixedwidthfonts/screen.r.7\
-sun-screen--r-normal---70-75-75-m---
```

Now rename the file, and move it into a font directory:

```
venus% mv - -sun-screen--r-normal---70-75-75-m---\
/usr/lib/X11/fonts/misc/-sun-screen--r-normal---70-75-75-m---.bdf
```

Finally, run mkfontdir (on this directory only — nothing has changed elsewhere) and tell the server to re-read the directories to see what fonts are available now:

```
venus% mkfontdir
venus% xset fp rehash
```

and finally, check that the font really is available:

```
venus% xlsfonts "*-sun-screen*"
-sun-screen--r-normal---70-75-75-m---
```

All is OK.

Caution: your fonts may be stored in places other than the defaults, and anyway the file protections of the directories may not allow you to alter them — check with your system administrator.

13.6 Using X Colours

We have used colours quite a lot already, without saying very much about them. This has been possible because **X** lets you refer to colours by every-day names. In this section we describe some other ways of specifying colour, explain how that naming mechanism works, and how you can set up some colour-names of your own.

13.6.1 RGB Colour Specs

Instead of using colour names, you can also specify colours in terms of their RGB (red, green, blue) components. I.e. you say that the colour you want displayed is to have r units of red, g units of green, and b units of blue. These specs take the form

    #<r><g><b>

and the following rules apply:

- The spec must begin with a sharp-sign (#).

- The elements of the spec refer to the red, green, and blue components in that order.

- You must specify all three (red, green, blue) elements.

- Each element is a hexadecimal number, consisting of one to four digits. A value of ffff means the corresponding colour is to be at its maximum intensity, a value of 0 means none of that colour. E.g.

      #0000ffff0000

  is the brightest green possible, and no red or blue at all. Similarly you have:

#000000000000	*black*	*(no colour at all)*
#ffff0000ffff	*magenta*	*(full red and blue)*
#ffffffffffff	*white*	*(all full on)*

  Note that while #rgb and #rrrgggbbb have the same relative intensities of the three components, the second is much brighter.

- Each element can have one to four digits, but they must all have the same number (so you can't use #rrbbbbgg, for example).

You can use these colour specs just as you do colour names, e.g.

    xclock -fg #3d7585 -background pink

This form of colour spec is very dependent on your display, and is not very portable.

13.6.2 The X Colour Database

To get over the lack of portability of the #rgb colour specs, and to make the system easier to use, X uses a database of colour names and the corresponding rgb values.

Unless it was explicitly changed when your system was installed, a plain text copy of the database is held in the file */usr/lib/X11/rgb.txt*. The first few lines of the file look like:

```
112 219 147    aquamarine
50 204 153     medium aquamarine
50 204 153     MediumAquamarine
0 0 0          black
0 0 255        blue
95 159 159     cadet blue
. . .
```

On each line, the three numeric fields represent the rgb components, but here the values are in decimal, and must be in the range 0-255, where now 255 means "colour full on". The fourth part of the line is the colour name, which may contain spaces.

You translate this text file into an internal form with the program $TOP/rgb/rgb in the **X** distribution tree. (It is *not* installed in a standard place in your system when **X** is built). So, to add new colours to your database, enter the colours into the *rgb.txt* file with any text editor, and then:

```
venus% cd /usr/lib/X11
venus% $TOP/rgb/rgb < rgb.txt
```

In fact rgb doesn't recreate the internal database from scratch each time — it just adds entries (or amends duplicated ones), so you could just type in colour entries on rgb's standard input if you wanted:

```
venus% $TOP/rgb/rgb
255 50 50 mypink
. . .
```

However, this gets your internal database out of step with *rgb.txt*; as there are no standard tools for querying the server about what colour names it understands, it is better to use *rgb.txt* always.

13.7 Conclusion

In this chapter you have seen how **X** names and stores fonts, how you can find out what fonts are available and what they contain, how to use fonts in **X** applications, and how you can add fonts to your system.

The concluding sections described **X**'s colour naming rules, the colour database and how to add your own colours to it.

The facilities described here are only those included in the **core** distribution. Again, the **contrib** distribution contains a lot more software, particularly for vendor-specific aspects like converting native fonts to **X** formats. It also includes a good selection of actual fonts of various types. And for colour, there is a very useful demo program called xcolors, which creates a window and in it displays all the named colours on your system.

The impact of multiple fonts and colours on your screen is striking. You are continuing to get more value and functionality out of the window system, and are starting to tailor it to suit your taste and way of working.

In the next chapter we continue with customising the system, and tell you how you can create, edit and use images using **X**'s *bitmap* facility.

Chapter 14 Defining and Using Bitmaps

A *bitmap* is a little picture. More precisely, it is a representation of a picture in which each pixel is represented by a single bit. The bit has the value 1 if the pixel is to be "black" and 0 if it is to be "white". X has a number of facilities for manipulating bitmaps of this type: you can create them, edit them, and store them in a variety of ways. Several user programs let you use them directly. (Many more programs use them internally, and there are facilities within the **X** programming libraries which make it easy to use them in user-written programs).

This chapter starts by describing the tools for working with bitmaps, and then describes a practical use: the xsetroot program, which lets you customise your screen, setting the background to a bitmap or colour of your choice and specifying a bitmap to be used as cursor.

14.1   The System Bitmap Library

You are provided with a library of bitmap files as part of the system. By default these are stored in the directory:

    /usr/include/X11/bitmaps

but this may differ in your site – check with the installer of your system. We use some of these files in the examples in this chapter, and assume the directory is the standard one.

14.2   Interactively Editing a Bitmap – bitmap

The bitmap program is a tool to let you create or edit bitmaps interactively. It displays the bitmap in a rectangular grid of squares, where each square represents a pixel. You can set or clear pixels using the mouse.

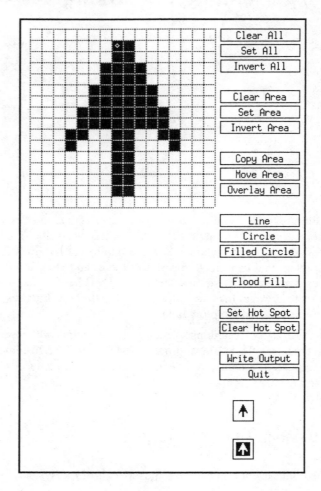

Figure 14.1 The bitmap editor

14.2.1 **Starting** bitmap

With bitmap you can edit an existing file containing a bitmap, or create a bitmap from scratch, and save it to a file. However, whichever you want to do, when you start bitmap you must always give it the name of a file – either the existing file, or the file you will want to dump the new bitmap into when you are done.

When creating a new bitmap you may optionally specify the size (as *width* x *height* in pixels); if you don't, the default size of 16x16 is assumed. E.g., if we are creating a new bitmap of a large cross, say, we might start bitmap with the command

```
bitmap big-cross 40x50 &
```

14.2.2 **Using** bitmap

As an example, we'll edit an existing file. Start the program with the command:

```
bitmap /usr/include/X11/bitmaps/cntr_ptr
```

and the window shown in Figure 14.1 appears. The large grid is what you operate on with the mouse, and at the bottom right the current state of the bitmap is shown actual size, once in normal video and once in reverse. The other boxes down the right-hand size perform commands when you click on them.

The simplest way to edit the picture is with the three mouse buttons:

To set pixels : click on a pixel with the LEFT mouse button. Or, press the LEFT button and drag it: every pixel square it enters is set, until you release the button.

To clear pixels : exactly the same, but use the RIGHT mouse button instead.

To invert pixels : click the MIDDLE button on a pixel and it is inverted (i.e. black pixels are cleared and white ones are set). If you press MIDDLE and drag, each time you enter a pixel square, it is inverted.

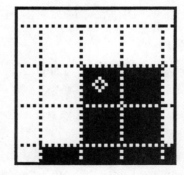

Figure 14.2 The "hot spot" in a cursor.

Bitmaps contain another feature: if you look very closely at the tip of the arrow (an enlarged view is shown in Figure 14.2) you will see a small diamond in one square. This marks the *hotspot*, which applies when the bitmap is used to construct a cursor: the hotspot is where the cursor is actually pointing. For pointed cursors, the hotspot is usually at the tip, and for square and round cursors it's usually at the centre. (You can alter the position of the hotspot, or remove it altogether with the $\boxed{\text{Set Hot Spot}}$ and $\boxed{\text{Clear Hot Spot}}$ commands).

When you have finished your changes, you can save the bitmap back to the file by clicking on $\boxed{\text{Write Output}}$. (This doesn't exit you from the program).

To exit, click on Quit. If you have edited the bitmap at all and try to quit without saving, you will prompted to make sure you know what you are doing.

14.2.3 Drawing Shapes

bitmap has several functions to make drawing easier:

To draw a line : click on Line: the cursor changes to a big black dot. Click this on one end of where you want the line drawn, and click it again on the other end: bitmap draws the line.

To draw a hollow circle : click on Circle: again, the cursor changes to a big black dot. Click this where you want the centre of the circle, and click it again anywhere on the circumference of the circle you want: bitmap draws the outline of the circle.

Drawing a filled circle : as above, but click on Filled Circle.

14.2.4 Working with Rectangular Areas

The commands Clear Area, Set Area and Invert Area operate on rectangular areas which you specify by pressing any mouse button on the top-left corner pixel of the area you want, and dragging to the bottom-right corner. As you drag, the area currently defined is highlighted by marking each square with an X.

You can also copy, move, and overlay areas. You specify the source area by dragging, as above, and the destination by clicking on the top-left corner. The actions of the commands are:

Copy : The destination area is cleared, and then all pixels corresponding to black pixels in the source area are also set.

Move : The source and destination areas are cleared, and then pixels in the destination corresponding to black pixels in the original source area are set.

Overlay : pixels in the destination area corresponding to set pixels in the original source area are set; everything else is unchanged.

14.2.5 Format of a bitmap File

A bitmap is stored in a file as ASCII text, in the form of a C-language program fragment. E.g. the file */usr/include/X11/bitmaps/cntr_ptr* contains:

```
#define cntr_ptr_width 16
#define cntr_ptr_height 16
#define cntr_ptr_x_hot 7
#define cntr_ptr_y_hot 1
```

```
static char cntr_ptr_bits[] =
0x00, 0x00, 0x80, 0x01, 0x80, 0x01, \
0xc0, 0x03, 0xc0, 0x03, 0xe0, 0x07,
0xe0, 0x07, 0xf0, 0x0f, 0xf0, 0x0f, \
0x98, 0x19, 0x88, 0x11, 0x80, 0x01,
0x80, 0x01, 0x80, 0x01, 0x80, 0x01, \
0x00, 0x00;
```

The *name_x_hot* and *name_y_hot* are included only if a hotspot is to be designated.

A more precise description is included in the bitmap(1) manpage. However, you never need to deal directly with bitmaps in this form: anything you need to do can be done with the tools described here, which insulate you from the complication of the low-level representation.

14.3 Other Ways to Edit Bitmaps

The bitmap program is very convenient when you are working on a small picture which you have created yourself. However it has a number of disadvantages:

- It doesn't accept input files in a simple pictorial format, such as might be produced by scanning an existing image.

- It must be run interactively, and has no facilities for procedural editing of pictures.

- It can't be run on non-**X** systems which you might be using to generate some of the bitmaps you want to display.

All of these problems are got over by allowing you to create bitmaps in the form of character pictures, and providing programs to convert between this format and bitmap's format. The character picture format is very obvious: each line of pixels is represented by a line of characters in the picture, black pixels are represented by one nominated character (default: #) and white pixels by another (default: −). E.g. the cntr_ptr used in the example above can be represented as shown in Figure 14.3.

You can edit these pictures with a text editor (e.g. Emacs's "picture mode" is especially good) or any other suitable program on any system. They could also be generated as output from a scanner, or other imaging equipment.

14.3.1 Converting Between Character Pictures and X Bitmaps

X provides two programs for converting between the bitmap format and the character-picture formats:

```
----------------------------
--------##----------
--------##----------
-------####--------
-------####--------
------######-------
------######-------
-----########------
-----########------
---##--##--##---
---#---##---#---
--------##----------
--------##----------
--------##----------
--------##----------
----------------------------
```

Figure 14.3 A bitmap in "Character picture" form.

atobm : converts a picture into a standard bitmap

bmtoa : converts a standard bitmap file into a character picture.

Both programs let you specify which characters to use for the black and white pixels.

14.4   Customising your Root Window – xsetroot

xsetroot lets you set a number of characteristics of your root window, i.e. the window which provides the (usually coloured or textured) background on your screen. You can change the colour and/or pattern displayed, and the cursor to be used in the window, i.e. when the pointer isn't in any application window.

14.4.1   Setting a Background Bitmap Pattern

You can specify any bitmap as the background for your screen (as long as it is in the **X** standard format), using xsetroot's command-line option -bitmap followed by the name of the bitmap file. E.g. the command

```
xsetroot -bitmap /usr/include/X11/bitmaps/mensetmanus
```

gives the very elaborate background shown in Figure 14.4. (The Latin phrase *Mens et Manus* ("mensetmanus") is MIT's motto, and the two figures shown are a simplified rendering of the MIT logo).

14.4.2 Setting a Background Cursor

If you don't want the default big-X cursor, you can specify a different one with the option
-cursor *cursorbitmap maskbitmap*, where both arguments are the names of bitmap files.
E.g. to set the cursor to the pointer we've seen above, you would use the command:

```
xsetroot -cursor /usr/include/X11/bitmaps/cntr_ptr\
/usr/include/X11/bitmaps/cntr_ptrmsk
```

The bitmaps cntr_ptr and cntr_ptrmsk are shown side by side in Figure 14.5 for comparison.

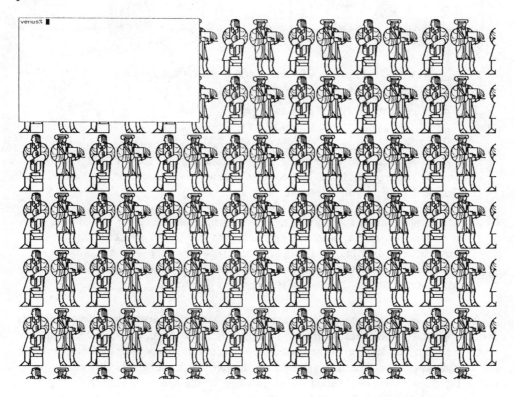

Figure 14.4 Root window pattern set to *mensetmanus* bitmap

The *maskbitmap* determines which pixels of the *cursorbitmap* are actually displayed:
only the cursor pixels whose corresponding mask pixel is black are used — the other
cursor pixels are not shown. So effectively, the mask determines the shape of the cursor,
whereas the cursor bitmap determines the colour of the pixels within that shape. (By
"colour" in this instance we mean black or white). The mask and cursor bitmaps must
be the same size.

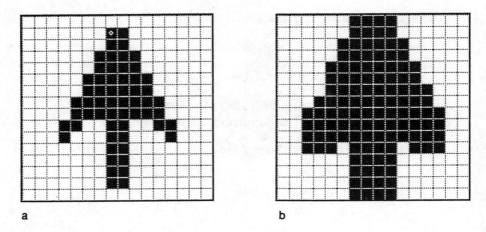

Figure 14.5 Cursor and mask bitmaps

This mask mechanism is useful in two ways:

1. It allows non-rectangular cursors to be shown neatly, without being surrounded by excessive white space. E.g. without a mask, the cntr_ptr would show as an arrow within a 16x16 white square which would often obscure a lot of the object you wanted to point at.

2. By setting the mask appropriately, you can ensure that the cursor will always be visible, no matter what background it is on. E.g. the cntr_ptrmsk above is one pixel bigger all round than cntr_ptr, so the cursor is always surrounded by a thin white area. If the mask matched the cursor exactly, the cursor would be invisible when it is in a black area.

You *can* use exactly the same bitmap for the mask and cursor: the cursor shape is defined perfectly well (because the mask determines the shape, and it is the shape we want) but what you lose on is the contrasting border around the cursor: because mask and cursor now coincide exactly, there is no border. So it will work OK, but as noted above the cursor may be difficult to see in areas of the same colour. In fact, not all the bitmaps in */usr/include/X11/bitmaps* have corresponding masks defined, and if you want to use them as cursors, you *have to* use the cursor as the mask.

For fun, try ***mensetmanus*** as cursor and mask. (The hotspot is the top left corner).

14.4.3   Other Background-Setting Options

You can set the background to a solid colour with the command-line option -solid *colour*. (Only black and white are sensible on monochrome displays). You can set it explicitly to a shade of grey with -grey or -gray. (NB: not -solid gray). Or you can set it to a grid pattern with -mod *x y*, where *x* and *y* are integers in the range (1,16) — experiment with the values to see what effects you get.

14.4.4 Resetting to the Default Background and Cursor

If you don't like what you've set up, you can revert to the default cursor and background with either of:

```
xsetroot -def
xsetroot
```

14.5 Summary

In this chapter you have seen how to edit bitmaps interactively, how to save them, and how to convert them to and from other formats so they can be manipulated by other (non-window) programs. You have used bitmaps in conjunction with xsetroot in the first step towards customising the system to your own taste: setting your root window background in a variety of ways, and changing the cursor.

In the next chapter, we continue with customising, and look at the mechanism you use to set default options for X programs.

Chapter 15 Defining Default Options for Applications — Resources

Most **X** programs accept command-line options to let you specify your choice for foreground and background colours, fonts, initial geometry, and so on. This is partly out of a desire to make the program customisable, but also partly out of necessity: on a given machine certain fonts, say, may not be available, so you can't really hard-code font names into the program.

It would be unmanageable to have to specify all the necessary options on the command line every time you run the program — there are just far too many possibilities. So instead, **X** provides a general mechanism called *resources* for passing default settings to application programs. When reading the manpages, you may already have noticed references to resources, and wondered what they were; that is what we are explaining here.

Almost all the customisation that you do to your system will involve resources. Virtually every option you choose for an application is set using resources, from simple items like colours or fonts, through to customising your keyboard, or controlling how work sessions on your display are to be managed. It is a very powerful facility, and is used throughout the system.

So, in this chapter we describe what resources are, with a little background information on how they developed. Then we describe the **X** Toolkit, which makes very full use of the resources mechanism, and move on to tell you in some detail how resources work, how you specify them, and the type of settings you can use them for.

This is quite a long chapter, and there are several new concepts involved, so don't be worried if you find the going a bit heavy to begin with. In fact, the resources mechanism is very simple in principle — just on first sight a lot of "magic" notation seems to be involved. It might be worthwhile overviewing the whole chapter quickly first, and then re-reading it in detail.

15.1   What are "Resources"?

In the **X** documentation you will find the term "resources" used in two contexts. First, at a relatively low level it means something which is created or managed by the server, and which is used by an **X** program. Windows, cursors, fonts and so on are all *resources* in this sense.

But there is another meaning, which you typically find in the manpages for the various applications: it is a method of passing default settings, parameters, and other values to application programs. In this chapter we are concerned only with this higher-level meaning of "resources". To explain how the present system works, it will useful to look back at earlier versions of **X** and see how this function was handled then, because the present mechanism has evolved from there.

15.1.1   The Background to "Defaults"

In earlier releases of **X**, there was a simple way to set your own default selections for items like the colour of the window background, the colour of the window border, the font to be used by the application, etc.

The format for default settings was straightforward. You specified a window attribute and the default value it was to take. E.g.

    `.Border: red`

meant that all windows would have a red border, (unless you over-rode that with an explicit command-line option setting the border colour). You could also prefix the attribute with a program name; in this case it applied only to the nominated program. So, combining the spec

    `xclock.Border: blue`

with the previous one would mean: by default all windows should have a red border, except xclock, which should have a blue one.

Once you had set the defaults, programs picked up the values automatically, so you didn't have to specify your own choices each time. It allowed you to use fonts which suited your way of working, whether you wanted small fonts to maximise the amount of information displayed, or larger ones to enhance readability. It let you choose colours for particular applications. And you could define startup positions for applications, so you could layout your initial screen with little manual intervention. Because many of the defaults — fonts, colours, etc. — were resources in the strict sense, the term "resources" gradually took on its wider meaning of "default settings", or "setting default options".

15.1.2   Resources Pass Information to Application Programs

As **X** developed, and the application programs expanded, there was a need for a facility to pass a lot of information to programs to customise or specify their behaviour, and not just information about fonts or colours. E.g. you might want to tell xbiff how often it is to check for mail, or xterm that function-key 12 is to insert a particular string of characters, or xedit that a double click of the MIDDLE button should select the current paragraph of text.

So gradually, the resource/defaults facility has developed, until now it is a general-purpose mechanism for passing any information at all to an application. You specify the information as a text string, and the application interprets that internally: whether it treats the string as the name of a mouse button, or a colour, or a function to be invoked depends on the application and how the "resource" is specified.

The mechanism has also become more sophisticated (but more complicated too) and it lets you specify very precisely where default values are to apply. Before, you could only specify "all programs", or "this particular program". With the present system you can set defaults like those, but also for e.g. "menu items in terminal windows", or "in all window labels", or even "for function buttons in boxes of buttons in all editor windows except xedit".

This enhanced precision has been made possible by the use of the *X Toolkit*, which makes very comprehensive use of resources. To use the resource mechanism properly, you need some understanding of what the Toolkit is, and that is covered in the next section.

15.2   The X Toolkit

As we mentioned before, **X** does not determine the user interface: it merely provides mechanisms which can be combined (by the application system designer) to make any style of interface required. In the abstract this is very desirable — it makes the system a general-purpose tool and places no limitations on its use. But from another point of view, it has big disadvantages:

- The various different application programs which one person uses may have very different user interfaces. Not only can it be difficult to learn and remember all the different modes required, but the applications may not work smoothly together (e.g. can't cut and paste between windows). Instead of a uniform and co-operative *system*, you end up with a collection of separate, isolated, programs.

- From the programmer's standpoint, it means everything above the basic window system has to be written from scratch. Menus, scrollbars, clocks, function buttons, etc., all have to be produced. And even on a single

product, different programmers may do things slightly differently, leading
to more incompatibilities.

To overcome these problems, the idea of the *Toolkit* was introduced.

To some extent, the Toolkit does determine the user interface style. However, to
minimise this effect, and to leave user interface developers as much choice as possible,
the Toolkit is divided into two parts:

1. A set of basic mechanisms and functions for constructing user-interface
   elements. This is called the Toolkit *Intrinsics*. This can be used by any
   toolkit, no matter what interface it provides, so we can consider this to be
   "fixed", i.e. not replaceable.

2. A set of elements providing a particular user interface (or style of interface).
   These elements are called *widgets*, and this second part of the Toolkit is
   called the *widget set*. We consider this to be replaceable: different interfaces
   would be provided by different Widget Sets, even though they are all using
   the same Intrinsics.

The next two sections describe these two component parts in more detail.

15.2.1 Part 1 of The Toolkit — The Intrinsics

The *Intrinsics* define entities called *widgets*, and provide all the facilities needed to
create, manage, and destroy them. In the abstract, a widget is an element of a user
interface which behaves in a particular way. In reality, a widget is an **X** window plus
the rules and functions which determine its input and output behaviour, i.e. how it
reacts to the user.

To help explain the concept of widgets, we'll give a few examples. But note! these
are *not* part of the Intrinsics — they are part of a particular widget set which we'll
describe later, and are only included here for purposes of illustration:

Command Widget : This is a rectangular "button" (i.e. a small window) on
the screen that contains some text. When the pointer is in the button, the
border is highlighted, and when a mouse button is clicked in the widget, a
software routine (specified by the programmer) is executed.

You have already used Command Widgets several times: in the Command
Menu in xedit, and in xman's main options window.

Scrollbar Widget : again, you have used these many times, for scrolling the
text in xterm and xedit, and scrolling text and directory listings in xman.

The Intrinsics provide the *basic* mechanisms — those which are needed by virtually
any higher-level software providing an interface — and address the following areas
(amongst others):

- Creating and destroying widgets.

- Managing groups of widgets as a unit.

- Handling geometry issues, i.e. positioning, both at top level (i.e. an application's -geometry operation), and lower down (managing the internal positioning of sub-widgets within an application). You can see this in operation by resizing xman's main option window: make it wide and short, and the boxes Help, Quit, etc., and the "Manual Browser" title will be rearranged in a horizontal line, to fit).

- Handling events, e.g. calling the appropriate procedures when a mouse button is clicked in a widget, managing window exposures, and handling input from the keyboard.

- Managing resources and defaults for each widget.

15.2.2   Part 2 of The Toolkit — Widget Sets

Broadly speaking, the Intrinsics only supply a framework on which you can construct a user interface. It is a *Widget Set* which actually provides a given interface, and different sets will provide different styles of interface. Generally it is expected that one system will adhere to a consistent set of widgets, although there is nothing to prevent mixing of widgets to any extent desired.

Only one widget set is supplied in the **core X** release; we describe it in the next section.

The Athena Widget Set

Most of the MIT **core** applications use the Toolkit and the *Athena Widget Set*. (So called because it was developed at MIT, where the **X** development grew out of Project Athena). It is this which defines the widgets which you have used in other various applications.

We've mentioned the Command Widget and Scrollbar Widget above. Others in the Athena Set include:

Label Widget : this is much as you would imagine - a string or picture displayed in a window. (Example: the "Manual Browser" title in xman's main options menu).

Text Widget : this is the "building block" we mentioned when describing xedit back in Chapter 10. It is this which provides the editing functions we used.

Viewport Widget : a window with a scrollbar along one side and/or the top or bottom, which allow you to scroll the contents in the "viewport". xman uses one of these to display its directory of manpages.

Box Widget : This manages the layout of its sub-widgets within a box of a specified size, and tries to pack the sub-widgets as closely as possible. E.g. it is a box widget which arranges xmh's $\boxed{\text{Reply}}$, $\boxed{\text{Forward}}$, etc. command buttons.

VPaned Widget : this manages sub-widgets, keeping them in a vertical stack, and displaying a *grip* on the dividing lines between each child widget. The grip optionally allows you to change the size of one widget, with a corresponding change in size of another. E.g. the major elements of xman's window which we saw in Figure 10.12 are managed by a VPaned widget.

Form Widget : another way of managing a set of sub-widgets, but giving more flexibility by allowing some choice in positioning.

List Widget : This manages a "list" of strings, arranged in rows and columns. Any of the strings can be selected by clicking on it: that string is high-lighted, and a specific function is called to perform the necessary action. xman uses a list widget to handle its list of manpages in a manual section.

We can see how a required functionality can be obtained by combining widgets, again using xman as the example. xman's directory of manpages at its lower level is a list widget, to handle the list of manpage names, and this is itself contained within a viewport widget (to allow the user scroll to the required location in the list). In turn this, together with the manpage widget, is contained in a VPaned widget so in fact there is a hierarchy of widgets, each performing its specialist function. All applications which use the Toolkit have this tree-structure of widgets within them.

15.2.3 Widgets: Names and Classes

The resource and defaults mechanism works on the basis of widget names, so we will conclude our look at the Toolkit with an overview of the naming process, and then move onto the resources proper.

The Toolkit provides a type of object-oriented programming system to the programmer. It defines *classes* of *objects*, i.e. specifies what properties the objects will have when they are created, how they operate, and so on. These objects are widgets, and the system ensures that they interact with other widgets and other parts of the application software in well-defined ways.

When a programmer creates a widget of a particular class, it is called an *instance* of that class. (Broadly, a class is an abstract definition, and an instance is something real which fits that definition). The created widget has a name, which was specified by the programmer. (E.g. the program code might effectively say "Create a widget, of the class Box Widgets, and call it **topBox**"). The widget can in some circumstances also be referred to by the name of its class.

In summary, a widget has an instance name and a class name (or more simply, a name and a class).

15.3   How Resources are Manipulated – The Resource Manager

Let's just remind ourselves what we are trying to achieve with resources. We want to be able to pass information to an application, telling it to modify its normal behaviour in some way, e.g. show its window border in pink instead of black, or use some specific font.

X handles this as follows. You set up a database of *resource specifications*. Each resource spec names some characteristic of an application and a value that the characteristic is to take by default. I.e. a spec is something of the form

> *characteristic* : *value*

When applications start running, they query this database to see if any of the *characteristic*s in it match items the applications want settings for, and if so they use the corresponding *value*. E.g.

```
xclock*foreground: blue
```

says that the value blue should be given to the characteristic xclock*foreground. The part of the system which determines whether a program's request matches anything in the database or not is called the *Resource Manager*.

Resource defaults can apply to objects (usually widgets) within an application, as well as to programs as a whole. (E.g. you can set a default colour specifically for the background of the command buttons in a specific sub-window of the application, not just for the background of all that application's windows). To be able to this, we need some precise way of naming the objects the defaults apply to.

15.3.1   Specifying what a Resource Default Applies To

It is the *characteristic* that the Resource Manager uses to decide if a default spec applies in a particular case. We can divide the characteristic into three parts:

1. The program *attribute* that you are setting the default value for. E.g. "background colour", or "font", or whatever.

   You *must* specify the attribute — that's what says what you are setting the value for. It's meaningless to give a resource spec which doesn't say what it is to apply to.

   Caution: in the X documentation and manuals, the attribute is often called a "resource" or a "resource name". "Resource" is also often used for what we term the *characteristic*.

   The other two parts of the characteristic specify where that default is to apply, e.g. whether it applies only in particular programs, or in specific types of objects, or both.

2. The name of the application program to which this spec applies. If you omit this, the spec applies to *all* applications.

3. A list of *restrictions*: the spec applies only to objects which match the restriction list. Restrictions are usually the names of widgets. You can specify any number of restrictions, from zero up. E.g. in

```
xclock*foreground: blue
xedit*row1*Command*Cursor: cntr_ptr
```

there are no restrictions in the first example, and two (row1 and Command) in the second.

These parts are arranged in the order

[*<program-name>*] [*<restrictions>*] *<attribute>*

and are separated from each other by special delimiters. We'll describe the delimiters in detail later, but first let's look at some examples of complete *characteristic*s. (For simplicity, we'll use only colour attributes in the examples).

Some Examples of Resource Specifications

- To specify that the foreground colour should default to yellow everywhere:

```
*foreground: yellow
```

We have not specified any application name, so the spec applies to all applications; we have not specified any restrictions, so it applies everywhere within an application. (The "*" at the start of the line is one of the special delimiters we mentioned).

- To specify that the foreground colour should default to pink only in the xclock application:

```
xclock*foreground: pink
```

This spec applies only to xclock, but it applies to all items within it which use an attribute called "foreground".

- Now, limiting the spec to a particular place within an application:

```
xman*topBox*foreground: blue
```

The spec only applies to xman, and within that only to the object named **topBox**, which is xman's main options menu. (In fact it applies to *any* object named topBox in xman, but there is only one).

- In the second (pink) example we included the application name, but omitted any restrictions. Here we do the reverse:

  *command*foreground: green

  i.e. we specify that the foreground colour in objects named command is to default to green, in every application.

15.3.2 Generalising Specifications Using Class Names

The examples above illustrate a lot of the functionality we want from the defaults mechanism. But there is a limitation: you have to know what name the application programmer gave to each of the widgets comprising the application. This information could be (and sometimes is) included as part of the program's manpage, but is frequently omitted.

However, the Resource Manager has a feature which minimises the problem: anywhere in a characteristic that you use an application name, restriction or attribute name, you can use a *class name* instead:

Application class name : describes the "type" of program this is. So, xterm might be of class TermEmul, xedit and emacs of class Editor. (But disappointingly, in reality they are not: xterm is of class XTerm, xedit of class Xedit).

Restriction class name : the restrictions are almost invariably widget names, so you use the widget class name here.

Attribute class name : attributes are instances of a type or class in the same way as widgets are.

By convention, all class names begin with an upper-case letter, other names begin with lower-case. So, e.g. the attribute "foreground" is of class "Foreground". Shortly we'll explain how you go about finding out the class names (and indeed the instance names) for items you want to specify. First, we'll look at some more examples, this time using classes, or a mixture of classes and instances.

Examples of Resource Specs Containing Class Names

These examples show how you use classes in resource specs, to set defaults in a more general way than before. They also illustrate how you can use a class to set up a default for a wide range of cases, and combine it with an instance to over-ride that default in a particular case.

- To specify that the foreground colour should default to yellow everywhere:

  *Foreground: yellow

This differs from the earlier example in that we are specifying the default for the Foreground class. The distinction is important because not all attributes which are of class Foreground have the instance name foreground. E.g. the colour of xclock's hands is determined by an attribute of class Foreground but whose instance name is hands.

- We can use the mechanism to help us identify the classes of objects if the documentation isn't clear, by setting defaults to improbable combinations:

```
xmh*Command*Foreground: khaki
xmh*Command*Background: maroon
```

This will highlight all command widgets in beautiful colours.

- To set up a default for all text widget windows, but to differentiate xedit windows:

```
*Text*Background: pink
xedit*Text*Background: navy
```

- or in a similar vein:

```
*Command*Background: green
xman*Command*Background: white
xman*manualBrowser*Command*Background: orange
```

Where to Find Instance and Class names

This is difficult. There is no simple and consistent documentation of widget names, classes, attributes, etc. We'll list the best sources for each, and give you some hints on how to get more information.

Application instance name : This one is easy — it's the name of the application program that you have run. If the program uses the Toolkit, you can explicitly specify a different application name with the command-line option -name *string*. Why would you want to do this? Because it lets you define more than one set of defaults for a single application, and you can switch between them just by using -name. E.g. you might define normal defaults for an xterm, but define a very big window size, and a large-size font, for the application named demo which you would invoke with:

```
xterm -name demo
```

giving you an xterm which you use for demonstrations or tutorial sessions.

Application class name : this is more or less undocumented. The easiest way to find it is to start the application and then use xprop on its window: the property WM_CLASS gives you both application instance and class names. E.g. for xterm you get

WM_CLASS(STRING) = "xterm", "XTerm"

Restriction/Object/Widget instance name : the program's manpage may list the names of the objects you are most likely to want to access. E.g. xman lists topBox, help, manualBrowser, etc. If the manpage doesn't give you the names, the only other option is to look at the program sources if you have them. (This is generally recognised as being unsatisfactory).

Restriction/Object/Widget class name : this is easier. Most manpages do tell you the class of the objects you might be interested in. Even if they don't, most of the objects are widgets from a standard set, and once you get used to the system you can often guess what class they are. (E.g. you will never be given the instance name of a scrollbar, but it's a 99.9% chance that it is a widget, of class **Scrollbar**).

Attribute name and class : most manpages list the names, and often give the class too, of attributes they use which are specific to themselves. The manpage for xclock is a very clear example of this.

However, programs written with the Toolkit often use standard widgets, whose attributes *aren't* listed in the manpage, but often consist of some or all of a set of standard attributes. To find these, you must look to the Toolkit documentation:

- Appendix E (*"StringDefs.h Header File"*) of the *"X Toolkit Intrinsics"* manual lists all the standard "resource" (i.e. attribute) names and classes. Instance name entries look like:

  #define XtNborderWidth "borderWidth"

  (all the names begin with XtN, followed by names beginning with lower-case letters), and the class entries are like:

  #define XtCBorderWidth "BorderWidth"

  (all beginning with XtC). The strings within the double quotes are what you are after, e.g. borderWidth is the instance name, BorderWidth the class name.

- Look at Section 2.3 (*"Common Arguments in the Widget Argument List"*) in the *"X Toolkit Athena Widgets"* manual, for a list of resources used by all widgets, giving name, type, default value, and a plain-text description. The name given is of the form you saw above, i.e. with the XtN prefix; strip this prefix off and you have the attribute name.

- Look up the description of the widget in *"X Toolkit Athena Widgets"* manual. Each widget lists the "resources" it uses, as above.

- If all else fails (and sometimes it will) you can look at the widget source code. The resources used are listed in the XtResource data structures. E.g. the code for the Athena Scrollbar widget contains:

```
static XtResource resources[] =
{XtNwidth, XtCWidth, ... },
{XtNheight, XtCHeight, ...}
...
```

The appendix *"Road-Map to the Documentation"* tells you where to find the source code for items like these.

Caution: the Resource Manager imposes no restrictions whatever on the format of the spec it will accept. There is no pre-defined list of valid attribute or component names or classes. The spec you give it may not mean anything, but that doesn't matter: it will be stored in the database just the same. So the fact that a resource spec is accepted does *not* mean that you got the spec right and have named valid attributes or objects or applications. However, a useful consequence is that you can define defaults for attributes before they have been set up.

15.3.3 Delimiters in Resource Specs — Overview

You separate the components of resource specs with the delimiters star (*) or period (.). So far we have used only the star, deliberately, because the two have specific and different meanings. Broadly, the star is more general, and lets you specify characteristics which match a range of cases; as we have seen,

```
xclock*foreground: pink
```

applies to anything in xclock which uses the foreground attribute, so in this case the star is effectively a *wildcard* for any number of restrictions. And the star is even more general in:

```
*Foreground: yellow
```

as it matches any application name as well. On the other hand, the period just separates components, and matches must be exact. So the spec

```
xman.Manual Browser.Help.background: black
```

does *not* apply to the command buttons, or to the various other widgets within xman's window. Before we describe more precisely the difference between the two types of delimiters, we need to look at the operation of the Resource Manager in more detail.

How the Resource Manager Operates

Earlier, we have said that an application queries the database of resource default specs to see if any of them match. Here we describe how that query process is carried out.

```
xedit (Xedit)
    vpaned (VPaned)
        row1 (Box)
            Quit (Command)
            Save (Command)
            Edit (Command)
            Load (Command)
            stringthing (AsciiString)
            Undo (Command)
            More (Command)
            Jump (Command)
        row2 (Box)
            << (Command)
            Search >> (Command)
            stringthing (AsciiString)
            Replace (Command)
            All (Command)
            stringthing (AsciiString)
        messageWindow (Text)
            scrollbar (Scrollbar)
        labelWindow (Label)
        editWindow (Text)
            scrollbar (Scrollbar)
```

Figure 15.1 Hierarchy of objects (widgets) within xedit

Resources apply to individual objects (usually widgets) within the application. The objects are arranged hierarchicallyixwidget +hierarchy, with the application at the top, then perhaps a widget managing the layout of other widgets such as text windows, command menus, etc. E.g. the application xeditixwidget hierarchy in +xprognxxedit has the structure shown in Figure 15.1. (Each line lists the name of an object with its class-name in parentheses).

For *each* object the application queries the resource database; it passes to the Resource Manager the full instance name and also the full class name of the object, a list of the attributes the object uses, and a list of the attribute class names. Thus for the $\boxed{\text{Save}}$ button, the application specifies:

full instance name	`xedit.vpaned.row1.Save`
full class name	`Xedit.VPaned.Box.Command`
attribute instance-names	`borderWidth, cursor, font, label, ...`
attribute class-names	`BorderWidth, Cursor, Font, Label, ...`

Then the Resource Manager checks every spec in the database to see if it matches both an attribute in the list passed by the application, and the object name passed by the application. The match can be on name *or* class. If a match is found, the value part of the spec in the database is returned to the application (with of course an indication of what attribute it is for).

It is in this matching operation that the distinction between the star and period delimiters is important. For simplicity we can consider that the Resource Manager is just matching text strings on the basis of "words" (where each component in a spec is a "word"). Then, the period is just a word separator. The star is also a separator, but in addition it is a wildcard which can represent any number of words, from zero up. The only restriction on the matching is that the attribute of the spec in the database *must* match the attribute passed by the querying application: you can't wildcard the attribute.

Now you can see how the various specs work:

   `*foreground: yellow`

applies to any object in any application because the star matches all applications and all restriction or object names.

   `*Command.Foreground: violet`

applies to any attribute of class Foreground in any Command-type object in any application.

   `xedit.vpaned.row1.Help.background: navy`

is a completely-specified characteristic and will only affect the attribute of the single object named in it. (In this example, in spite of the fact that it is capitalised, "Help" is an instance-name; its class is "Command").

Unless you have some very specific requirement, it is best not to use the period delimiter — always use the star instead. It reduces the likelihood of making a mistake, and insulates you to some extent from changes in the hierarchy structure if an application is re-written.

This simplicity of the matching mechanism explains why you can enter specs which are strange, or which are for resources and attributes not yet defined: meaning is attached to a spec only when an application queries the database, and even then the extent of the meaning is trivial — the spec matches the query or it doesn't.

15.3.4 Precedence Rules When Multiple Resource Specs Match

We now have a very flexible way for specifying resources for applications. But it is so general that often several specs in the resources database will match when an application queries it. How is this resolved?

Briefly, if more than one spec matches, the *most specific* one is used. The Resource Manager has a set of precedence rules which it uses to decide if one spec is more specific than another:

- Using the period delimiter is more specific than using the star. E.g. *Command.Foreground is more specific than *Command*Foreground.

- Instance names are more specific than class names. E.g. *foreground is more specific than *Foreground.

- Specifying a component is more specific than omitting it. For example, xmh*command*foreground is more specific than xmh*foreground.

- Components nearer the left (start) of the spec are more specific than others further right. E.g. xmh*foreground is more specific than *command*foreground.

These rules are fairly straightforward. Most of them are just another way of saying: "If one spec matches only a subset of the cases matched by another, then the first spec is more specific than the second".

15.3.5 "Application Resources" in Toolkit Programs

Usually an application uses the Resource Manager to define default attributes for widgets in that program's hierarchy. But sometimes there is a need to be able to set defaults (or pass values) for things which are not directly related to widgets.

To handle this, the Toolkit provides a facility for what it calls *Application Resources*. In principle it is similar to the non-Toolkit defaults feature — the application defines attributes of it own choosing. Class names can be used too (when the application defines the attribute, it specifies its class too), so apart from the fact that these attributes are not part of the usual hierarchy, you use them as normal.

xman uses this facility quite a bit. It enables you to specify a different file for text in the help window, to specify whether you want a window for the main options window or if the program should go straight into a manpage window when it starts up instead, etc. (Look at the manpage, in the *X Defaults* section: it explicitly lists its "application-specific resources").

15.3.6 Resources and non-Toolkit Applications

Not all programs use the Toolkit. But it is the Toolkit which handles almost all of the resource management for an application; in particular, the application's widget structure defines the hierarchy of objects and sub-objects, and queries the Resource Manager accordingly. So how can non-Toolkit applications use the Resource Manager?

The answer is that the applications just have to query explicitly for each of the attributes they are interested in. You will recall that earlier we said the Resource Manager places no limitations on resource specs. As a result, applications can use any attribute names they want, and as long as the program documentation tells the user what they are, they can be used just like any others.

The xcalc application is an example of a program which doesn't use the Toolkit and which handles its resource specs like this.

There are a few points to note:

- There are no classes for this type of default.

- Programs tend to use class-like names (i.e. initial letter capitalised) for their attributes. E.g. xcalc uses Background, Foreground, BorderWidth, etc.

- If you get the letter-case wrong, your spec won't work. E.g. the spec

    ```
    xcalc.foreground: green
    ```

    is ignored by xcalc.

- Even though these program-defined attributes aren't part of a hierarchy, you can still use the star delimiter. E.g. xcalc is quite happy with

    ```
    xcalc*Foreground: orange
    ```

15.4 Types of Resources — How You Specify Values

Until now we have looked exclusively at the "left-hand side" (characteristic) of resource specs, and have either ignored the value part, or just used colour names. Now we'll look briefly at the "right-hand side" or *value* part.

At its simplest, the value is just a text string which is passed on to the application, and that is all the Resource Manager is concerned about. After that, the application can do what it wants with the value. Of course, for the system to be usable, the application must do something sensible, and indeed the Toolkit handles most of this part of the work too, so you get a consistent interface.

So while we can pass anything we want as a resource value, in practice we use a small number of types. You've seen most of them already, and you use them in resource specs just as you do everywhere else:

Colours : we have used these extensively already — they need no more explanation.

Fonts : which we've described already in a general way. In resource specs, too, you can use either a full name or a wildcarded spec. E.g. the set of specs:

```
*Font: *-courier-medium-r-*-140-*
xterm*Font: 8x13
xterm*boldFont: 8x13b
demo*font: *-courier-medium-r-*-240-*
demo*boldFont: *-courier-bold-r-*-240-*
```

sets an overall default font, but specifies an explicit pair of fonts for use in a normal xterm, and a pair of bigger fonts to be used in the demo application (which might well be just an xterm -name demo).

Numeric quantities : in various situations. E.g.

```
xclock*update: 30
xload*update: 60
BorderWidth: 10
xlogo*Width: 120
xterm*saveLines: 200
```

Boolean values : specifying "yes" or "no". You can use any of yes, on, true, and no, off, false. E.g.

```
xterm*scrollBar: false
xman*bothShown: true
```

Cursor names : specify the name of the file in */usr/include/X11/bitmaps* containing the cursor you want. E.g.

```
xterm*pointerShape: cntr_ptr
```

Caution: If the cursor specified doesn't contain a "hot spot", you may get an error.

Geometry specs : full or partial. The specs

```
xcalc*Geometry: 180x240-0-0
xclock*Geometry: -0+0
```

set a default size for the calculator only, and default positions for both — top-right hand corner for the clock, bottom-right for the calculator.

Keyboard translations : i.e. assigning particular strings to keys, or assigning special (non-printing) actions to keys or buttons. These are quite complex in themselves, so all of Chapter 17 is devoted to them.

Pixmaps : *Pixmaps* are patterns like bitmaps used to texture (colour in) an area. Specify them like bitmaps or cursors. These can be very handy when you are working on a monochrome screen, and want to set backgrounds for various classes of widget so you can see where the application uses them. E.g. the following resource specs:

```
*Pixmap: mensetmanus
List*backgroundPixmap: scales
Box*backgroundPixmap: cntr_ptr
Command*backgroundPixmap: sipb
```

cause your applications to be visually horrible — you get very cluttered windows, with virtually every space patterned in some way — but they do work, and can be helpful at times. (The attribute backgroundPixmap is of class Pixmap).

15.5 Conclusion

In this rather involved chapter, you have seen what "resources" are, and how you use them to specify defaults and other values for applications. We outlined the Toolkit and its concept of a hierarchy of widgets, and how you can take advantage of the structure of the widgets or other objects in the application to set a wide-ranging set of defaults. From there we moved on to the idea of classes, which let you specify objects without knowing their individual names, and that led us to the Resource Manager and its rules for matching resource specs in its database to programs' queries for default values. To finish, we outlined the format used to specify the values themselves.

This chapter has concentrated on the principles behind the resources mechanism. Now it's time to tell you to how to use them in practice on your system. In the next chapter we tell you how and where you store the default specs, i.e. how to manage the "resource database" that we mentioned above. In the chapter after that, we explain how you can use resources to customise your keyboard.

Chapter 16 **Using Resources in Practice**

The previous chapter explained the principles of **X** resources — why you want them, how the mechanism works, and the format of resource specifications. In this chapter we continue with resources, but the emphasis is much more practical: we tell you how and where to set up resource defaults, to affect some or all of your system. At the end of the chapter we go through many examples, pointing out the sort of problems you are likely to meet, and how to overcome them.

In the examples we'll be using, we assume that your own workstation is called venus and you use this most of the time. From venus's display you run client applications on remote machines saturn and mars, which share a file system with venus, and on neptune which doesn't, as we described in Chapter 4.

As you work through these sections, remember what the resource mechanism is for: passing information to applications. Often the information passed is a preferred default value for a colour or a font, say, but as long as the application understands it you can use the facility to pass any information at all. So we will tend to use the terms "resource spec", "defaults" and "resource" to mean more or less the same thing.

16.1   Where You Store Resource Defaults

In the last chapter we just said that you enter resource specs into "a database", without telling you how to do it. In fact there are several different places where you can store defaults: most of these places are simple text files which you can alter with any editor, but there is one special location which needs special tools to set it up. We'll give you a quick overview of everything first, and then cover each in detail.

At first the scheme will seem very complicated: including command-line options there are *eight* ways of specifying resources! But there are two important points to note:

1. You tend to use only one or two of the facilities, and once you have done your initial setup, you will rarely need to change default settings.

2. The system is designed to handle many different modes of working, and to satisfy the needs of people who work on many different displays as well as those who use only one display and access remote machines from that.

In summary, the facilities are provided to make the system as flexible as possible, but at any one time you will want only a subset of the total.

16.1.1 Eight Methods to Specify Resources

Overall there are eight different ways to specify resources, but they divide sensibly into categories:

- **Application-specific resources**: lists of resources, held in files which are read only by the particular application.

- **Server-specific resources**: settings which apply, no matter which host the application is running on.

- **Host-specific settings**: settings relating to the host the application runs on, irrespective of where it's displaying to.

- **Command-line options**: for one-off settings, at run time.

Application-Specific Resources — Methods 1 and 2

Toolkit programs initially look for resources in two files which are directly related to the application. These files are read only by the particular application:

1 **Application-class resource file**: This file contains site-wide defaults for a class of applications, and is usually set up by the system manager. Its name is the application class name and in the standard installation it is stored in the directory */usr/lib/X11/app-defaults*. E.g. for xterm the file would be:

> **/usr/lib/X11/app-defaults/XTerm**

In the **core** release, there is one of these files for Xmh; look at it to see the type of settings used.

2 **Your own application-specific resource file**: This file has the same name as the one above, but is stored in a different place — in the directory specified by the shell variable $XAPPLRESDIR, or if that isn't defined, in your home directory. E.g. for Xmh-class programs, the file is one of

> *$XAPPLRESDIR/Xmh*
> *$HOME/Xmh*

You can use this to override settings that you don't like in the site-wide file, above.

Server-Specific Resources — Methods 3 and 4

These are settings which relate to the server (i.e. display) that you are currently working on. Keyboard settings are often server-specific (because different displays have different keyboards). Another server-specific characteristic is whether the display is colour or monochrome.

Resources concerning these items should apply to all applications connected to the display, no matter what host those applications are executing on. (E.g. if the display you are using is monochrome, it doesn't matter where your application program is running — you still don't want it to use colour).

The methods of storing the server-specific settings are:

3 **The server's RESOURCE_MANAGER property**: (You saw this in xprop's output in Chapter 12). Using the xrdb program described below, you can store resource settings in the RESOURCE_MANAGER property of the server's root window. The advantages of this are:

    (a) You can set defaults without editing any files. (Especially useful when you are experimenting with the system as you get to know it).

    (b) The resources are held on the server, so they are available to all applications, no matter what host they are executing on. In our example scenario, this is particularly useful in the case of neptune: even though it doesn't share a file system with our display machine venus, it still automatically picks up the resource settings for the display is it using.

4 **Your *$HOME/.Xdefaults* file**: (This is only used if the root window has no RESOURCE_MANAGER property defined on it). If you don't want to get to grips with xrdb yet, you can just use this file instead, but you may have to set one up on each machine you run client applications on.

Host-Specific Settings — Methods 5 and 6

In a way, host-specific defaults are the converse of server-specifics. What you are saying is that if an application is executing on this host, then these defaults apply, no matter which machine's display the application is using. You might use these for:

- Customising applications to take account of the different file systems available on the various machines, e.g. a data file read by an application may be kept in different locations on different hosts.

- Distinguishing between the windows of several hosts (which may be running the same application) displayed on the same screen. E.g. you might want the windows for all xterm's executing on mars to have red borders, and saturn windows to have yellow ones.

- Accommodating differences in the implementations of the same applications on the various client machines. E.g. the xterm on venus is the standard MIT version, but on neptune it is a third-party product tailored for that machine's architecture: the two versions may not be completely compatible.

Host-specific resources are stored in:

5 **The file named by** $XENVIRONMENT: if the shell variable $XENVI-RONMENT is defined, it is interpreted as a full path name of a file containing resource settings.

6 **Your file** *$HOME/.Xdefaults-thishost*: (This is only used if $XENVIRON-MENT is not defined). Note that this is not the same as the file we mentioned earlier — it has a hostname appended to it. E.g. if you are executing the application on neptune displaying to venus, (and assuming that the RESOURCE_MANAGER property isn't defined) the server-specific resources are read from:

   .Xdefaults

and the host-specific ones from:

   .Xdefaults-neptune

both in your home directory on neptune.

   Caution: in the various sections we have said things like "the server-specific resources are read from ...". This may be misleading: if you really want to, you can put *any* resource settings of any type into any of the files or databases mentioned. What we really mean is that this is where you *ought to* put resources which are machine-specific or whatever, and that if you do, then you will get the behaviour you require.

Command-Line Options — Methods 7 and 8

Finally, you can specify values for applications to use by means of command-line options. Once you have setup your defaults, you won't often need to use options to specify X-related settings for your programs. But you will use them for:

- One-off settings, e.g. you temporarily want an extra-small xedit on your screen.

- For differentiating between separate instances of the same application. You have already seen an example of this, where we used the command

   xterm -name demo

to set the application instance-name to demo, to make it pick up resources for application-name demo instead of for xterm.

Command-line options fall into categories:

7 **Application-specific options**: e.g. xclock's -chime, or xpr's -scale.

8 **Toolkit-standard options**: all applications which use the Toolkit accept a standard list of command-line options in addition to any particular ones for that application. We've seen most of these already, including -fg, -bg, -display, -geometry, etc. A list of these is included in Section 2.3 of the *"X Toolkit Intrinsics"* manual.

One of these options, -xrm, is important enough to have a section of its own.

The -xrm *Toolkit-Standard Option*

Many of the usual resources can be set with explicit command-line options, e.g. to set the window background colour, you can use -bg *colour*. However, there are other resources which don't have a corresponding option, and to get over this, the Toolkit provides a "catch-all" option, -xrm (for **X Resource Manager**").

-xrm takes as an argument a resource spec, in just the same form as you enter it in a defaults file. E.g. you can say:

```
xclock -xrm "*update: 30"
```

which is equivalent to

```
xclock -update 30
```

Use -xrm as many times as you like in one command-line, but only include one resource-spec in each. E.g.:

```
xclock -xrm "*update: 30" -xrm "*chime: on"
```

The benefit of -xrm is that you can use it to set *any* resource the application uses. There are some resources which have no corresponding command-line options, and you have to use -xrm for these. Some of the more useful of these are:

iconX, iconY : the x and y coordinates of where the top-left corner of the window's icon is to be positioned.

iconPixmap : the name of a bitmap to be used as the window's icon. With this, you can specify as icons for your applications any bitmaps you have been given, or have created yourself using the bitmap program. E.g. the command:

```
xedit -iconic -xrm "*IconPixmap: cntr_ptr" \
-xrm "*iconX: 500" \
-xrm "*iconY: 400"
```

starts xedit up already iconified: the top-left corner of the icon is at (500,400), which on many displays will be about mid-screen, and the bitmap to be used as the icon is cntr_ptr.

backgroundPixmap : specifies a bitmap to be used for the background.

borderPixmap : specifies a bitmap to be used for the window border. E.g.:

```
xclock -bw 20 -xrm "*backgroundPixmap: scales" \
-xrm "*borderPixmap: cntr_ptr"
```

runs xclock with a 20-pixel wide border (so you can see it), and patterns the window with fish-scales, and the border with cntr_ptr's.

All these resources can of course be specified by class, too (i.e. IconX, BorderPixmap, etc.).

  Caution: Remember, -xrm is available only in programs which use the Toolkit.

16.1.2 Summary of the Various Ways to Specify Resources

Now we'll summarise the eight ways you can specify resource settings for an application:

Application-specific resources : these are held in two files and are used only by the Toolkit. One file is usually setup by the system manager, the other is your own.

Server-specific resources : are stored either in the RESOURCE_MANAGER property on the root window, or in your *$HOME/.Xdefaults* file.

Host-specific resources : are stored in the file named by the shell variable $XENVIRONMENT if it is defined, or else in your *$HOME/.Xdefaults-host* file.

One-off settings : are specified using the application's own command-line options, and the Toolkit's standard command-line options, including the catch-all *-xrm*.

  They are processed in the following order:

```
if (this program uses the Toolkit)
    read the /usr/lib/X11/app-defaults/class file (1)
    read your $HOME/class file (2)
if (RESOURCE_MANAGER property defined)
    process the specs it contains (3)
else
    read your $HOME/.Xdefaults file (4)
if (shell variable XENVIRONMENT is defined)
```

```
    read the file it names (5)
else
    read your $HOME/.Xdefaults-host file (6)
 if (this program uses the Toolkit)
    process the standard resource options,
    including -xrm (7)
 process this application's own options (8)
```

Now we'll look in more detail at the one unfamiliar method — the one which is used to store resources in the server itself.

16.2   Storing Defaults on the Server – xrdb

Most of the mechanisms for defaults depend on files — when the application starts up, the various files are read and their contents are processed. The disadvantage of this scheme is that you want all clients using a particular server to share a set of defaults, but if thê machines on which the clients execute don't have a common file system, how can you achieve this?

The solution is to store the defaults on the server itself. The mechanism used is a general purpose one — X's property facility. (Remember, a *property* is just a named pieced of data with a known format, associated with a window, and stored in the server). The specs are loaded onto the RESOURCE_MANAGER property of the server's root window, and the system looks at this when starting applications. When the window system is started, the RESOURCE_MANAGER property is not defined: if you want to use this facility, you have to set it up explicitly (see below).

There is no general user-level tool for manipulating a property, so a specific program is provided for managing the resources property. This is xrdb (the **X** Resource **DataB**ase utility).

16.2.1   What xrdb Does for You

(For convenience, in the rest of this part of the chapter we'll just refer to the RE-SOURCE_MANAGER property and its contents as "the database").

xrdb's function is very simple: it lets you:

- Set up the database from scratch.

- See what resources are currently in the database.

- Add new resources to the existing database.

- Remove the database completely.

These are the basic operations, and they are easy to perform. There are also some more sophisticated features, to let you control your resource setting very precisely. First we'll cover the basic operations, and we'll move on to the fancy bits later.

16.2.2 Using xrdb's Basic Functions — Getting Started

xrdb operates like most Unix programs: it reads input either from a file or its standard input, and you control its mode of operations with command-line options. The input it reads is just a series of resource settings in the form we've seen already — what's special is that it loads these settings into the database. Let's look at the main functions in turn:

To set up a new database : enter either of the commands:

> **xrdb** *filename*
> **xrdb** < *filename*

to set up a database containing the settings contained in the file *filename*, or just use xrdb on its own if you want to type in settings directly on the standard input. Later on we'll give a comprehensive description of the file format xrdb accepts, but for now take it that you enter resource settings just the same way as you have done everywhere else, whether that was in the *.Xdefaults* files, or in arguments to -xrm. E.g. to define settings for xclock you could use:

> **venus% xrdb**
> **xclock*Background: pink**
> **xclock*update: 30**
> **xclock*backgroundPixmap: cntr_ptr**
> *<end-of-file>*

Usually you use a file as the input to xrdb. E.g. it is common practice to have xrdb load defaults from a file as part of your window-system initialisation. However, when you are experimenting, directly typing in settings may be easier.

To look at the contents of the existing database : enter the command:

> **xrdb -query**

and xrdb prints out the contents of the database in a plain text format. (-query can be abbreviated to -q).

(You may recall that you can also see the database contents by using xprop on the root window; however, xprop doesn't format the output neatly, and it gives you a lot of other information you don't need). If you want, you can capture xrdb's output in a file, edit it, and use it as input to xrdb again if you want to alter settings. (But the next item describes a better way of doing that).

Caution: To look at the database, you *must* use the option -query. If you omit this and just enter xrdb on its own, you clear out the database, and xrdb will wait for you to type in new settings on the standard input.

To add extra settings to the existing database : to add more settings to the database without completely removing what's already there use the command:

> **xrdb –merge** *filename*

(As above, -merge can be abbreviated to -m, and if you omit *filename*, xrdb reads from the standard input). xrdb reads the resource settings from the specified file, and *adds* them to the existing ones. New values for any resources already in the database override the existing values, but otherwise the previous contents of the database are not altered.

To remove the database completely : as indicated earlier, the database vanishes when the system closes down and isn't re-created unless you explicitly do so yourself. But if you want to remove while the system is still running use:

> **xrdb –remove**

That concludes our "getting started" introduction to xrdb, and it should let you do most of what you want. In the next sections we describe some more advanced features which you may want to use when you are proficient with the system.

16.2.3 xrdb's File Format

You already know most of the details of the format — you use standard resource-spec of the form

> *characteristic* : *value*

as you've seen many times by now. But xrdb has two extra rules as well:

1. Comments: lines which begin with an exclamation mark (!) are ignored, so you can use them for comments.

2. xrdb passes its input lines through the C preprocessor, by default.

Let's look at the preprocessing more closely.

xrdb *Pre-Processes its Input Lines*

Let's look at a typical problem you are likely to meet. In the usual scenario, you use the following displays:

venus   *colour screen, normal resolution*
saturn   *mono screen, normal resolution*
mars   *colour screen, high resolution*

all of which share a common network file system. When you start your **X** session on a display, you want to define defaults which reflect the characteristics of that display — e.g. on the hi-res screen you will probably want a larger default font, and you don't want to define colour defaults for the mono system.

How do you do this? Let's see if you can use the *.Xdefaults-host* file: in *.Xdefaults-venus* we include colour specs, and in *.Xdefaults-saturn* we put only mono-type parameters. Does this work? Yes, but only to a limited extent: it handles applications which execute on the server machine, but applications on other machines get their own host's file. So if you are using venus and start a remote client on saturn, it will pick up *.Xdefaults-saturn* and miss all the colour specs.

Can you use the plain *.Xdefaults* file to differentiate between the machines? No, because all three hosts share the same file system, so the *$HOME/.Xdefaults* picked up on venus is also picked up on the other machines.

The solution is to provide, somewhere in the resource-processing procedure, a mechanism that can identify some characteristics of the server in use; xrdb does this using a very simple idea. It first defines a few C-preprocessor symbols which specify the server characteristics of interest, then passes all its input through the preprocessor, and finally loads the processed data into the resource database. The manpage lists all the preprocessor symbols that xrdb defines, but the ones we want to use here are:

X_RESOLUTION=n : n is the number of pixels per metre across the screen. (According to our server, our normal resolution screen has a nominal 90 pixels/inch, equivalent to 3545 pixels/metre).

COLOR : defined only if the screen supports colour. (Note the spelling: "COLOUR" doesn't work).

WIDTH, HEIGHT : the width and height of the screen, in pixels.

Figure 16.1 shows how we can use these in xrdb's input file (which we name $HOME/.Xresources, and which we will use again later). This does exactly what we want – it handles all our displays correctly, whether they are colour, or hi-res, or both. A few points are worth noting:

- You can use all the preprocessor's facilities. E.g. we used its expression-handling capability in the line:

```
! resources file for low-/hi-res ; colour/mono
!
! first resolution - normal res is about 3550
!
#if X_RESOLUTION > 3600
   *Font:            *-courier-*-r-*-180-*
   XTerm*font:       *-courier-medium-r-*-180-*
   XTerm*boldFont: *-courier-bold-r-*-180-*
#else (x-res)
   *Font:            *-courier-*-r-*-120-*
   XTerm*font:       *-courier-medium-r-*-120-*
   XTerm*boldFont: *-courier-bold-r-*-120-*
#endif (x-res)
!
! now colour
!
#ifdef COLOR
   XTerm*BorderColour:  blue
   XTerm*Foreground:    yellow
   XTerm*Background:    #242
   *Command*Foreground: pink
#endif COLOR
!
! don't bother with anything if mono
!
! now for common items
!
demo*font:       *-courier-medium-r-*-240-*
demo*boldFont:   *-courier-bold-r-*-240-*
xload*Width:     WIDTH
xload*Height:    80
xload*Geometry: 0+0
xclock*chime:    off
```

Figure 16.1 Resources file utilising preprocessor commands

#if X_RESOLUTION > 3600

- You can use preprocessor symbols anywhere in the file, not just in the #-lines. E.g. when the line

  xload*Width: WIDTH

  has been run through xrdb on venus, it will read:

  xload*Width: 1152

  so by default xload's window will be the full width of the screen, 80 pixels high, right at the top of the screen.

Caution: most Unix preprocessors define a number of symbols related to their machine architecture and operating system, and these may interfere with what you are doing. In particular, the symbol unix is usually defined. Now xrdb defines HOST to be the hostname part of the displayname, so you might think you could use a resource spec like:

demo*title: X demo using display HOST

and expect that on venus say, this would evaluate to

demo*title: X demo using display venus

In fact on our machine we get:

demo*title: X demo using display 1

What has happened is that the displayname is unix:0.0, so the host part is unix. But the preprocessor has defined unix so the whole interpretation sequence is:

HOST -> unix -> 1

You can get over this using xrdb's -U option to undefine the symbol, viz:

xrdb -Uunix < *filename*

but even so, the host name will still be unix, unless you explicitly specify the display, as in:

xrdb -display venus:0 < *filename*

Another example of interference can be seen if you enter the spec

xedit*Font: *-sun-screen-*

using xrdb. Now do an xrdb -query, and you see the setting actually in the database is:

```
xedit*Font: *-1-screen-*
```

What has happened is that on our machine the preprocessor defines another symbol, sun. You are likely to get the same effect if you use names related to your machine. (If you decide you don't need the preprocessor facility, you can disable it by giving xrdb the -nocpp option).

16.2.4 How to Merge Database Settings Back into Your xrdb Input File

Let's say you have initialised the database by running xrdb on a file containing lots of preprocessor commands like the one above. Later on in the same session you make a lot of changes to the database, using xrdb interactively, and you now want to record these settings, and include them in the input file for the future.

If you use just xrdb -query, you get only the current settings: all the lines in the input file for conditions not met on this server are not included. E.g. running our file above on saturn, all the colour and hi-res settings, and of course the #-lines are omitted. To get over this, xrdb provides the -edit option. E.g. the command

```
xrdb -edit myresf
```

merges the values currently in the database into the existing contents of the file *myresf*. It does this by matching on the *characteristic* part of the resource specs: if a line in the file has the same characteristic as an entry in the database, the value part in the file is replaced by the value part in the database. This way, all the #-lines and conditionalised settings remain in the file.

Caution: the preprocessor is not used at all with the *-edit* operation, which causes problems. Let's see what happens when we are using venus, have initialised the database with the file above, and have changed it since with:

```
venus% xrdb -merge
XTerm*font: *-courier-medium-r-*-140-*
<end-of-file>
```

and then use the command:

```
xrdb -edit myresf
```

to put the altered setting back into the file, we find two things:

1. Preprocessor symbols in value parts of specs have been replaced by literal values. E.g. we now have:

    ```
    xload*Width: 1152
    ```

    instead of

    ```
    xload*Width: WIDTH
    ```

2. Values in *all* specs whose characteristic parts match the changed one are altered, even if they are in conditionalised sections which don't apply to the current case. E.g. in the file above, both lines setting XTerm*font (one in the hi-res section, one in the normal) are changed to the new value, even though we only wanted the setting for normal case changed.

16.3   Some Common Mistakes and How to Fix Them

Especially when you are new to the system, resources can seem quite complicated. When something doesn't work it can seem that the system gives you no help at all in finding out what is happening, or where you have made your mistake. Here is a list of common mistakes, with some hints on how to fix them.

- If you don't specify an application name or class, make sure you prefix the resource spec with a star. (If you omit the star, nothing will ever match this spec). This error is particularly common when you are using -xrm, e.g.

      xclock -xrm "update: 3"   *wrong*
      xclock -xrm "*update:3"   *correct*

- Not all applications use the Toolkit. Non-Toolkit programs don't use classes, and their attribute names may be different. E.g. the spec

      *geometry: 300x400+500+600

  works for xclock, xlogo, etc., but has no effect on xcalc because it doesn't use the Toolkit, and it uses the attribute-name Geometry (with initial uppercase "G"). Because, by coincidence in this case, the Toolkit class name is the same as xcalc's attribute-name, the single spec:

      *Geometry: 300x400+500+600

  does work for all these applications.

- You may be using the wrong name for the attribute or for some widget in the spec. It is especially easy to get class and instance names mixed up; e.g. both the following are wrong:

      xclock*Update: 10
      xclock*interval: 10

  Another common error is something like:

      xterm*Text*background: blue

which doesn't work because xterm doesn't use a Text widget; its normal and Tektronix windows use widgets of class **VT100** and **Tek**, respectively. Finally, when you know what class a widget is, you may have wrongly assumed the instance name, either for the widget itself or one of its attributes. Try specifying the class name instead, to see if this fixes the problem.

- Even if you have specified real widget and attribute names or classes, the application may be using them in a way you didn't expect. E.g. you might specify the following:

```
xterm*Width: 40
xterm*Height: 10
```

with the intention of starting up xterm with a smaller window than usual, but it doesn't work. xterm applies these values to its Tektronix window, not the normal window.

- You may have everything specified perfectly correctly, but still nothing happens. E.g.

```
xmh -xrm "*inc.Label: Include"
```

is a valid way to run xmh while specifying that the label for the ⌐inc⌐ box should be "Include". However, on the standard system as distributed, it has no effect. What is happening is that xmh has an application-specific defaults file, */usr/lib/X11/app-defaults/Xmh* set up, and it contains the line:

```
Xmh*inc.label: Incorporate New Mail
```

This spec is more specific than ours (because it specifies the application) and so takes precedence.

- Including the spec:

```
*Width:200
```

on its own in the database will cause most Toolkit programs to fail on startup with a message saying that their "shell widget has zero height or width". If you specify one of height/width, you must specify the other too.

- If you have created a resource file with an editor, you may have omitted the final newline. This will cause the whole file to be ignored when you try to load it with xrdb. To avoid this, when loading resources, use a command line like:

```
xrdb resfile; xrdb -query
```

If xrdb doesn't print out what you have in *resfile*, you have a syntax problem.

- You may forget that the argument the -xrm option takes is a resource spec. Occasionally people put the resource specs in a file, and use the filename as -xrm's argument, expecting it to read the resources from the file.

- Lastly, a very human error. When you run into problems, you often end up in a cycle: edit resource file ... save it ... load resources into database ... run application and see what happens. It is surprisingly easy to omit the "load resources into database" step when you have got very confused about what is happening with the resources.

16.4   Conclusion

In this chapter you have seen all the different places you can specify resources, why there are so many different methods, and how to decide which settings to put where. You saw how to use the xrdb program to store defaults actually on the server, where they can be accessed by all clients of the server, even those executing on remote machines. And finally, there were a few practical hints about mistakes that are easy to make, telling you what to watch out for.

You are now in a position to really use resources, and to tailor your system to your taste in a big way. The resource mechanism is very powerful and almost infinitely flexible, so it should let you customise anything you want. At the beginning, try simple settings like colours or fonts, and move on to more sophisticated examples only when you have become comfortable with the basic mechanism.

In the next chapter we tell you how to use a particular type of resource settings, called *Translations*, to tailor your keyboard for specific applications.

Chapter 17 Customising Your Keyboard and Mouse — "Translations"

Computer keyboards usually have lots of "special function" keys, so that in some unspecified way you can "program" them to perform particular functions to suit your way of working. For example, you might want to define keys to enter commands you use a lot, e.g. to monitor the contents of the printer queues, or within an editor, e.g. to enter some program fragment with a single keystroke.

In **X**, you can program not only the function keys, but all the other keys as well, and the mouse buttons. For each application you can assign particular functions to keys, or to buttons, or to combinations of both. (E.g. in xedit you might want Shift and RIGHT mouse button to move you forward a word). All programs using the **X** Toolkit let the user perform these definitions, using a facility called key *translations*, and these definitions are passed to the application with the normal resources mechanism. (Other, non-Toolkit, applications could implement the same facility, but it has to be programmed into each and so is not generally available. From now on, we assume that whenever we are talking about translations, we are dealing with Toolkit programs).

Like all resources, translations are managed within each application as it executes. So for example you could have several instances of xedit with different translations set up, all running at the same time. (You might have one xedit tailored for editing text, another for editing program code, and a third for documentation).

This chapter describes translations — the format used to define them, how you specify them to applications, and the range of functions they cover. It starts with a practical introduction, which leads you gradually through the various aspects involved. Then we backtrack a little, and describe translations more formally and in more detail. And finally, we list some mistakes you are likely to meet when you use translations, and we give some hints on how to get over your problems.

17.1   Translations in Practice

At its simplest, the Toolkit *translations* mechanism allows you to program the keys of your keyboard. E.g. when you are using xterm just as a window to run a normal shell in, you might want to define several special function keys to enter commands which you often use, and you'd like to specify some correspondence like:

> *When I press   I want this string*
> *this key ...   to be typed*
>
> **F1   rm core * . tmp** *⟨newline⟩*

The way you do this with Toolkit programs is by specifying a value for a resource in the widget where the translation is to be used. This value is processed by the Toolkit's *Translation Manager* to set up the necessary customisation within the application. The resource attribute is of class Translations, and almost always the instance name is translations.

In the next section you look at the format of the value we give the resource.

17.1.1   How to Specify Translations for an Application

For the xterm example above, we define (in the resource database, or in some resource file which will be read by the application) a spec like:

```
xterm*VT100*Translations: (contd.)
<Key>F1: string("rm core *.tmp")     Incomplete!!
```

This says that in any xterm widget of class VT100, when key F1 is pressed, insert the string "rm core *.tmp".

Unfortunately, it's not as simple as that: the translation manager takes the above spec as meaning "remove *all* existing translations, and insert ...". So all normal bindings, like "key A should insert an A" are lost. To get over this you have to use some special syntax called a *directive*, which you insert at the beginning of the resource value, viz:

```
xterm*VT100*Translations: #override (contd.)
<Key>F1: string("rm core *.tmp")
```

Almost always you will want to leave most of the existing bindings as they are and just over-ride the ones you are explicitly setting values for, so almost always you will specify #override in your translation table.

The spec we have now works: try it by starting an xterm and passing the spec (enclosed in single quotes to protect it from the shell) as an argument to the -xrm option:

```
xterm -xrm 'xterm*VT100*Translations: ...etc.'
```

and press the F1 special function key. You will notice that the text is inserted OK, but no newline is included. You can get over this too with a little more syntactic sugar, like:

```
xterm*VT100*Translations: #override (contd.)
<Key>F1: string("rm core *.tmp") string(0xd)
```

This illustrates a couple of points:

1. The string() action is flexible about its arguments. You can enter text directly (e.g. string(lpq)) but if the text contains whitespace or non-alphanumerics you must surround it with double quotes. If the argument begins with "0x" it is taken as a hex number, and the corresponding ASCII character is inserted. (E.g. 0xd is RETURN).

2. The function you specify can consist of more than one action. Above, we have invoked the string() action twice, and if we knew of other actions, we could bind those in too.

Defining Many Translations Together; Syntax

You can define as many translations as you want in the one table. Suppose that, in addition to the earlier translation we want to add bindings for:

When I press this key ...	*I want this string to be typed*
F2	**lpq -Plpa3** *<newline>*

The translation for this on its own is:

```
<Key>F2: string("lpq -Plpa3") string(0xd)
```

so we can just append this to the table defined above. But the Translation Manager's format rules say we must separate one translation from the next with the sequence "\n" giving the single line:

```
xterm*VT100*Translations: #override(contd.)
<Key>F1: string("rm core *.tmp") string(0xd) \n(contd.))
<Key>F2: string("lpq -Plpa3") string(0xd)
```

This becomes very unmanageable when you have a lot of translations, and you can make it more readable by including "hidden newlines", i.e. newlines preceded by a backslash:

```
xterm*VT100*Translations: #override \n\
<Key>F1: string("rm core *.tmp") string(0xd) \n\
<Key>F2: string("lpq -Plpa3") string(0xd)
```

You can put in as many hidden newlines as you want, almost anywhere you want; they are just ignored. (As far as the translation manager is concerned, you can even split a word with them with no bad effects. But don't use them in the resource characteristic part of a spec: that is interpreted by the resource manager which doesn't work the same way). If you find this confusing, don't worry — it is a bit of a jumble. What's happening is a minor conflict in the syntax required by various parts of the system. The resource mechanism demands that the "value" part of a resource spec be all on one line; the translation manager wants each binding on a separate "line" (i.e. terminated with \n), and humans want each thing on a separate physical line to make the whole lot readable! The practical rule of thumb is: *End every translation line except the last with "\n\"*.

17.1.2 Translations Can Bind Many Types of Action

All the xterm examples above show how you can cause an arbitrary, literal, string to be inserted when you press a key. But the translation mechanism is much more general than that — it can bind to keys *any* action supported by the widget you are writing the translations for. Let's look at these "actions" in more detail.

With xterm we mapped keys F1 and F2 onto the string() action which is implemented in xterm's **VT100** widget. We'll stay with xterm, and use some more of the actions it implements.

Look up the xterm manpage, and under the headings **KEY TRANSLATIONS** and **KEY/BUTTON BINDINGS** you will find several actions listed. We'll define a translation to map key F3 onto the insert-selection() action, so that we can paste the last cut text, using the keyboard instead of the mouse. The documentation tell us that this action requires an argument; from the listing of the default bindings, we can see that the default cut-and-paste mechanism is using CUT_BUFFER0, so we'll use CUT_BUFFER0 as the argument. Our resource spec is:

```
xterm*VT100*Translations: #override\n\
<Key>F3: insert-selection(CUT_BUFFER0)
```

So far, this is just a minor convenience. However, let's say you spend a lot of time working on text documents, which you format with tbl; you preview them on your screen with nroff, and typeset them with troff, sending the output to your own printer with a (supposed) filter tr2printer. Set up the translations:

```
xterm*VT100*Translations: #override\n\
<Key>F3: string("ed ") insert-selection(CUT_BUFFER0)\
string(0xd)\n\
<Key>F4: string("tbl ") insert-selection(CUT_BUFFER0)\
string("| nroff -man") string(0xd)\n\
<Key>F5: string("tbl ") insert-selection(CUT_BUFFER0)\
string("| troff -man -t | tr2printer") string(0xd)
```

Make sure they are loaded into the database with xrdb, or are in a resource file that xterm will process. Now when you have started xterm, with the mouse "cut" the name of the file you want to work with. After that, press F3 to edit it, F4 to preview it, and F5 to typeset it on hardcopy.

More Examples of Widget Actions — xbiff

Look up xbiff's manpage: under the heading **ACTIONS** you will find the list of actions supported by the **Mailbox** widget. The only default translation is to lower the mail flag (action unset()) when you press any button. We'll set up translations so you can explicitly invoke each of the actions using the keyboard, mapping actions onto three keys: the "?", and the up and down cursor-control keys, as follows:

?	check()	*is there any new mail?*
UP	set()	*raise the mail flag*
DOWN	unset()	*lower the mail flag*

Here is the corresponding translation table:

```
xbiff*Mailbox*Translations: #override\n\
<Key>?: check()\n\
<Key>Down: unset()\n\
<Key>Up: set()
```

Try this out: load these settings onto your resource database with xrdb, then start xbiff, and position the pointer in its window. Pressing the up and down cursor control keys raise and lower the mail flag, respectively.

Finding Out What Actions Are Provided

With widget actions you have a problem similar to the one we had with resource and widget names: how do you find out what actions a widget provides, and what they do? Again, there is no perfect solution, but here is a sensible way to proceed:

1. Look up the manpage for the application. Most applications which have their own specific actions document them fairly clearly. E.g. xbiff has a section called **ACTIONS** and xterm has two sections relating to translations and actions — **KEY TRANSLATIONS** and **KEY/BUTTON BINDINGS**.

2. The original manpage may give you hints, or even tell you directly, what class of widgets it is using, so you can look up the particular widget in the documentation for its widget set. (The only widget set provided with the **core** release is the Athena one, so you can't go far wrong here). Even if the manpage doesn't tell you what class of widget it is, once you get used

to the system you will have a good idea whether a widget is one of the standard types. However, if that fails ...

3. Look at the source code of the program, to see which class of widget is used, and of the widget, to see what actions are supported.

17.1.3 Translations Bind Actions to Events, Not Just Single Keys

You have seen that translations let you specify actions apart from just inserting. The mechanism is also flexible in what you bind the action to: it can be a single key, or a sequence of keys, or in fact a sequence of any X events.

Let's stay with xbiff, and see how we can translate a sequence of keyboard characters. E.g. we'll define translations for strings of characters as follows:

```
look    check()
raise   set()
lower   unset()
```

This is the corresponding translation table:

```
xbiff*Mailbox*Translations: #override\n\
<Key>l,<Key>o,<Key>o,<Key>k:  check()\n\
<Key>r,<Key>a,<Key>i,<Key>s,<Key>e: set()
<Key>l,<Key>o,<Key>w,<Key>e,<Key>r: unset()
```

Again, try this — load the settings and start xbiff. Position the pointer in its window. Now you can raise and lower the flag by typing the full strings too, e.g. entering the five characters r, a, i, s, and e in order raises the flag. There are some points worth noting in the two tables we've used for xbiff:

- The names of the keys are specified in various ways. Normal printing characters are specified directly (as in "<Key>w"), and other characters have their names spelled out in full (as in "<Key>Down"). The appendix *"Road-Map to the Documentation"* tells you where you can look up the names of the keys, but a much easier way is described in the section below.

- For a string of characters, you specify each in turn, separated by commas (as in "<Key>l,<Key>o,<Key>o,<Key>k").

- Translations can have keys in common, e.g. "look" and "lower" both begin with "lo". The translation manager has no problems with this.

Finding Out the Names of Keys

The easiest way to find out the name of a key you want for a translation is to run xev, position the pointer in its window, and press the key you want. The name you need is contained in parentheses preceded by the string keysym and a hex number. E.g. pressing the DOWN cursor control key in xev's window gives you the output shown in Figure 17.1, from which you can see that it is

(keysym 0xff54, Down)

i.e. its name is Down.

```
KeyPress event, serial 14, synthetic NO, window 0x200001,
    root 0x8006b, subw 0x0, time 939363390, (55,105), root:(874,150),
    state 0x0, keycode 120 (keysym 0xff54, Down), same_screen YES,
    XLookupString gives 0 characters:  ""

KeyRelease event, serial 14, synthetic NO, window 0x200001,
    root 0x8006b, subw 0x0, time 939363450, (55,105), root:(874,150),
    state 0x0, keycode 120 (keysym 0xff54, Down), same_screen YES,
    XLookupString gives 0 characters:  ""

venus% ▌
```

Figure 17.1 xev output shows key names

You Can Use Any Type of Event in Translations

So far, all the translations we have written bind actions to the pressing of keyboard characters. But we said that the mechanism binds actions to events: you can specify *any* event you are interested in, not just key-presses. There is a large set of possible event types, but we'll only mention a few here:

Type	Meaning
<Key>	pressing a key
<KeyDown>	pressing a key (just a different name)
<KeyUp>	releasing a key
<BtnDown>	pressing a mouse button
<BtnUp>	releasing a mouse button
<Enter>	pointer entering the window
<Leave>	pointer leaving the window

We've already used key-press events. Let's bind xbiff actions to mouse buttons instead:

```
xbiff*Mailbox*Translations: #override\n\
<BtnDown>Button1: unset()\n\
<BtnDown>Button2: check()\n\
<BtnDown>Button3: set()
```

You can see the syntax for specifying the event is similar to what we had above: you give the general *event type*, e.g. <Key> or <BtnDown>, and follow it by an *event detail* field specifying which particular event of that type you want, e.g. s and Button3. (Buttons 1, 2, and 3 are left, middle and right, respectively).

Translations for Sequences of Events

Just as we defined a translation for sequences of key-press events (set, unset, and check), so we can use sequences of mouse events, too. In fact the sequence of events you translate can consist of any events at all — you can arbitrarily mix the event types on the left-hand side of a translation. So you could define the following (rather ridiculous) translation table:

```
xbiff*Mailbox*Translations: #override\n\
<BtnDown>Button1, <Key>?, <BtnDown>Button3: check()\n\
<BtnDown>Button1, <Key>u, <BtnDown>Button3: unset()\n\
<BtnDown>Button1, <Key>s, <BtnDown>Button3: set()
```

i.e. to invoke check() you have to press button 1 (LEFT), then the key ?, then button 3 (RIGHT) in order. This example is far-fetched, but you could use translations like these where the action to be taken is critical or irreversible (say deleting a file, or overwriting the contents of a buffer) and you want a very deliberate command sequence to invoke it so the user can't enter it by accident.

Translations Using non-Keyboard, non-Mouse Events

Usually you define translations for pressing or releasing mouse buttons or keyboard keys. But as we said, you can specify translations for *any* event, e.g. the pointer entering or leaving a widget's window. Let's illustrate this using xman's main options window (Figure 10.3) as an example. This is a rather artificial example because it doesn't do anything useful: however, we have chosen it because it's very easy to see what is happening in its operation, and there aren't yet very many other applications in the **core** release which use translations).

Look up the xman manpage: under the heading **X DEFAULTS** you will find listed (very concisely) the classes and names of the widgets which xman uses: the name of the main options window widget is **topBox**, and there is a hint that it is of class Command. This would also be a good first guess anyway, because of the way the boxes in the menu operate. (We can confirm that it is correct using the techniques we mentioned in Chapter 15: run the program with the command:

```
xman -xrm "*Command*backgroundPixmap: scales"
```

and all Command widgets will have a scaly background).

This differs in an important respect from what we've done before: we are using actions which are not specific to particular applications but which are provided by standard widgets (in this case the **Command** widget, described in the *"X Toolkit Athena Widgets"* manual).

Before we define anything ourselves, let's look at the default behaviour of the widgets so we can understand better what is happening, and see what the various widget actions are doing. Start xman, and move the pointer into Help: you see the box outline is highlighted — that is the highlight() action. Move the pointer out again: the border goes back to normal — that is the unhighlight() action. Move the pointer into Help again: press a mouse button, and keep it pressed. The box colours invert (the text is displayed in the default background colour, and the window background in the default foreground colour). This is the set() action. Still keeping the mouse button pressed, move the pointer out of the window: the colours revert to normal — this is the reset() action. The normal sequence for "clicking on" Help is:

1. Move the pointer into the box: highlight() highlights the border.

2. Press a button: set() inverts the box's colours.

3. Release the button: notify() is activated, causing the program to create the help window. While this is happening, the box colours remain inverted. When the window has been created, reset() reverts the window colours to normal, but the border remains highlighted.

4. Move the pointer out of the window: unhighlight() un-highlights the border.

(If you don't have a geometry specified for xman, you may not see the last couple of steps clearly, as you will have to use the pointer to position the help window when it is created).

Now that you have seen what the actions do, we'll define some translations to change the actions associated with entering or leaving a window:

```
*Command*translations: #override\n\
<EnterWindow>: reset()\n\
<LeaveWindow>: set()
```

With this (strange) translation table, when you initially enter the box with the pointer nothing appears to happen, but when you leave it, the colours are inverted. If you enter the box again, the colours are reset to normal. Clicking works as before.

Using Modifiers to Qualify Event Specifications

Sometimes you want to specify a translation not just for an event, but for that event only when one or more *modifiers* are pressed too. E.g. you want to bind an action to a key only when META is pressed, or to a mouse button when CTRL and SHIFT are pressed. So far we don't have any way of specifying this. We can't use event sequences to do it, because those are (by definition) sequential, whereas we want to specify things which are simultaneous, e.g. "pressing key X while CTRL is simultaneously down".

To specify modifiers in the translation, you just prefix the event with the names of the modifier(s) you want. E.g. in xterm, to define meta-i to paste the last cut text, use:

```
*VT100*Translations: #override\
Meta <Key>i: insert-selection(PRIMARY, CUT_BUFFER0)
```

Because this combination of modifier/event-type is so common, the translation manager allows an abbreviated form. Exactly equivalent to the second line above is:

```
<Meta>i: insert-selection(PRIMARY, CUT_BUFFER0)
```

We can do the same with mouse events. Let's define translations for xedit so that we can conveniently move around the text using only the mouse. Our first attempt might be something like:

```
*Text*Translations: #override\
Shift <Btn1Down>: forward-character()\n\
Shift <Btn2Down>: forward-word()\n\
Shift <Btn3Down>: next-line()\n\
Ctrl <Btn1Down>: backward-character()\n\
Ctrl <Btn2Down>: backward-word()\n\
Ctrl <Btn3Down>: previous-line()
```

However, if you try this, strange things happen — the cursor seems to have a will of its own, and pieces of text are selected and unselected. What's happening is that the **Text** widget's default bindings are still active, and these contain translations like:

```
<Btn1Up>: extend-end(PRIMARY, CUT_BUFFER0)
```

You might think that this wouldn't affect you, because you always have the SHIFT or CTRL key pressed when you release the buttons. But it does in fact: the translation manager takes the absence of modifiers to mean that you don't care whether they are in effect are not, so releases of Button1 match the spec above. To get over this we define translations for all the button-releases we are going to generate inadvertently, and bind a null action to them. These are more specific than the default spec, and if they are matched, the default one isn't. With the **Text** widget we add two more lines, giving the complete table:

```
*Text*Translations: #override\
Shift <Btn1Down>: forward-character()\n\
Shift <Btn2Down>: forward-word()\n\
Shift <Btn3Down>: next-line()\n\
```

```
Ctrl <Btn1Down>: backward-character()\n\
Ctrl <Btn2Down>: backward-word()\n\
Ctrl <Btn3Down>: previous-line()\n\
Shift <BtnUp>: do-nothing()\n\
Ctrl <BtnUp>: do-nothing()
```

This illustrates a few points:

- We have used abbreviated syntax for the mouse events, viz <Btn1Down>, whereas in earlier examples we used the explicit syntax <BtnDown>Button1. The translation manager allows a few abbreviations like this. (We have already seen the <Meta> abbreviation for modifier and an event type).

- We have used do-nothing() as a dummy action, as listed in the documentation for the **Text** widget. In fact this action doesn't exist, and causes warning messages, but as we didn't want it to do anything anyway, this doesn't matter.

- For the dummy actions we specified just the one event <BtnUp>, instead of explicitly listing all three buttons. In the same way that the translation manager takes absence of modifier specs to mean "any at all", absence of a *detail field* in an event (e.g. "Button1" in the full spec "<BtnUp>Button1") is interpreted as "any detail at all".

  A very common use of this is in translations of the form

  ```
  <Key>: ...
  ```

  No detail is specified, so this applies to *all* key-press events, i.e. to all keys. In fact one of the default translations for the **Text** widget is

  ```
  <Key>: insert-char()
  ```

  where the insert-char() action inserts the ASCII character corresponding to the key pressed.

17.1.4 Multiple Translation Tables (and More Examples)

So far we have applied all our translations to entire classes of widgets. But you can specify them for individual widgets, just like any other resource. Here we'll define more translations for xman. We'll use only keyboard events with the [Help] widget (mapping the actions onto mnemonic characters), and only window events with [Quit]. To do this we explicitly name the widget to which the translations are to apply. For this, then, our translation table is:

```
*Help*translations: \
<Key>h: highlight()\n\
<Key>u: unhighlight()\n\
<Key>n: notify()\n\
<Key>s: set()\n\
<Key>r: reset()\n\
<Key>Linefeed: set() notify()

Quit*translations: #override\n\
<EnterWindow>: reset()\n\
<LeaveWindow>: set()
```

There are a few extra syntax points to note:

- Here we are specifying different translations for different widgets of the same class, so we need to know the instance names. Unfortunately, these instance names (**Help, Quit, Manual Page**) aren't obvious. If they aren't documented (and in this case they aren't), you have to try and guess what they are (!!), or else go and look at the source code (which is what we did).

- For **Help**, we have omitted the usual #override, because we don't want *any* of the default bindings for this widget. In particular, we don't want the widget to be highlighted when the pointer enters the window, just so we can see exactly what effects our translations have.

- Having omitted the #override, we move the first translation spec onto the first line. (If we didn't do this, and ended the first line with \n\ we would get the error:

      **X Toolkit Warning: translation table syntax er-
      ror: Missing ':'after event sequence.
      X Toolkit Warning: ... found while parsing ''**

  because the \n is only used to separate translation specs or directives like #override). The alternative would be to insert a hidden newline before the first spec, like:

      ***Help*translations:\
      <Key>h: highlight()\n**
      ...

  which is a little neater.

- The last translation, for Linefeed, contains multiple actions. We saw something similar — multiple string() actions — in xterm, above.

With that we have about covered the everyday translations that you are likely to want. The basic ideas are simple, and the mechanisms used to implement them are not very complex either, but they can be very confusing. This is largely because it is a developing system, and not very much documentation comes with the release. In the next sections we recap most of what we've covered above, but whereas so far we have introduced the concepts gradually and by means of examples, now we will describe the rules for translations more formally.

17.2   Translations — Formats and Rules

Translations are a general mechanism provided by the Toolkit to let the user specify which *action* a widget is to perform when certain events are received by that widget. The part of the Toolkit which handles translations is called the *Translation Manager*.

The translations are specific to a widget, indeed to each instance of a widget. A set of translations for a widget is called a translation table, and the table is passed to the application by means of the standard resource mechanism. Widgets (those for which translations are meaningful) have a resource attribute of class Translations, usually with an instance name translations. This translation resource expects a value which is a translation table. Just like all other resources, you can specify different values for different widgets in the same application, and you can specify them by class name, or instance name, or a mixture.

Each widget defines which actions it supports, and these can vary enormously, both in number and in the types of thing they can do.

Translations can be specified for all the different types of events, not just key and mouse actions. Arbitrary sequences of events can be handled, as well as just single events.

Translations and translation tables are described very concisely and cryptically in Section Appendix B of the *"X Toolkit Intrinsics"* manual. That is not a good place to start looking at translations, but it does contain complete lists of event types, modifier names, etc., which we don't duplicate here.

17.2.1   Format of Translation Tables

A translation table has the following overall format:

> [*optional-directive*\n] *list-of-translations*

Each *list-of-translations* consists of one or more translations which have the format:

> *event-sequence* : *list-of-actions*

This specifies that the widget is to perform the *list-of-actions* when *event-sequence* occurs. If there is more than one translation in a list, they must be separated from each other using the syntax "\n".

First we'll look at the optional directive, and then look in detail at the *list-of-translations*.

17.2.2 Translation Directives — #override, etc.

The optional directive tells the translation manager how it is to process this set of translations in relation to any already set up for the corresponding widget.

#replace : clear out *all* existing mappings, and install only those in this table. (Use the new ones only).

#override : leave existing mappings in force, but also add in those in this table. If any in this table are already set, the old ones are overridden, i.e. are superseded by the new ones. (Combine old and new, but the new ones are more important).

#augment : leave existing mappings in force, but also add in those in this table. If any in this table are already defined in the existing set, use the old ones and ignore the corresponding new ones. (Combine old and new, but the old ones are more important).

If no directive is specified, it defaults to #replace.

17.2.3 Format of Individual Translation Specifications

Each translation is of the form

> *event-sequence* : *list-of-actions*

Let's look in turn at the two parts of this spec.

Format of Events and Event-Sequences

An event sequence consists of one or more *event-specs*, each of which has the format:

> **[***modifiers***]** <*event-type*> **[***repeat-count***] [***detail***]**

where everything is optional except the *event type* (which must be enclosed in < >).

modifiers : these are a refinement of the basic scheme; we'll deal with them in the next section.

event-type : specifies the type of event we are interested in, e.g. whether it is a key-press (<KeyDown>), a button-release (<BtnUp>), or pointer leaving the window (<Leave>), etc.

detail : this specifies which one of the possible many of this type we are interested in. If you omit the detail field, the event spec will match any detail; thus, <Key> on its own matches all key-press events. The format is specific to each event type. Detail fields for specific event-types are:

- For <Key>, <KeyUp> and <KeyDown> events, the detail is either the name of the key, (e.g. "<Key>s" above) or the *keysym* of that key expressed as a hex number starting with "0x". (Keysyms are explained in the next chapter — they needn't concern us much now).

- For button-events, the detail is the name of the button, i.e. one of Button1 ... Button5. E.g. we used "<BtnDown>Button1" above.

type/detail abbreviations : some combinations of event-type and detail are used so often that the translation manager allows you to abbreviate them:

Abbreviation	*Full Equivalent*
`<Btn1Down>`	`<BtnDown> Button1`
`...`	
`<Btn5Down>`	`<BtnDown> Button5`
`<Btn1Up>`	`<BtnUp> Button1`
`...`	
`<Btn5Up>`	`<BtnUp> Button5`

repeat-count : this specifies how many of these events are required. If specified, the repeat count must be enclosed in parentheses. E.g.

    `<Btn1Down>(2)`

specifies a double click with button-1. If you add a plus-sign (+) after the count, it means any number of clicks equal to or greater than the number specified. E.g.

    `<Btn1Down>(3+)`

means three or more clicks. The default repeat-count is one.

An *event-sequence* consists of one or more *event-spec*'s, separated by commas. When this sequence of events occurs in the widget, the corresponding action list is invoked.

Several rules determine whether the translation manager is satisfied that the sequence has occurred. We'll look at this more closely using an example: assume you define translations for the two character sequences set and unset:

- Broadly, the translation manager is satisfied if the individual events have happened in the specified order; other events (such as keys you haven't specified) occurring in between the specified ones do not necessarily prevent this sequence being satisfied. E.g. `set` is matched by `sweat` and `serpent`.

- However, if any of the intervening non-specified events are the start of another event-sequence in this table, the translation manager abandons this sequence and starts trying to satisfy that other one. E.g. `set` is not matched by `sauerkraut` — the `u` switches the translation manager to matching `unset`.

- If a set of events occurs in more than one event-sequence in a table, the translation manager only applies one translation:

  - If one sequence matches the end (right-hand side) of another, the shorter is applied only if it does not occur in the context of the other. So if `unset` is matched, the translation for `set` will not be actioned.

  - If one sequence occurs in the middle of another, e.g. if you defined sequences `at` and `rate`, the longer will never be successfully matched.

Event Modifiers

Modifiers are keys or buttons which you are saying must be pressed when the main event takes place if the translation manager is to take account of it. You can specify modifiers for key, button, motion and enter/leave window events. The most common modifiers are:

```
Button1  ...     Button5
Ctrl     Shift   Meta
Lock
```

If you don't specify any modifiers, the translation manager takes this as meaning "it doesn't matter which modifiers are set or not when the event happens — accept it anyway". E.g. `<BtnDown>` is satisfied when you press a button even if SHIFT and/or META are depressed at the time.

If you really want to specify "accept this event only when no modifiers are in force" specify the pseudo-modifier None. E.g. None `<BtnDown>` is not satisfied if META is down when a button is pressed.

Specifying some modifiers for an event means "match this translation if these modifiers are as specified: the state of the other modifiers doesn't matter" — it does *not* mean "when these and only these are in force". E.g. Ctrl `<Key>a` is satisfied if you press `meta-ctl-shift-a`.

If you really want to specify "these modifiers and only these", prefix the modifiers with an exclamation mark (!). E.g. ! Ctrl <Key>a is *not* satisfied if you press `meta-ctl-shift-a`.

To qualify a (possibly empty) set of modifiers with the constraint "but only if these other modifiers are *not* in force", enter these others in the modifier list, but with each of them prefixed with a tilde (˜). E.g. Shift˜Meta <Key>t is satisfied with `ctl-shift-t` but not with `meta-shift-t`.

Matching of key events usually ignores case. If you want case-sensitive matching, precede the modifiers with a colon (:). E.g. <Key>H is matched by either H or h, but : <Key>H is matched only by H.

In addition to abbreviations for common event-type/detail pairs, the translation manager also supports abbreviations for common modifier/event-type pairs:

Abbreviation	*Full Equivalent*
`<Ctrl>`	`Ctrl <KeyDown>`
`<Shift>`	`Shift <KeyDown>`
`<Meta>`	`Meta <KeyDown>`
`<Btn1Motion>`	`Button1 <Motion>`
...	
`<Btn5Motion>`	`Button5 <Motion>`
`<BtnMotion>`	*any button* `<Motion>`

Format of Actions and Lists of Actions

Each translation binds a sequence of one or more events onto a list of one or more actions. Individual actions in a list are just concatenated, and may optionally be separated by white space. (They should *not* be separated by commas — that causes an error).

The format of individual actions is:

action-name (*parameters*)

Even when no parameters are specified, the parentheses after the action-name must be entered, as in:

`start-selection()`

If you leave any space between the action name and the opening "(" you get an error.

The *action-name* can contain only the alphanumeric, dollar ($), and underscore (_) characters. Each widget supports its own set of actions (if any) and contains within itself a hard-coded list of the names for these actions.

The *parameters* are a list of zero or more character-strings, separated by commas. The meaning of the parameters is specific to the particular action (and in fact most actions don't take any parameters). The parameter strings can be unquoted, e.g.

```
insert-selection(PRIMARY)
```

or double-quoted, typically to include whitespace or a comma, e.g.

```
string("plot <x,y>")
```

There is no general way to include a double-quote anywhere in a parameter string, although a quote in the middle of a string, as in string(ab"cd) is handled OK. Nor does the syntax allow you to have both a double-quote and white space in the same parameter string. Because of this, some widgets may add their own syntax conventions when interpreting their parameters, e.g. for the string action in xterm's **VT100** widget, if an unquoted string begins with "0x", the string is interpreted as a hex number representing an ASCII character.

That concludes our description of the rules and formats for translations. With these, you should be able to understand the translations listed in the various **X** manuals, and to write translations of your own. To help your further, the next section lists some problems you are likely to meet, and how to overcome them.

17.3 Common Problems in Translation Specs

Translations are simple in concept but messy in practice. The syntax is complicated and opaque, although you get used to it in time. Anyway, when you are beginning, the best approach is to take what somebody else has done and use it as a basis for your own translations. There are several examples of translations in the manpages for xbiff, xdm (which you haven't met yet — see Chapter 20) and xterm, which you may find helpful.

If you do find that something is going wrong with your translations, here are a few points worth checking:

- Translations apply only to programs which use the Toolkit. If you try to define translations for non-Toolkit applications, everything will seem to be OK but the translations simply don't take effect.

  Let's see why this is, using translations for xcalc (which is non-Toolkit) as an example. You define a translation table for a resource named something like *xcalc*translations, and load it onto your database with xrdb. xrdb won't complain, because it doesn't know which applications use what resources — it only sets up the database, to be interrogated later by the Resource Manager. Now you run xcalc: it knows nothing about translations, so it doesn't interrogate the database for them, so it never complains either!

- Don't omit the #override unless you really know what you are doing. If you omit it by mistake, e.g. in xedit, you will find that none of your keyboard keys print anything (because the default translation "<Key>: insert-char()" has been lost).

- Check that you have terminated each line properly. If you omit the "\n\" or "\n" from a line in the middle of a translation table, all translations after it are ignored. And if you *do* end the last line with a backslash, or omit the final newline in the file, the whole table is ignored. (This is a problem with xrdb, not the translation manager).

  These errors are especially common where you are editing an existing table and moving entries around within it.

- Strange behaviour may be due to a conflict between the translations you have defined and the default ones. In particular, with mouse button events, for each press or "Down" there is a corresponding release or "Up" event, and the part you haven't explicitly specified may have a default binding. (Keyboard keys have press/release pairs of events, too). So:

  1. Check the documentation for the default bindings.
  2. If you specify a translation for only half of a press/release pair, make sure the other half isn't part of a default translation; if it is, explicitly specify a translation for it too.
  3. If you still can't work out what is happening, temporarily remove the #override from the table. This removes all the default translations, and lets you see if the problem was due to unexpected interactions, or just that your translation table is wrong.

- The Translation Manager isn't very good about telling you that you have syntax problems. E.g. if you have a translation like:

      <Key>F6: string("abc""def")

  the parameter syntax is invalid, and you will get no action from the F6 key, but you get no error message either.

- If you are translating a sequence of events, and want a modifier to apply to each, you must explicitly specify it for each. E.g. if you want a translation for ctl-X ctl-K use:

      Ctrl <Key>X, Ctrl <Key>K: ...

  If, instead, you used:

      Ctrl <Key>X, <Key>K: ...

  you would be specifying ctl-X K

- Check that the widget you want has the name or class you have specified. E.g. for xterm you might specify a table beginning:

```
xterm*Text*translations: ...
```

but this will do nothing, as xterm's normal window widget is of class
VT100. As usual, neither xrdb nor the Translation Manager will complain,
because neither sees anything wrong.

- The translation may be specified correctly, and be working too, but the
  action may not be doing what you expected. E.g. this translation for
  xterm:

```
Meta Ctrl <Key>m: mode-menu()
```

is fine, and takes effect. However, mode-menu() actually checks to see
whether it was the LEFT or MIDDLE mouse button that invoked it, and
does nothing otherwise.

- Not specifying modifiers in a translation does *not* mean that if modifiers
  are in force, the translation is not to be satisfied. What it really means is
  "I don't care about modifiers". If necessary, be more precise, and use the
  "None", " " or ! notation. Be careful about this when checking if default
  translations are going to interfere with your own.

- Translations are widget-specific, and all the actions in the translations must
  be supported by that widget. It is easy to forget this where you specify the
  translation resource name fairly loosely. E.g. a table like:

```
xman*translations: \
<EnterWindow>: reset()\n\
<LeaveWindow>: set()
```

will cause a lot of errors: the set() and reset() actions are defined only for
Command widgets, but xman has several other types of widgets which accept translations, and the Translation Manager complains that these widgets
do not support set() and reset(). The solution is to specify the resource
name more fully, e.g. xman*Command*translations in this case.

- For any given resource, the Resource Manager only passes a single value
  back to a widget when the resource database is interrogated; the value
  passed back is the one whose "characteristic" (resource-name) part most
  closely matches the widget's and attribute's full class/instance name. So
  you *can't* specify a generic translation for all **Text** widgets, and then a more
  specific add-on set just for xedit, say, and expect to have them combined:
  only one translation table is ever passed to the widget. E.g. with these
  tables:

```
*Text*Translations: #override\
```
"generic" translations for Text

```
...
xedit*Text*Translations: #override\
```
"specific" translations for xedit's Text
```
...
```

you get only the "specific" translations in xedit, and only the "generic" ones elsewhere.

The source of the confusion is the #override, whose meaning is "add these translations to the existing ones". But this is handled only within the Translation Manager, and by the time it has reached the Translation Manager the decision on which single value to pass to the widget has already been made by the Resource Manager. To the Resource Manager, #override is just another text string which is part of a value to be passed to a widget.

Because you use resources to specify translations, errors may occur in either area. To reduce the scope for error, when you are experimenting with translations it is worthwhile explicitly printing your resource database after you have loaded in the translation resource. E.g. if you are writing translations for "xprog", and have the translations in the file *mytrans*, run the program with the command:

```
xrdb mytrans ; xrdb -q ; xprog ...
```

17.4   Conclusion

This long and involved chapter has covered the standard Translations mechanism used by the **X** Toolkit to allow you to specify what effect pressing any key or button is to have. These translations are specific to each widget, and you pass translation tables to widgets with the standard resource mechanisms. You have seen how to specify translations for normal keyboard keys, and for mouse buttons, and for other events such as pointer entering a widget. Then we moved on to defining very precisely the events we want translated, by specifying what state the various modifiers are to be in if the translation is to take effect.

The second part of the chapter covered much the same area, but more formally, and explained the very detailed syntax which can be involved in translation specs, particularly for modifiers.

Finally, we gave a brief list of problems often met when using translations, and some suggestions on how to solve them.

We have covered a lot of material. There are few concepts involved, but the syntax is complicated and error-prone, and far from transparent. If you find it difficult at first, don't worry. Just start with some simple translations (probably in xterm), and where possible use somebody else's translation table or examples from the manpages as a basis on which to develop. As you gain experience you will progress very quickly: you'll be able to look right through the syntax and see what is happening behind it.

Chapter 18 Keyboard and Mouse —
Mappings and Parameters

In the previous chapter we looked at the Translations mechanism provided by the Toolkit; it let you customise your keyboard and mouse for individual instances of an application. In this chapter we look at a second, lower, level of customisation which is managed by the server, called *mapping*; in effect you tell the server that you want your keyboard laid out differently, and that this is to apply to every application connected to your server. E.g. instead of the usual QWERTY layout, you might want the keys arranged ABCDEF ... , to suit users who are not accustomed to using keyboards, (and you would of course change the symbols painted on the keyboard buttons to match). You can also specify which keys are to act as "modifiers" — Control, Shift, etc. For the mouse buttons, too, there is a corresponding mapping of "logical" button to physical. Overall, you are likely to use these key and mouse mappings much less frequently than translations.

Finally, there is a third, more everyday, type of customisation available: you can set various parameters relating to your keyboard and mouse, e.g. how loud the bell is to be, whether the keys are to click or not when you press them, and so on.

In this chapter we first describe the keyboard, mouse, and modifier mappings, with the tools for managing them, and then we describe the xset program which you use to define keyboard preferences like key click, etc.

18.1 Keyboard and Mouse Mappings – xmodmap

The server itself handles one level of keyboard and mouse customisation which applies to *all* applications using that server or display: this is *keyboard mapping*.

Each key has a unique, arbitrary, code to identify it, called a *keycode*. The correspondence between key and keycode is absolutely fixed. (In a loose way, you could say "The keycode is the key").

Associated with each keycode (or key) is a list of *keysyms*. A keysym is a special numeric constant which represents the symbol painted on the top of the key. In the default state, most keys only have one keysym associated with them, e.g. SHIFT, A, B, Delete, Linefeed, etc. Keysyms are *not* ASCII or EBCDIC characters, nor does the server maintain any correspondence between keysyms and characters. You can have more than one keysym per key. In the default mapping, many keys have two associated keysyms, e.g. Colon with Semicolon, 7 with Ampersand, etc. In the list of keysyms attached to a key, the first keysym is what pressing the key indicates when no modifier (like SHIFT, CTRL, etc.) is in force. The second keysym is what pressing the key indicates when SHIFT (or Lock) is already depressed; if there is only one entry in the list, and it is an alphabetic, the system assumes a second entry of the corresponding upper-case alphabetic. No special meaning is attached to entries beyond the first two. This association between keycode and list of keysyms is called the *keyboard mapping*.

That is as far as the server goes with handling normal keys and keysyms. It attaches no significance to keycodes, and it doesn't itself use the mapping from keycode to keysym: it just passes the information to the client application. In particular, the server has no concept of ASCII (or any other) character sets; it merely says "key ... was pressed, the modifiers ... were in force at the time, and that keysym list ... is associated with the key". It is the client (typically using the standard **X** library) which attaches meaning to keysyms and modifiers: e.g. it decides that if keysym A is generated while Ctrl is pressed, it should be interpreted as the ASCII character hex 0x1, i.e. ctl-A. Particular clients may decide to take special account of other modifiers; e.g. in xterm, when you press a key while META is in effect, the program converts this to ESC followed by the character pressed. (I.e. if you press meta-A, what is actually generated is the two characters ASCII 0x1b, ASCII 0x41).

The server does provide one extra facility in this area. You can define which keycodes you want to server to interpret as modifiers. E.g. "when the key whose keycode is ... is down, this is to mean that the CONTROL modifier is in force". These definitions are not exclusive: if you define the key labelled F7, say to be a Shift modifier, this doesn't take away the modifier meaning from any existing shift key. This facility is called the *modifier mapping*. **X** supports eight modifiers, Shift, Lock (caps-lock), Control, and Mod1 through Mod5. Conventionally, Mod1 is interpreted as Meta.

Finally, there is a similar *pointer mapping* for the mouse buttons. For each physical button you can specify which logical button-number it is to correspond to.

In effect, if you change your keyboard or mouse mappings, you are saying that the manufacturer didn't layout your input devices correctly, and that you are going to do it right yourself. (A common opinion). Of course, if you change the keymap, you ought to change the symbols painted on the tops of the keys; usually, however, people change only control and modifier keys, so that isn't very necessary. On the other hand, if you were changing the mapping so that the keyboard layout agreed with a nation-specific standard (e.g. French or German) you *would* change the symbols on the physical keys.

As you can see, changing the key mapping is a relatively rare thing — you might set it up once and never change it again. In the following sections we'll cover fairly quickly how to look at the current mappings and how to alter them, using the program xmodmap.

18.1.1   Looking at the Existing Mappings

You use xmodmap for listing the current mappings as well as for changing them. You specify various command-line options to select which of the different mappings you want printed:

List the current key mapping : specify the -pk option.

List the current modifier mapping : specify -pm (or no options at all because this is xmodmap's default action).

List the current pointer (button) mapping : specify -pp.

E.g. to print out all the mappings together, use the command:

```
xmodmap -pm -pk -pp
```

Sample listings of key, modifier, and pointer maps are shown in Figure 18.1, Figure 18.2 and Figure 18.3 respectively. (Only a part of the key map is shown — the full map is too long).

18.1.2   Running xmodmap to Change Mappings — General Options

When used to change or set maps, xmodmap processes one or more expressions specifying the action to be taken. You can enter these in a file, and have xmodmap read that file, called *myfile*, say, with either of the commands:

```
xmodmap myfile
xmodmap - < myfile
```

The dash in the second line is necessary; without it, the program will just perform its default action (listing the modifier map). Instead of entering the specs in a file, you can specify them directly on the command-line by preceding each of them with the option -e, as in:

```
xmodmap -e expression
xmodmap -e expression-1 -e expression-2 ...
```

To get more information about what xmodmap is doing, specify the "verbose" option, -v or -verbose. You can get the same printout without actually changing the maps by specifying the -n option. (This is identical in function to the -n option in the Unix make command: it says "pretend you are doing what I asked you, and tell me exactly

```
There are 2 KeySyms per KeyCode; KeyCodes range from 8 to 129.

    KeyCode        Keysym (Keysym) ...
    Value          Value  (Name)  ...

        8          0xffc8 (F11)
        9
       10          0xffc9 (F12)
       11
       12          0xffbe (F1)
       13          0xffbf (F2)
       14
       15          0xffc0 (F3)
...
       36          0xff1b (Escape)
       37          0x0031 (1)        0x0021 (exclam)
       38          0x0032 (2)
       39          0x0033 (3)        0x0023 (numbersign)
       40          0x0034 (4)        0x0024 (dollar)
       41          0x0035 (5)        0x0025 (percent)
       42          0x0036 (6)        0x005e (asciicircum)
       43          0x0037 (7)
       44          0x0038 (8)        0x002a (asterisk)
...
       59
       60          0xff09 (Tab)
       61          0x0051 (Q)
       62          0x0057 (W)
       63          0x0045 (E)
       64          0x0052 (R)
       65          0x0054 (T)
       66          0x0059 (Y)
       67          0x0055 (U)
...
```

Figure 18.1 Sample listing of the keyboard mapping

how you go about it, but don't actually perform the actions"). These extra options are very useful when you are a beginner, or are not sure that what you are doing is correct.

The syntax for each expression is different, but the general form is:

keyword target = value(s)

(where there is a space on either side of the "=").

18.1.3 Changing the Pointer Map

The pointer map is a list of logical button numbers. (Logical button-1 is what we call LEFT, logical button-2, MIDDLE, etc.; physical button-1 is the button on the left of the

```
venus% xmodmap -pm
xmodmap:  up to 3 keys per modifier, (keycodes in parentheses):

shift       Shift_L (0x6a),  Shift_R (0x75)
lock        Caps_Lock (0x7e)
control     Control_L (0x53)
mod1        Meta_L (0x7f),  Meta_R (0x81)
mod2
mod3
mod4
mod5        ▮
```

Figure 18.2 Sample listing of the modifier mapping

```
venus% xmodmap -pp
There are 3 pointer buttons defined.

    Physical        Button
    Button          Code
       1               1
       2               2
       3               3
      ▮
```

Figure 18.3 Sample listing of the pointer mapping

mouse, button-2 the next, etc., so by default the logical buttons correspond with the physical ones). The first item in the list is the logical button which is to be associated with physical button-1, the next with physical button-2, and so on. E.g. to reverse the button order, use the command:

xmodmap −e "pointer = 3 2 1"

so pressing the button on the right-hand side of the mouse is interpreted as LEFT.

18.1.4 Changing the Key Map

xmodmap lets you associate a new list of keysyms with a key (i.e. with a keycode), using the expression:

keycode *keycode* = *keysym-1* [*keysym-2* ...]

assigning *keysym-1* to the key with no modifiers, *keysym-2* to the key when SHIFTed, the next keysym (if any) to the third slot in the list for *keycode*, etc. (Remember, the system attaches no special meaning to the keysyms after the first two; the application can if it wants to).

Let's take a practical example. Some keyboards place some of the non-alphanumeric keys in non-standard places, so let's assume you want to redefine the key F6 to mean "9" when unmodified, and " (" when shifted. To write the xmodmap expression you need to know three things: the keycode for F6, and the keysyms for "9" and " (". As we mentioned in Chapter 12, you can get all of these by running xev: press each of the three current keys (F6, 9 and () and you get the keycode and keysym for each. Then put them into your expression. E.g. on our system we would use the command:

```
xmodmap -e "keycode 21 = 9 parenleft"
```

To make it easier, so you often don't have to look up the keycode, xmodmap lets you use the format

keysym *target-keysym* = *keysym-1* [*keysym-2* ...]

which means "attach this list of keysyms to the key (keycode) which currently has this *target-keysym* attached to it". E.g. for our earlier example we could have said:

```
xmodmap -e "keysym F6 = 9 parenleft"
```

If you have the same keysym attached to several keys, xmodmap can get confused, so in cases like that you should stick to the keycode ... notation.

18.1.5 Changing the Modifier Map

The modifier map in the server is a set of lists, one list for each modifier. The list for a modifier contains all the keys (keycodes) which when pressed mean this modifier is in force. xmodmap lets you add entries to a list, remove entries, or clear out a list completely. The formats for the three operations are:

add *modifier* = *list-of-keysyms*
remove *modifier* = *list-of-keysyms*
clear *modifier*

Unfortunately, the syntax is a little confusing, because instead of specifying the keycode you want, you have to specify the keysym attached to that keycode.

An example: let's say you want to have a second Ctrl key, on the right-hand side of your keyboard. On our keyboard we have an Alternate key which we don't use for anything, so we'll alter that. The command is:

```
xmodmap -e "add Control = Alt_R"
```

To illustrate a few more aspects, let's assume you don't have a "spare" key, but that you have a second Meta key on the right-hand side of the keyboard, and you want to use that. We must first remove it from the Mod1 map (you have to use the name "Mod1" — "Meta" doesn't work) and then add it into the Control map. (If we really wanted to, we could have it in both maps, so that it would in effect be a combined

Control-Meta key, useful for some editors). So put the commands:

```
remove Mod1 = Meta_r
add Control = Meta_r
```

in a file, ***mymaps***, say, and execute the command xmodmap mymaps. This works, but it's confusing if you do an xmodmap -pm — you have a Meta and a Control mixed — so it would be better to change the keysym on the key as well:

```
remove Mod1 = Meta_R
add Control = Meta_R
keysym Meta_R = Control_R
```

There are several more examples of modifier alterations in the xmodmap manpage.

Caution: when adding a key to a modifier map, the keysym is used only to specify to xmodmap which key you are talking about. It is completely local to xmodmap and is just a notation: only the corresponding keycode is passed to the server, which actually alters the map. Similarly, the keysym and keycode expressions have absolutely no effect on the modifier mappings. A common mistake is to execute a command like:

```
xmodmap -e "keysym F1 = Control_R"
```

and expect the F1 key to act like a control key. It won't — all you have really told the system is "I have painted this symbol on the top of my F1 key". What you ought to have done was:

```
xmodmap -e "add Control = F1"
```

on its own (or in conjunction with the first command if you want to make the map listings a bit clearer).

That concludes our description of manipulating all the various mappings.

18.2   Keyboard and Mouse Parameter Settings – xset

Finally we have come to the more commonplace facilities for setting various parameters for your keyboard, mouse, and screen. These are set using the xset program (which we used already to control the server's font search path). In the descriptions below we only show xset with one set of arguments, but you can specify as many together as you want to define many different settings simultaneously.

Controlling the Terminal Bell

With xset you can enable/disable the bell, and set its pitch, and its duration (assuming your machine supports these operations):

To disable the bell	**xset -b**
	xset b off
To enable the bell	**xset b**
	xset b on
To set the bell volume	**xset b** *vol*
. (to *vol%* of its max).	*e.g.* **xset b 50**
To set bell volume, and	**xset b** *vol p*
pitch, in Hertz	*e.g.* **xset b 50 300**
To set bell volume, pitch,	**xset b** *vol p d*
and duration, in milliseconds	*e.g.* **xset b 50 300 100**

Controlling Key-Click

To disable keyclick	**xset -c**
	xset c off
To enable keyclick	**xset c**
	xset c on
To set the click volume	**xset c** *vol*
(to *vol%* of its max).	*e.g.* **xset c 50**

Controlling Key Auto-Repeat

If autorepeat is enabled, keeping a key depressed causes the corresponding character to be generated repeatedly, until you raise the key.

To disable autorepeat	**xset -r**
	xset r off
To enable autorepeat	**xset r**
	xset r on

Mouse Parameters — Acceleration and Threshold

The motion of the pointer on the screen is proportional to the motion of the mouse. The *acceleration* is a multiplier applied to the pointer motion, e.g. if your acceleration is four, the pointer moves four times as fast as normal when you move the mouse. (Or if you prefer, if the pointer would normally have travelled *n* pixels, it now travels *n*x4).

Having a relatively high acceleration is handy when you want to move the pointer large distances on the screen, but it can be awkward when you want to do some fine positioning — the pointer seems to leap around. To overcome this, the server supports a *threshold*: the acceleration is brought into play only when the pointer moves more than *threshold* pixels at once.

To set mouse acceleration, to *a*	**xset m** *a* *e.g.* **xset m 5**
To set acceleration, and threshold to *t*	**xset m** *a t* *e.g* **xset m 5 10**

Controlling the Screen-Saver Mechanism

The *screen saver* is a facility intended to reduce the probability of a constant pattern burning permanently into the phosphors of your screen. The idea is that damage is most likely where the system is left idle for a long time, so the screen saver comes into effect if there has been no input for a specified period, either blanking the screen totally, or displaying a varying pattern.

If you choose a varying pattern rather than blanking, the root window background covers the whole screen, a big X appears on the screen, and it moves periodically. The X changes size each time it moves, and the background is shifted randomly too. (You won't notice this with a fine-grained background pattern, but with a large one you can see it jump).

If you find that repainting the application windows when the screen-saver has finished takes too long, you can specify that it should come into effect only if the server can re-paint the screen without generating any exposure events (i.e. without having to ask applications to re-paint their windows themselves). This applies only to the varying-pattern case: blanking the screen is a purely hardware action and doesn't affect the applications.

To enable the screen saver	**xset s**
To disable the screen saver	**xset s off**
We prefer screen blanking	**xset s blank**
Allow activation only if no exposure events	**xset s noexpose**
Allow activation even if exposure events	**xset s expose**
We prefer varying pattern	**xset s noblank**
Screen saver to activate when system idle for *t* seconds	**xset s** *t* *e.g.* **xset s 600**
and pattern to vary every *p* seconds	**xset s** *t p* *e.g.* **xset s 600 10**

Let's combine these, assuming that we want the screen saver to come in after 80 seconds idle, we want varying pattern, with a period of three seconds, and we don't mind if exposure events are generated:

```
xset s noblank s 80 3 s expose
```

Caution: the value on is not supported for xset s.

18.3 Conclusion

The first part of this chapter told you how to change the mapping of physical keys and buttons to logical ones, which can then be interpreted by client applications. You saw how to use xmodmap to list or change each of the mappings for keyboard keys, modifiers, and mouse buttons. These mappings are maintained in the server and so apply to every application using the server. This mechanism gives you the freedom to alter the layout of your keyboard, whether out of personal preference or to meet an external standard.

In the second part of the chapter you saw how to use xset to specify settings for more commonplace characteristics such as key-click, terminal bell, screen saver, and mouse speed ("acceleration").

Chapter 19 More About uwm and How to Customise It

In Chapter 6 you learned how to use uwm to perform the basic window-configuration tasks necessary just to be able to use windows in a comfortable way. Now we continue with uwm, looking at two main areas:

1. Some extra useful features the program supports, in particular:

   - Configuring windows directly with the mouse, without using menus.

   - Some more menu selections we haven't described yet.

   - Editing the titles of existing icons.

2. How to customise uwm, including:

   - Defining your own menus for any commands you want.

   - Binding different window manager functions to the mouse buttons and modifier keys (SHIFT, CTRL, etc).

19.1 New Features of uwm

The facilities we are going to describe here are standard uwm functions — we omitted them before so as to keep the introduction to window managers as simple as possible.

19.1.1 Managing Windows Without Using uwm's Menu

Up to now you have relied on uwm's menu for configuring your windows — moving them, resizing them, etc. Using the menu all the time is a fairly slow business, so uwm gives you the option of performing any of its functions directly.

You specify the function you want to perform, and which window it is to operate on, using the mouse buttons and the keyboard *modifier* keys. By now you ought to be quite familiar with the meaning of the various window manager functions and how they work, so we'll run quickly through them just telling how to select them outside the menu.

Move : To move a window:

1. Press META and keep it pressed.
2. Position the pointer in the window to be moved.
3. With the RIGHT button, drag the window to its new position.

Resize : To resize a window:

1. Press META and keep it pressed.
2. Position the pointer in the window to be resized.
3. With the MIDDLE button, drag the window outline to its new shape.

Lower : To send a window to the bottom of the stack:

1. Press META and keep it pressed.
2. Click on the window to be lowered with the LEFT button.

Raise : To raise a window to the top of the stack:

1. Press META and keep it pressed.
2. Click on the window to be raised with the RIGHT button.

Circulate up : To raise to the top the lowest obscured window, you have two options. *Either*

1. Press META and keep it pressed.
2. Click the RIGHT button on the *root* window.

or

1. Press META and SHIFT and keep them pressed.
2. Click the RIGHT button anywhere on the screen.

Circulate down : as for *Circulate up*, but use the LEFT button.

Iconify : As before we have two styles of iconify, one for windows which have been iconified before (and therefore have an icon location defined), and the other for "new" windows.

To iconify a new window:

1. Press META and keep it pressed.
2. Position the pointer on the window you want to iconify.
3. Press the LEFT button, and keeping it pressed ...
4. ... Drag the icon outline to where you want it positioned.
5. Release the button (and META).

Note that the only difference between this and the procedure for *Lower* is that here you *press ... drag ... release* the mouse button, and for *Lower* you just *click* it.

To iconify a previously iconified window:

1. Press META and CTRL and keep them pressed.
2. Click the LEFT button on the window you want to iconify.

(If you do this on a window which hasn't been iconified before, or which hasn't had an icon position specified via the resource mechanism, the icon is positioned where the pointer is).

De-Iconify : To change an icon back into its window (at its original position):

1. Press META and keep it pressed.
2. Click the MIDDLE button on the icon.

If you find these bindings of function to mouse button awkward, or difficult to remember, don't worry: lots of people do. But even better: the bindings are completely configurable by you — what we have listed are only default settings. You can change any or all of them if you want, and we'll tell you how to do that in the second half of this chapter. For now though, we'll look at some functions in the standard menus and what they can do for us.

19.1.2 Some More uwm Menu Selections

These are the selections in the standard menus which we didn't explain in Chapter 6.

Focus : lets you set the keyboard *focus*, i.e. attach the keyboard to a window, so that keyboard input is always directed to that window, no matter where the pointer is on the screen. Normally the input is directed to the application window that the pointer is currently in.

> **To set the focus to a particular window** : select **focus**, giving the hand cursor, and click this on the window you want to direct the input to.

> **To reset focus to normal** : select **focus**, but click on the background window.

Restart : stops uwm, and causes it to restart, re-reading its configuration file (see below) as it does so. Use this selection when you have changed the configuration and want the new settings to come into force immediately (rather then waiting until you start a new session again).

Freeze : pauses all display to windows. You might use this when you want to photograph your screen. To enable displaying again, use ...

UnFreeze : enables display again, and all windows update themselves immediately.

Exit : aborts uwm. Use this when you want to kill off uwm, e.g. prior to starting a different window manager.

The Preferences Menu

As we mentioned in Chapter 6, there are two ways of calling up uwm's **WindowOps** menu — pressing the MIDDLE button on the background window, or holding down META and SHIFT and clicking MIDDLE anywhere. Using the second method lets you call up a second menu, headed *Preferences*, by moving the pointer sideways out of the *WindowOps* one.

The selections in *Preferences* just invoke the xset program to set mouse and keyboard options.

Caution: the selections **Lock On** and **Lock Off** are historical, and may cause an error message to be printed in your console window.

19.1.3 Changing the Title on Existing Icons

uwm's default icons — grey boxes with a name inside — have the disadvantage that if you are running many copies of the same application, e.g. three xterm's, it is not obvious which icon is which. To get over this, uwm lets you edit the string in the icon to anything you want. (This only applies to uwm's own default icons — e.g. you can't edit a string into xclock's special icon).

To edit the name in an icon:

1. Position the pointer in the icon.

2. Type in any text you wish.

3. You can remove text — whether it was there previously, or you've just typed it in, as follows:

   To remove the last character : press DELETE.

   To remove the whole name : press ctl-U.

19.2 Customising uwm

uwm is highly configurable. You can store a whole range of parameters and definitions in a configuration file which uwm reads when it starts up. And as we mentioned above, you can change the file in mid-session and tell uwm to re-read it by selecting **Restart** in the **WindowOps** menu.

uwm's Configuration Files

By default, uwm uses two configuration files, one of them

/usr/lib/X11/uwm/system.uwmrc

is typically set up by the system manager and is read in first and the other

$HOME/.uwmrc

is your own. Neither file need exist, and uwm has its default settings hard-coded in.

Caution: if you setup a configuration file with incorrect syntax, when uwm reads it you will get an error like:

```
uwm: /usr/nmm/.uwmrc: 38: syntax error
uwm: Bad .uwmrc file...aborting
```

and uwm will not start at all. When starting a new session, this isn't too much of a problem. However, if you are resetting uwm in mid-session you can end up with no window manager and no xterm or editor window in which to edit the bad file or start another window manager. If this happens, to close **X** down you must login from another terminal or machine, or else crash your system.

uwm's Command-line Options

If you don't want the system file, and don't want any of the default settings, you can suppress them by giving uwm the command-line option -b.

If you want to use another file, as well as the two standard ones, you can specify it with *-f filename*.

19.2.1 Binding Functions to Buttons and Keys

uwm lets you define what function is to be invoked when you press a particular mouse button, e.g. that a window is to be raised to the top of the stack when you click MIDDLE on it, say. This binding mechanism has no connection whatever with the Toolkit translations — it is implemented entirely by uwm itself.

To make this mechanism more useful, you can specify other conditions for invoking the function, perhaps a modifier key (like META) must be depressed, or the action is to happen only if the pointer is positioned on an icon but not an application window or the background window. We've already seen examples of this in practice:

This function is to occur	*... only if these modifier keys are pressed, and ...*	*... only if pointer is in this type of window and ...*	*... when this mouse event occurs*
Resize	META	**normal**	MIDDLE **pressed and moved**
WindowOps menu	*none*	**background**	MIDDLE **pressed**
WindowOps menu	META **and** SHIFT	*doesn't matter*	MIDDLE **pressed**

You specify bindings by including binding specs in your *.uwmrc* (or other configuration file). Specs are formatted almost as written in the table above, viz:

> *uwm-function* = *modifiers* : *window context* : *mouse events*

where the components are:

uwm-function : the name of one of uwm's inbuilt functions. E.g. the function *f.move* is what you have been using all along to move windows, *f.lower* lowers a window, etc. The functions are described more fully below.

The function-name *must* be followed by an equals-sign (=).

modifiers : a list of modifier keys which must be depressed when the specified *mouse-event* occurs for this function to be invoked. Valid modifier names are:

> **ctrl** (or c), for the CONTROL key.
>
> **meta** (or m or mod1) for META.
>
> **shift** (or s) for the SHIFT key.
>
> **lock** (or l) for CAPSLOCK.

The case must be exactly as shown. You use one or two modifiers; if you use two, separate them with an | symbol.

You can omit the modifier list completely (and the function will be invoked only when the mouse event occurs and no modifier keys are pressed) but you must always enter the trailing colon (:).

window context : restricts the invoking of this function: it is invoked only if the pointer is in a specified type of location on the screen. Valid contexts are:

window (or w): the pointer must be positioned in an application window.

icon (or i): the pointer must be positioned on an icon.

root (or r): the pointer must be positioned on the root or background window.

You can specify any number of contexts, separated by a | symbol. If you don't specify any, the function is invoked no matter where the pointer is positioned.

mouse event: which mouse action is to invoke the function. Specify the event as a button-name — any of

left (or l)

middle (or m)

right (or r)

followed by an action:

down : invoke the function when the button is pressed.

up : invoke the function when the button is released.

delta : invoke the function when the button is moved more than a small threshold number of pixels.

You have actually used all of these in practice — the bindings for some of the actions described at the beginning of this chapter are:

```
f.resize = meta : window : middle delta
f.iconify = meta : icon : middle up
f.raise = meta : window|icon : right down
```

showing each type of mouse action, and a few contexts. The default bindings for uwm are listed in the file *$TOP/clients/uwm/default.uwmrc*, which is shown in Figure 19.1.

uwm's Built-In Functions

The uwm manpage lists the available functions. You have met most of them already, and from Figure 19.1, you can see which function corresponds to which selection in the **WindowOps** and **Preferences** menus.

However, one set of functions you haven't met are those concerned with *pushing* windows (**f.pushleft**, **f.pushup**, etc). Pushing is just what it says: you move a window in a specified direction, but it is moved a fixed distance. This is different from the

```
# $Author $
# $XConsortium $
# Copyright (c) 1987 by the Massachusetts Institute of Technology.
#
# This is a startup file for uwm that produces an xwm lookalike,
# but adds two useful menus.  It is patterned on the public
# distribution ../lib/X/uwm/jg.uwmrc file by Jim Gettys.
#
resetbindings
resetvariables
resetmenus
noautoselect
delta=5
freeze
grid
zap
pushabsolute
push=1
hiconpad=5
viconpad=5
hmenupad=3
vmenupad=0
iconfont=fixed
menufont=fixed
resizefont=fixed
volume=0

# FUNCTION        KEYS     CONTEXT          MOUSE BUTTON ACTIONS
f.newiconify=     meta     :window|icon:    delta left
f.raise=          meta     :window|icon:    delta left
f.lower=          meta     :window|icon:    left up
f.raise=          meta     :window:         middle down
f.resize=         meta     :window:         delta middle
f.iconify=        meta     :icon:           middle up
f.raise=          meta     :window|icon:    right down
f.move=           meta     :window|icon:    delta right
f.circledown=     meta     :root:           left down
f.circleup=       meta     :root:           right down
f.circledown=     m|s      ::               left down
f.menu=                    :root:           middle down   : "WindowOps"
f.menu=           m|s      ::               middle down   : "WindowOps"
f.menu=           m|s      ::               middle down   : "Preferences"
f.circleup=       m|s      ::               right down
f.iconify=        m|c      :window|icon:    left down
f.newiconify=     m|l      :window|icon:    left down
f.raise=          m|l      :window|icon:    left up
f.pushright=      m|l      :window|icon:    right down
f.pushleft=       m|c      :window|icon:    right down
f.pushup=         m|l      :window|icon:    middle down
f.pushdown=       m|c      :window|icon:    middle down
```

Figure 19.1 The default .uwmrc configuration file

```
menu = "WindowOps" {
New Window:        !"xterm&"
RefreshScreen:     f.refresh
Redraw:            f.redraw
Move:              f.move
Resize:            f.resize
Lower:             f.lower
Raise:             f.raise
CircUp:            f.circleup
CircDown:          f.circledown
AutoIconify:       f.iconify
LowerIconify:      f.newiconify
NewIconify:        f.newiconify
Focus:             f.focus
Freeze:            f.pause
UnFreeze:          f.continue
Restart:           f.restart
" ":               f.beep
KillWindow:        f.kill
" ":               f.beep
Exit:              f.exit
}
menu = "Preferences" {
Bell Loud:         !"xset b 7&"
Bell Normal:       !"xset b 3&"
Bell Off:          !"xset b off&"
Click Loud:        !"xset c 8&"
Click Soft:        !"xset c on&"
Click Off:         !"xset c off&"
Lock On:           !"xset l on&"
Lock Off:          !"xset l off&"
Mouse Fast:        !"xset m 4 2&"
Mouse Normal:      !"xset m 2 5&"
Mouse Slow:        !"xset m 1 1&"
}
```

f.move function, where you interactively specify how far and in which direction the window is to be moved.

By default, **f.pushdown** is bound to pressing the MIDDLE button with CONTROL and META down. Try it a few times, and you'll see your window moves very slightly — the push functions are very useful for fine-positioning of windows.

Another function is **f.moveopaque**. This moves a window, but unlike *f.move*, it doesn't give you a grid to indicate the new position of the window: you drag the whole window itself. This can make screen management clearer, but it is much slower and jerkier than the normal window-move.

19.2.2 Defining Your Own Menus

One very powerful uwm function is **f.menu**: this lets you define your own menus. Menus can invoke uwm's own functions, or arbitrary shell commands, or a special action which inserts text in a cut buffer.

You define a menu in your configuration file in a two step process. First you define the binding which will invoke the menu, and second you define the contents of the menu itself. The binding is just like we used before, but there is an extra field at the end which is the menu name. E.g. for the **WindowOps** menu (called by pressing the MIDDLE button on the background window) the binding is:

```
f.menu = : root : middle down : "WindowOps"
```

The menu name here is both the name displayed on the menu when it is invoked and a link to the menu-contents spec later in the configuration file.

The format for the menu contents is simple: you include a line for each selection, giving the "name" of the selection as it is to appear on the menu, and the action to be taken when it is selected. And around the set of lines making up one menu you have to include a little bit of "syntactic wrapping". Let's look at an abbreviated definition for **WindowOps**:

```
menu = "WindowOps" {
New Window : !"xterm &"
RefreshScreen : f.refresh
Redraw : f.redraw
Move : f.move
}
```

From this you can see that the syntax is:

```
menu = "menu name" {

   . . .

selection lines

   . . .

}
```

where the *menu name* is the same as you specified in the bindings line (and should be quoted). The selection lines consist of the selection name, the colon delimiter (:), and the action to be taken. The action can be one of three things:

1. A uwm function: just use its name, as in the "move" line in the example above.

2. A shell command: enclose the command in quotes (specifying with the shell's & syntax that it is to run in the background) and prefix it with an exclamation mark (!). E.g. the "xterm" line in the example. (If you omit the ampersand, uwm will hang, waiting for the command to complete, and in turn this will cause trouble if the program is an **X** application which needs uwm to position its window).

3. A text string: this is inserted into a cut buffer, from which you can paste it as usual.

Multiple Menus on the Same Key-Binding

Usually you bind only one menu to a particular key/button combination, but you can have multiple menus on the same binding: if you don't select anything from one and move the pointer sideways out of it, you get the next menu. You have seen this already in practice: clicking MIDDLE with META and SHIFT down first gives you the **WindowOps** menu, and then the **Preferences** one.

Binding multiple menus is trivial — just define each binding as though none of the others were present — and define the menus' contents in the standard way. E.g. uwm's default settings include the bindings:

```
f.menu = meta | shift :: middle down : "WindowOps"
f.menu = meta | shift :: middle down : "Preferences"
```

Note that you define a menu only once, but you can use it in as many bindings as you wish. (Look at the default setup: you will see that the **WindowOps** menu is defined once but used twice).

Specifying Colours for Menus

You can specify colours to be used in a menu. For each selection item you can specify a foreground and background colour, a foreground and background for the menu's name-heading, and a foreground and background colour to be used to highlight the selection the pointer is currently in, i.e. the one which will be selected when the mouse button is released. The syntax is a little bit strange — you embed the colour specs in the rest of the menu definition — so a colour menu is of the form:

menu = *"menu name"* **(***head-fg* : *head-bg* : *hilite-bg* : *hilite-fg***)** {
...
selection-name : **(** *item-fg* : *item-bg* **)** : *action*
...
}

As a concrete example, you could make your **WindowOps** more colourful with:

```
menu = "WindowOps"(yellow : blue : red : green) {
New Window : !"xterm &"
RefreshScreen : f.refresh
Redraw : (navy : magenta) : f.redraw
Move : f.move
}
```

The header will be yellow on blue, most of the items will be black on white (the default) except "Move", which will be navy on magenta, and the currently pointed-at selection will be shown in red on green.

19.2.3 Parameter Variables which Control uwm

So far you have been able to change which functions are invoked when you use particular mouse and key sequences, whether using a menu or not. There is another type of customisation of uwm: you can alter the mode or "style" in which many of the in-built functions operate, e.g. you can specify that for resize or move operations, the grid to indicate the new position should be just an outline, instead of the nine-square type you have used so far. The manpage lists all the variables and their meanings, but here we'll mention some particularly useful ones, and explain a few of the more obscure ones.

To over-ride settings in the default configuration files : uwm has no mechanism to suppress reading of the system and user configuration files. (-b doesn't affect *$HOME/.uwmrc*). To "undefine" settings contained in an earlier file, include the uwm variables resetbindings, resetmenus, and resetvariables to undo the previous definitions of the bindings, menus and variables, respectively. (Make sure you put these at the top of your file — otherwise they will undo anything that comes before them in the file).

To confine windows and icons to within the screen : X allows you to position your windows anywhere, even partially (or fully!) off the screen, which can sometimes be awkward. uwm doesn't offer any help when you are creating a window. But when you use f.newiconify to de-iconify an icon, if variable normalw is set, then the window is positioned fully on-screen, as close as possible to where you specified with the pointer. (The same applies to icons if you have normali included).

To control the push **action** : by default, the f.push*xxx* functions push a window one pixel in the appropriate direction. You can make them push *num* pixels by specifying push=*num*. You can also change the mode of operation completely: instead of pushing a fixed number of pixels as usual (which is called pushabsolute), you can specify pushrelative: in this case the window is pushed by one *num*'th the size of the window. E.g. if you specify

```
push=5
pushrelative
```

then a f.pushup will move the window up by a distance equal to a fifth of the window's height.

To prevent uwm **functions locking-out applications** : by default, certain uwm operations like resize and move cause all other client applications to freeze, i.e. prevent them outputting to their windows. You can over-ride this by specifying nofreeze.

This is necessary if you want to take window-dumps of some of uwm's own transient windows (such as the resize dimensions box in Figure 6.6). It also has the side-effect that the outline grid displayed during resizing and moving flashes a lot and is harder to see.

19.3   Conclusion

This chapter has shown you how to use some more features of uwm, now that you are more experienced with the system and can make use of them. In particular, you have seen how to configure windows without using the default menu, which lets you work much more rapidly.

The second part of the chapter outlined how you can customise uwm: how to attach uwm built-in functions to specific combinations of modifier keys and mouse actions, how to define general menus, and how to use uwm's parameter variables to tailor modes of operation.

Just as an aside before we finish, it is worth noting that uwm is just a client of the server, as xclock or xterm or xedit are. So, it is possible to run uwm remotely, e.g. execute uwm on saturn, but specify -display venus:0 so it is the window manager for venus. This illustrates how deeply the network elements are ingrained into the system; on normal workstations this is just a curiosity, but with **X** terminals (which don't support general-purpose processes) it is actually a necessity.

We are now nearing the end: you have really all the functionality you need to run your window system. You have window manager, applications, convenience tools, window-related utilities, and a wide range of facilities for tailoring all these to suit your display, the configuration of your network, and just how you prefer to work. To finish off, in the next chapter we will bring together all you have learned so far, showing you how to manage your complete working sessions, and we will include practical examples of defining uwm menus and preferences.

Chapter 20 Putting It All Together — xdm

Now we have covered all the individual items you need to use **X**. You know how to start the system, how to set a window manager running, how to run applications, how to customise all the various aspects of the system, and finally, how to shut it down.

In this chapter we bring all these separate parts together, and describe a complete set of files to customise the system for the machine environment we have used for all our examples. As part of this we introduce the last **X** tool we are going to look at: the *display manager*, xdm, which provides a clean and elegant way to start **X** sessions on your machine.

20.1 What We Want to Do

When we start up, we want our screen laid out so that the applications we use all the time are already running. Some we use only occasionally, and we want these to come up initially as icons. We want the window manager to be running, and there are a few miscellaneous settings which we want set up too. In detail then, we want the following programs:

- A "console" xterm, in the top left corner of the screen.

- uwm running in the background.

- A full-screen xterm window for our (normal) editor, iconified on startup.

- A (smaller than usual) clock in the top right corner.

- xbiff below the clock.

- A calculator in the bottom right corner.

- An iconified xterm using the smallest font we have, the full height of the screen.

- Load average displays for the remote machines we use frequently, aligned below xbiff.

and items other than programs:

- Set the background window to a light grey.

- Enable key-click on the keyboard.

- Allow access to our server from all our usual network hosts.

- Load our server-specific resources, in the file *$HOME/.Xresources* which we defined in Chapter 16, onto the root window RESOURCE_MANAGER property, for all clients to use.

- Enable a *screen saver*.

and we want uwm to have menus to allow us to:

- Access other hosts on the network easily.

- Change some keyboard and mouse settings, and set the background window colour.

- Start up **X** applications which we use only occasionally.

- Start up some selected demos.

All this is specific to ourselves; other users on our network want different initial setups. So we want an arrangement where individual users can set up their own preferences, and ideally, they ought to be able to do this on their own, without the assistance of the system manager. In the next section we see how the program xdm can help us do this.

20.2   An Overview of xdm — The X Display Manager

xdm manages one or more displays, which can be on the same machine that xdm is executing on, or on remote machines. It does all that xinit does, but a lot more as well. The idea behind it is that it should control a complete "session" of you working on X. In the same way that a "login session" is all the work you do from when you login to the system until you logout, here a session is from when you enter the window system until you finish. (With xinit, the session starts when you run xinit and ends when you logout of your initial xterm window and the server closes down).

xdm goes further than this: you can have it run an indefinite cycle of sessions. As one finishes, it gets ready to start the next, and so on. In effect, it lets you dedicate a display permanently to X if you want to.

xdm replaces xinit completely. You can forget about xinit from now on, and you need never use it again. We only used xinit in the first place because it makes it easier to see and understand how the system is operating.

xdm is a very flexible program, and you can configure it almost any way you want. Before going into it too deeply, let's look at its default behaviour in a sample session. Then we can move on, and see what else you can do to improve the initial interface a user sees when entering the X system.

20.2.1 A Sample Session with xdm

We are going to use xdm to set X running on our machine. Your machine is up, but no window system is running at this point. Start xdm with the command:

```
xdm
```

xdm runs, and you get your shell prompt again almost immediately. Then the screen background changes to the usual grey pattern, and you get the big X cursor, so you know the server has started.

Welcome to the X Window System

Login: mansfiel
Password: |

Figure 20.1 xdm's authentication widget

Next there is a long pause — this can easily last 15 seconds or more — and suddenly a window appears with a welcoming banner, asking you for your login name and password, as shown in Figure 20.1. (This is xdm's *authentication widget*). Type in your username and password, there is another pause, and then you get an xterm window in the top left corner, just as you did in Figure 5.3. From now on you work just as you did before — start your window manager, run applications and so on.

When you want to finish, you close down the same way as before, too: logout of the initial xterm window. But this is where xdm differs from xinit. Instead of the server closing down, and returning you to the non-**X** environment, the screen reverts to the startup grey background, and after a pause you get the **X** login-window again. In fact, xdm is running a repeating cycle of sessions.

Caution: like many Unix programs, the authentication enforces a maximum login-name length of eight characters — if you enter more than this the login will fail. (This may be surprising if your real login program lets you use longer names).

Closing Down xdm

At some time you may want to close down **X** altogether. To do this, you close down xdm.

The servers in the MIT release follow the convention that if they receive the Unix signal SIGTERM, they will terminate. xdm makes use of this: if you send *it* a SIGTERM, it shuts down all the servers it is controlling, and exits. That's how you shut the system down.

To shut down xdm in practice then, in an xterm window (or elsewhere on your machine) use ps to find the xdm's process-id, and send it SIGTERM using kill. (You will see several xdm processes running: the one you want is the youngest, i.e. with the lowest process-id). E.g. on our machine we did a shutdown with:

```
venus% ps ax | grep xdm
1997 ?  IW   0:00 xdm
1998 ?  IW   0:00 xdm
2000 ?  IW   0:00 xdm
2078 p0 S    0:00 grep xdm
venus% kill -TERM 1997
```

All your applications are aborted, and the server closes down.

Caution: when everything relating to **X** has finished, your screen may end up with just the usual **X** background grey pattern, without any shell prompt or anything else. Don't be fooled: your shell is ready for your commands — press RETURN and you'll see. (What has happened is that the shell has already given you your prompt: it gave it to you after the interactive xdm command you entered finished, so it's not going to repeat it now — unless you press RETURN).

20.3   More About xdm

What we've described above is xdm's default mode of operation. So far it doesn't seem to offer very much more than xinit, but it does really. If you are using a normal workstation or display, some aspects won't be of great interest. However, an increasingly popular device is the *X-terminal*, and xdm greatly simplifies administering such systems. As the X-terminal usually doesn't have a file-system of its own, and can't support general purpose programs, the controlling software — including the window manager and display manager for the terminal — have to be run elsewhere in the network, and that is where xdm becomes so necessary.

xdm has advantages over xinit in the following areas:

- It can control multiple servers. By implication, some of these are remote servers, perhaps on X-terminals or on fairly small workstations.

- It provides password access control to the system. Again, this is very useful on X-terminals (but a bit of a nuisance of ordinary workstations where you have logged in already).

- It supports indefinite cycles of **X** sessions. You can configure displays to operate permanently within **X**, so users don't have to worry about how to start up the system.

- It is highly configurable. The system manager can setup site-specific start- and end-procedures, to handle such items as accounting, authorisation, file-system management, etc., and yet leave individual users full scope to tailor their own environment as they require.

- From the user's point of view, it provides a clean, simple, way to start the system.

So overall, xdm is primarily a system-administration tool, but it also provides a uniform and consistent framework in which ordinary users can customise their system as they wish.

The xdm manpage contains a lot of tutorial information and guidelines on how to use the program, which we won't duplicate here. However, what we will describe in the following sections is how exactly you configure xdm to provide the environment which, at the beginning of the chapter, we said we wanted.

xdm really is very flexible, and you can select settings in many different ways. We will use the simplest approach while trying to stay broadly consistent with the descriptions given in the manpage. Occasionally we use different names for some files, to emphasise that the names are not hard-coded or otherwise special.

As we work through this, bear in mind that we are really doing two separate jobs: the first is as system manager, setting up xdm for anyone using the system, and the second is as a normal user, setting up what we want for ourselves.

20.3.1 System-Manager's Configuration for xdm

By default, xdm looks for the file

> */usr/lib/X11/xdm/xdm-config*

and if it exists, treats it as a resource file which specifies several other parameters. We will use this, because it simplifies our task.

The manpage lists all the parameters you can set via the ***xdm-config*** file, but the ones we are interested in are:

- The name of a file containing a list of the servers which xdm is to manage.

- The name of a file in which xdm is to record any errors it encounters.

- The name of a file containing resources relating to the startup of the system.

- The name of the program to be run for you after the server has started. This program defines your "session" — when this program terminates, xdm takes it to mean that your session has ended, and goes back into its login sequence. By default, the program used is xterm; here, just as we saw before when using xinit, your session lasts until you logout of your initial xterm.

Here are the settings we have defined on our system:

```
DisplayManager.servers:        /usr/lib/X11/xdm/our-servers
DisplayManager.errorLogFile:   /usr/lib/X11/xdm/errors
DisplayManager*resources:      /usr/lib/X11/xdm/our-resources
DisplayManager*session:        /usr/lib/X11/xdm/our-session
```

(We have chosen to keep all the xdm-related files in the directory */usr/lib/X11/xdm*; this is only a convention — you could use any directory you like).

So you can see that the way we are using ***xdm-config*** is really a two-step process: first we define, in ***xdm-config*** some filenames, and second, we go and setup the files we've just named. Let's now look in turn at each of the resources we are defining in ***xdm-config***.

xdm*'s List of Servers*

The file specified by the DisplayManager.servers resource contains a list of servers managed by xdm. Each line contains the name of a server (i.e. display), its *type*, and a type-dependent entry.

The type specifies whether the display is local or remote, and whether an indefinite cycle of sessions, or only a single session, should be run on that display. (See the xdm manpage for a full list). We will use type localTransient — single session on a local display — because that way, if anything goes wrong, we won't get into an infinite loop. Later on, when we have everything setup and working, we can change the type to local, and run a cycle of sessions.

The type-dependent information, for a local display, is the name of the server program to run for this display, and any necessary arguments. For a remote display, the information is ignored, but you still must enter a dummy program name.

So, we create our file */usr/lib/X11/xdm/our-servers* containing the one line:

```
:0 localTransient /usr/bin/X11/X :0
```

(If we were happy to run with a cycle of sessions, this file wouldn't be necessary at all — the default setting does what we want — so we wouldn't define the DisplayManager.servers resource in the configuration file).

xdm's Error Log File

This file receives all error messages from xdm and xdm's session program, and if you are having trouble getting your xdm setup to work, this is the first place to look.

When you are just setting up your system, set the permission of this file so that everyone can write to it — otherwise errors may not be recorded because the offending program isn't allowed write-access to the file.

Resource File for Starting-Up Time

This file contains a list of resources which are loaded by xrdb just *before* the authentication widget starts. Consequently, you can use it to specify resources for that widget. (You can of course put any other resource specs into it too, but usually the user-specified part of the session program will load resources which over-ride these, so it doesn't make sense to put other specs in here).

The default settings for the authentication widget resources are fine for most cases, but for the sake of example we'll specify a slightly different banner for the login; we create our file */usr/bin/X11/xdm/our-resources* containing the one line:

```
xlogin.Login.greeting: X-Window on the Planets network
```

xdm's "Session" Program

You can nominate any program you want as your "session", but as soon as it terminates your session is over too, so you usually choose a program which enables you to start other programs. You can rely on xdm's default setting, which is to run xterm; but that way you still have to do all your setups by hand once xterm is running. We want to define our own session program which will do all our setups, and which will stay active (i.e. not terminate) until we are finished. But remember, we would like users to be able to define their own session program if they want, so we will use a two-stage process. As system manager we will set up a general purpose, basic, session program which will invoke a user's own program if that exists, but otherwise will run a sensible default. As individual user, we will define our own specific session which will be executed by xdm's general purpose one (but we'll cover that in a separate section).

Our basic site-wide session program is very simple. We will use the convention that if the user has setup the file $HOME/.Xsession, then we do nothing except execute that. Otherwise, we will run a sensible default — start uwm and then pass control to an xterm which we position in the top left corner of the screen. But before doing that, we check to see if the user has setup the file $HOME/.Xresources (another convention) and if so, we load it with xrdb. A full listing of the program is shown in Figure 20.2.

20.3.2 Our Own Configuration for xdm

Now we change roles: we are no longer system manager, but just another user. We could rely on the default session the system manager has defined, but we prefer to define our own session so that we get the initialisations that we said we wanted.

Our Sample .Xsession

We have created our own *$HOME/.Xsession*, which is shown in Figure 20.3, and the initial configuration of the screen after it has run is shown in Figure 20.4. The operation of the script is very straightforward, but there are a few points to watch when setting up your own, and when you are creating the site-wide session program too. We are assuming here that your session program will be a shell script: it doesn't have to be, but it almost certainly will be (unless you want to write an elaborate replacement for xterm or some such).

- Order the commands in the file so that the very last one to run is a program which is to last for the whole of your session (because, when this program finishes, the session program finishes and everything else comes to an end too).

- Run all commands except the last in the background, i.e. end the command line with an ampersand (&). If you don't do this, the session will never get past any program which runs indefinitely. E.g. in our sample program, if we omitted the ampersand on the uwm line, uwm would start, but execution wouldn't continue to the next line until uwm had finished, i.e. never.

- The last command should be exec'ed, so it continues to run and so keeps your session active. (If you ran it in the background like the others, it would start alright, but the session program would then have reached the end of the file and terminate, thus finishing off the session. If you didn't exec it, but omitted the ampersand, it would run and the session would remain and work prefectly OK; you would just be running one process more than

```
venus% pr -147 /usr/lib/X11/xdm/our-session


Jan 26 22:52 1989  /usr/lib/X11/xdm/our-session Páge 1


#!/bin/sh
#
own_session=$HOME/.Xsession
own_resources=$HOME/.Xresources

#
# if the user has setup her own session
#
if [ -f $own_session ]; then
        #
        # if it's executable
        #
        if [ -x $own_session ]; then
                #
                # run it directly
                #
                exec $own_session
        else
                #
                # it's presumably a shell script
                #
                exec /bin/sh $user-session
        fi
#
# user hasn't setup her own session,
# so use a sensible default
#
else
        #
        # if user has setup own resources file, load it
        #
        if [ -f $own_resources ]; then
                xrdb $own_resources
        fi
        uwm &
        exec xterm -geometry 80x24+0+0 -ls
fi



venus% ▮
```

Figure 20.2 The program /usr/lib/X11/xdm/our-session

```
#!/bin/sh
#
# .Xsession - my own session program
#
uwm &
xrdb $HOME/.Xresources
xhost +
xset            \
        c on    \
        s blank \
        s 300   &
xsetroot -bitmap /usr/include/X11/bitmaps/light_gray &
xclock  -geometry 100x100-0+0   &
xbiff   -geometry       -0+100 &
xcalc   -geometry       -0-0   &
xterm   -geometry   80x90+400+0
                -sf                         \
                -fn "6x10"                  \
                -iconic                     \
                -xrm "*iconX:1000"          \
                -xrm "*iconY:60"            \
                -name demos                 \
                -title demos                &
xterm   -geometry   120x56+0+0
                -sf                         \
                -fn "*-courier*-r-*-14-*"   \
                -iconic                     \
                -xrm "*iconX:1000"          \
                -xrm "*iconY:100"           \
                -bw 30                      \
                -bd white                   \
                -name editor                \
                -title editor               &
rsh saturn  xload -display venus:0 -geometry 100x100-0+200 &
rsh mars    xload -display venus:0 -geometry 100x100-0+300 &
rsh neptune xload -display venus:0 -geometry 100x100-0+400 &
exec xterm -geometry    +0+0
                -C                          \
                -ls                         \
                -fn 9x15                    \
                -xrm "*iconX:1000"          \
                -xrm "*iconY:140"           \
                -name console               \
                -title console
```

Figure 20.3 The program $HOME/.Xsession

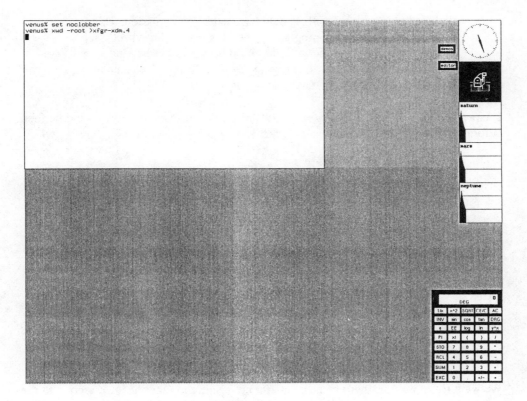

Figure 20.4 Screen after our initialisation

you need, as you still have both the last program and the session program itself).

- Specify geometry specs for all the programs which create windows — otherwise you'll have to position them by hand when they start up.

- The last program in the script is usually for starting xterm. Because the life of this defines your session, this window will always exist when you are running **X**, so you usually specify two special options:

  1. Make this a "console" xterm by using the -C option, so that system messages appear in its window.

  2. Make its shell a login shell by specifying the -ls option. This causes the shell to read your *.login* or *.profile*, so your environment variables are setup properly. (If you don't do this, you only have a few defined: DISPLAY, HOME, USER, PATH and SHELL).

3. The session program file should have execute permission. Using the site-wide session program above, this isn't strictly necessary for the user session script, but with others it might be, and it is essential for the site-wide program itself. (If that isn't executable, you just get xdm's default startup).

It is a good idea to try out your .Xsession by starting it from an xterm window first, before installing it and relying on it to start your window session.

20.4 **Our Own** uwm **Configuration**

```
f.menu       = m | s :             : left down    : "Hosts"
menu = "Hosts" {
   vt100:     !"xterm -name vt100 -title vt100 &"
   saturn:    !"rsh saturn  xterm -display venus:0 -name saturn  -title saturn &"
   mars:      !"rsh mars     xterm -display venus:0 -name mars    -title mars    &"
   neptune:   !"rsh neptune xterm -display venus:0 -name neptune -title saturn &"
   "/ mars":  !"rsh mars     xterm -display venus:0 -name mars    -title mars -geometry +0-0 -e login root &
}
```

Figure 20.5 Hosts menu, in *$HOME/.uwmrc*

We want to set up four uwm menus: one for connecting to other hosts, a second to run some **X** applications, a third to setup some keyboard and mouse parameters (rather like the default **Preferences** menu), and a fourth to run demos.

For our "hosts" menu, we now want to be able to start an xterm on any host just by selecting its name in the menu. We often have to do some system management on mars, so we will set up selections logging us in as the super-user (root) on that, too. We will always create the super-user window in the bottom-left corner, but for the ordinary xterms, we omit the geometry spec so we can position them explicitly when they are created. We'll bind this menu to META-SHIFT-LEFT. So in our *$HOME/.uwmrc* we include the lines shown in Figure 20.5.

The other three menus we won't use so often, so we'll bind them all to META-SHIFT-MIDDLE. There is nothing special in these, but note that **Misc.** does contain a mixture of uwm built-ins and shell commands. The *.uwmrc* entries for these are shown in Figure 20.6.

The remaining part of *.uwmrc* (shown in Figure 20.7) we have setup to customise the bindings and parameters for the usual window configuration operations (move, resize, etc.). Note a few points:

• We have chosen a font which is slightly bigger than the default (with "menufont=fixed", and have reduced the amount of white space between menu

```
f.menu       = m | s :              : middle down  : "Tools"
f.menu       = m | s :              : middle down  : "Misc."
f.menu       = m | s :              : middle down  : "Demos"

menu = "Tools" {
  xman:        !"xman -notopbox -geometry -0-0 &"
  xedit:       !"xedit -geometry 300x600-200-0 &"
  xmag:        !"xmag &"
}

menu = "Misc." {
  "zap":        f.kill
  "Click on":   !"xset c 100 &"
  "Click off":  !"xset c off &"
  "gray":       !"xsetroot -gray"
  "gray-L":     !"xsetroot -bitmap /usr/include/X11/bitmaps/light_gray"
  "white":      !"xsetroot -solid white"
  "black":      !"xsetroot -solid black"
  "Reset uwm":  f.restart
}

menu = "Demos" {
  maze:        !"maze &"
  puzzle:      !"puzzle &"
  "O.O.":      !"xeyes &"
}
```

Figure 20.6 Other menus, in *$HOME/.uwmrc*

selections (with "vmenupad=1") so the menus aren't so large. (menufont may not be described in the manpage).

- We have specified that all menus, bindings and variables are to be reset (with resetmenus, etc). This clears out uwm's configuration, so we don't end up with a mixture of the default configuration and our own.

- Where possible, we bind the functions to mouse UP events rather than DOWN: this way you can change your mind and abort the operation, by pressing another button before releasing the first. (But you can't bind a move operation to an UP event).

- We have included some of the functions that are in the default uwm menus — one to kill off application windows, and one to restart uwm. They are not essential, but useful to have when you are experimenting with the system.

```
resetmenus
resetbindings
resetvariables
menufont=fixed
vmenupad=1
normali
normalw
grid
resizerelative
nofreeze
normalw

f.circledown  =  meta : root        : left    up
f.circleup    =  meta : root        : right   up
f.iconify     =  meta : window|icon : middle  up
f.lower       =  meta : window|icon : left    up
f.move        =  meta : window|icon : right   delta
f.newiconify  =  meta : window|icon : left    delta
f.raise       =  meta : window|icon : right   up
f.resize      =  meta : window      : middle  delta
f.moveopaque  =  m | s : window|icon : right   down
```

Figure 20.7 Bindings and parameter settings in *$HOME/.uwmrc*

20.5 Conclusion

You're done! You have covered just about all the user-level programs in the **core** release, and how to use them.

You now have a system which you can set up and tailor to your own requirements. Most of the tailoring is confined to just three files in your home directory — *.Xsession*, *.Xresources* and *.uwmrc* — so it is easy to control your environment, and work within whatever scheme your system manager has setup.

We have covered a lot of material, and there are many new concepts involved, so you won't have absorbed it all yet — that's not to be expected. Now that you have used the system for a while, go back and read the conceptual overview of the system again. You'll find that you understand a lot more of it, and you can see the motivation behind the features of the system.

As you use the system more and more, you will find there are some features which you'd like, but which the system doesn't have. And there are some tools and window-related programs which would simplify your work, and some applications which would benefit a lot from the interface **X** provides, but which aren't included in the release. Don't despair! — look in the **contrib** software instead. Now that you know the capabilities and limitations of the basic system, see what other people have already made available and there is a good chance that what you want is there.

This purpose of this book was to get you started — it is not intended to be a complete reference manual. In some places we have left out some details of programs which are not often used, or which would be confusing or complicated at the beginning. But now you *can* go back and read the documentation supplied with the system. The manpages and other material are very largely reference material: if you know what you are doing and just want to refresh your memory on a particular point, or find out how exactly something works, you will find it in there somewhere. Now that you have used the system and seen how it hangs together, you can make sense of the reference manuals. To help you find your way through the documentation, we have included an appendix which lists the material included in the release, tells you what to find in which place, and how to delve further into the system.

So all that remains to be said is, *Bon voyage!*

Part 4

Appendices

Appendix A **Road-Map to the Documentation**

A.1   Manuals Supplied with the Release

The manuals listed below are supplied in hardcopy form as part of the full MIT release of **X**.

   The document sources for these manuals are included on the software tapes, and the corresponding filenames are given in parentheses. To print hardcopy versions, use nroff or troff, with option -man for manpages, or -ms for the tutorial or other manuals. For some of the longer manuals, formatted files already translated to PostScript are also included; because of their large size, these are compressed, and have to be decompressed using uncompress. (If you don't already have uncompress, it's included on the release tape in *$TOP/util/compress/*, along with instructions on how to use it).

1. The release notes, including installation instructions and description of what the release contains. Almost all of this is reproduced here, in Appendices B, C and D. (*$TOP/doc/releasenotes/**; PostScript in *$TOP/hardcopy/releasenotes/relnotes.PS*).

2. The program manual pages, or "manpages(1)". The sources are stored not in one location but with the corresponding program sources. As part of the default installation procedure, they are installed in the system manpage directories so they can be read using man. (*$TOP/.../*.man*; PostScript in *$TOP/hardcopy/man/*.PS.Z*).

3. The manual pages for the Xlib functions; "manpages(3X11)". (*$TOP/doc/Xlib/Xman/**).

4. The manual pages for the Toolkit Intrinsics functions; "manpages(3Xt)". (*$TOP/doc/Xt/Xman/**; PostScript in *$TOP/hardcopy/Xt/man.PS.Z*).

5. The book *"X WINDOW SYSTEM, C Library and Protocol Reference"*, by Scheifler, Gettys and Newman (Digital Press, 1988). This includes:

- The *"Xlib — C Language Interface"* manual. (*$TOP/doc/Xlib/**; PostScript in *$TOP/hardcopy/Xlib/*).

- The *"X Window System Protocol, X Version 11, Release 3"* manual. (*$TOP/doc/Protocol/*).

6. The *"X Toolkit Intrinsics"* manual. (*$TOP/doc/Xt/**; PostScript in *$TOP/hardcopy/Xt/intrin.PS.Z*).

7. The *"X Toolkit Athena Widgets"* manual. (*$TOP/doc/Xaw/*; PostScript in *$TOP/hardcopy/Xaw/index.PS.Z* and *$TOP/hardcopy/Xaw/widgets.PS.Z*).

8. The *"Bitmap Distribution Format"* manual. (Document source, in Scribe format, with PostScript illustrations, in *$TOP/doc/bdf/*; complete PostScript in *$TOP/hardcopy/bdf/bdf.PS.Z*).

A.2   Other Documentation Contained in the Release

1. Description of Font Naming Conventions. (*$TOP/doc/fontnames/fnames.txt*).

2. Several small tutorials on various aspects of **X**:

   - Using colours in **X** programs you write. (*$TOP/doc/tutorials/color.tbl.ms*).
   - Converting widgets from **X**11 release 2 to release 3. (*$TOP/doc/tutorials/r3widgets.ms*).
   - Using resources. (*$TOP/doc/tutorials/resources.ms*).
   - Correspondence of Xlib functions in **X** version 10 to those in **X** version 11. (*$TOP/doc/tutorials/x10equiv.txt*).

3. Notes on porting the MIT servers to different systems.

   - "Godzilla's Guide to Porting the **X** V11 Sample Server". (*$TOP/doc/Server/gdz.tbl.ms*).
   - Definition of the Porting Layer for the **X** v11 Sample Server. (*$TOP/doc/Server/ddx.tbl.ms*).
   - Strategies for Porting the **X** V11 Sample Server. (*$TOP/doc/Server/strat.ms*).
   - **X**11 server extensions. (*$TOP/doc/Server/ext.doc*).

4. "Inter-Client Communication Conventions Manual", often referred to as IC-CCM. This would have been included in the release, in *$TOP/doc/conventions/*, but was being revised at the time of the release and so was omitted. You may be able to get a copy via electronic mail — see the **xstuff** section in the *"X Network and Electronic Mail Services"* appendix.

5. Tutorial on writing **X** programs, first using only the basic **Xlib** functions, and then using the Toolkit. (*$TOP/doc/HelloWorld/*).

A.3 Other Sources of Information in the Release

For some items, such as names of widgets, resources and actions, you have to look at the source code:

- Widgets provided as part of the Intrinsics. (*$TOP/lib/Xt/*).

- Widgets in the Athena Set. (*$TOP/lib/Xaw/*).

- Client-program sources. The sources for each client are stored in a separate directory, *$TOP/clients/program-name/* or *$TOP/demos/program-name/*.

Appendix B **Installing** X

This appendix contains some hints on installing the release, as well as detailed installation instructions.

B.1   Hints on Installing X

- Get a copy of all the documentation as soon as possible, ideally before starting to install the system. (You can print it off yourself from the files included on the distribution tape, or order it from one of the suppliers listed in Appendix E).

- At first, change as little as possible in the files which specify the build configuration. If you are installing X for the first time, we recommend *very strongly* that you use the default settings for the directories into which the various parts of the distribution are installed. Only when you are used to how the system operates should you consider re-installing it in the directories you really want. (If you don't do it this way, when something goes wrong you won't know whether there is a real problem or you've just made a mistake in the installation).

  If you are building for one of the standard systems supported by this release, you can almost certainly perform the installation without changing anything at all — the configuration files are already set up correctly. (The release notes may be a little misleading on this point; you might get the impression that you *have to* make a lot of changes no matter what system you are using).

- For many systems you don't have to specify the system type explicitly when you start the installation: the build relies on the C preprocessor to define the system name, and this is picked up automatically.

- Don't install the **contrib** software until you are familiar with the **core** release — it takes a long time to install, there may be problems with the installation, and once you become familiar with the system you may want to alter some of the configuration parameters anyway.

- If you really have to use different configuration from the default, read the document *$TOP/util/imake.includes/README* for information on what to change. (This also gives an outline of the imake tool — a front-end to the normal Unix make — which is used to build the release).

The remainder of this chapter consists of the installation instructions supplied as part of the release.

B.2   Building the Release

This documentation is reproduced from sources included in the MIT distribution.[1]

The software in this release is divided into two distributions: one for the core software that is supported by the staff of the X Consortium, and one for everything else. Great pains have been taken to make the core distribution easy to reconfigure, build and install on a wide range of platforms. The user-contributed distribution, on the other hand, has not been compiled or tested by the staff of the X Consortium and will require building by hand. The *ximake.sh* in *util/scripts/* may be useful for creating *Makefiles* from *Imakefiles*.

Almost all *Makefiles* in the core software are generated automatically by a utility called *imake*. Initial versions of all of the Makefiles are included for those sites that cannot use *imake* (they will undoubtedly require patching for the specific machine). On many systems, X should build correctly right off the tape. However, it can be reconfigured by simply setting various parameters in the files *site.def* and **.macros* in the directory *util/imake.includes/*.

---

[1]*X Window System* is a trademark of MIT.

B.2.1 Installation Summary

To load and install this release of the **X** Window System, you will need to:

1. Finish reading these Release Notes.

2. Create a directory into which you will read the distribution tapes (usually named something like */usr/local/src/X* or */src/R3/*). You will need roughly 30 megabytes to hold the core software and up to 80 megabytes for the user-contributed software.

3. Unload the core tape into the directory created in step #2. Since the user-contributed software must be built by hand, you may wait and load it in later. Each of the tapes contain one (very large) UNIX *tar* file stored at 1600 bits per inch.

4. Read the file *util/imake.includes/README* for instructions on how to con-figure the build for your particular site. Also, make sure that you follow the directions in *README* files in *server/ddx/* directories for which you plan to build servers.

5. If you plan to compile the release on more than one machine and have a distributed file system, you may wish to use the script *util/scripts/lndir.sh* to create symbolic link trees on each of the target machines. This allows all of the platforms on which you wish to run **X** to share a single set of sources. In either case, the phrase *build tree* will be used to refer to the directory tree in which you are compiling (to distinguish it from the *source tree* which contains the actual files).

6. If you are building on a Macintosh II under A/UX 1.0, make sure that you have run the *R3setup.sh* from the *server/ddx/macII/* directory. This builds a new C preprocessor from the public domain sources in *util/cpp/* and fixes several misplaced system files. If you are building on a Sun, make sure that you set the four *OS* parameters at the top of the file *util/imake.includes/Sun.macros*. These enable workarounds for bugs in var-ious SunOS compilers. If you are building on an Apollo, make sure that you are running rev 9.7.1 or later of the C compiler; otherwise, the server will not compile correctly.

7. Make sure that you have followed all machine-specific directions and that *imake* has been configured for your machine (see the blocks of #ifdefs at the top of *util/imake.includes/Imake.tmpl* in the source tree).

8. Once you are satisfied with the configuration, you are ready to build the core distribution. Look at the *.macros* file in *util/imake.includes/* that applies to your system. There should be a line near the top that sets a *make* variable named BOOTSTRAPCFLAGS. If this variable is left blank, you may use the following command to start the build:

```
% make World >& make.world &
```

If it is not blank, you should append that definition to the command line. This is used by *imake* to set particular *cpp* symbols for all compilers (if you are porting to a different platform, see *util/imake/imake.c*). Of the systems for which macro files are provided in the core distribution, only A/UX needs this flag:

```
% make BOOTSTRAPCFLAGS=-DmacII World >& make.world &
```

Do not call the output file *make.log* as the *make clean* done by *make World* removes all files of this name. This will rebuild all of the *Makefiles* and execute a *make -k all* to compile everything in the core distribution. This will take anywhere from 2 to 12 hours, depending on your machine.

9. When the *make* is done, check the log file for any problems. There should be no serious errors. A/UX users may ignore compiler warning about enumeration type clashes and Apollo users may ignore optimizer warnings.

10. If you are satisfied that everything has built correctly, test the various critical programs (servers, *xterm*, *xinit*, etc.) by hand. You may need to be root to run the server or *xterm*. A second workstation or terminal will be useful if you run into problems.

11. Make backup copies of your old **X** header files, binaries, fonts, libraries, etc.

12. Go to the top of the build tree and type

```
% make install >& make.install
```

You will either have to do this as root, or have write access to the appropriate directories (see DIRS_TO_BUILD in the top level *Imakefile* and *util/imake.includes/Imake.tmpl*). The *xterm* program should be installed setuid to root on most systems and the *xload* program should be installed setguid to whatever group the file */dev/kmem* belongs to (it is installed setuid to root by default).

13. If you would like to install the manual pages, type the following at the top of the build tree:

```
% make install.man
```

14. If you would like to create and install lint libraries, type the following at the top of the build tree:

```
% make install.ln
```

If you are installing **X** for the first time, you may also need to do some of the steps listed below. Check the various README files in the *server/ddx* directories for additional instructions.

15. Add device drivers or reconfigure your kernel.

16. Create additional pseudoterminals. See your operating system script */dev/MAKEDEV* and site administrator for details.

17. Read the manual page for the new Display Manager *xdm*. This program provides a portable way of running **X** automatically and has many hooks for creating a nice interface for novice users. This supersedes the support in *xterm* for running the terminal emulator from */etc/init*.

18. Make sure that all **X**11 users have the BINDIR directory (usually */usr/bin/X11*), in their search paths.

Release 3 of Version 11 of the **X** Window System should now be ready to use.

B.2.2 Operating System Requirements

One of the reasons why **X** is so popular is that is operating system-independent. Although this distribution only contains sample implementations for Unix-based platforms (because that's all we have), support for many non-Unix operating systems is available from a wide variety of vendors. The servers in this release have been built on the following systems:

4.3+tahoe
Ultrix 3.0 FT2 (also compiles under Ultrix 2.0)
SunOS 3.4
HP-UX 6.01
Apollo Domain/IX 9.7 (and 9.6 according to its developers)
IBM AOS 4.3 (according to its developers)
A/UX 1.0

If you are using versions prior to these, you may run into trouble. In particular, the server will not run on IBM 4.2A release 2. The *README* files in the various *server/ddx/* describe particular requirements such as compilers, libraries, preprocessors, etc. As was noted above, A/UX 1.0 users will need to build a new version of the C preprocessor and Apollo users will need the 9.7.1 C compiler.

You should verify that your networking and interprocess communication facilities are working properly before trying to use **X**. If programs such as *talk* and *rlogin* don't work, **X** probably won't either.

B.2.3 Reading in the Release Tapes

This release may be obtained electronically from the DARPA Internet, the UUNET Project, several consulting firms, and various UUCP archive sites. In addition, a set of three 2400 foot, 1600 BPI magnetic tapes is available from the MIT Software Distribution Center (please do not ask SDC for cartridge tapes or floppy disks).

Each tape from MIT contains one large *tar* archive with source for the software and documentation for part of the release. If you have a limited amount of disk space, you should load the core tape, prune out any servers that you don't need, and generate listings of the user-contributed tapes for later retrieval. All filenames are given as relative paths (i.e. beginning with a period instead of a slash) so that the release may be placed anywhere in your file system.

Before reading in the tapes, make sure that you have enough disk space. The chart below shows the amount of space you will need for each tape:

Distribution	Contents	megabytes	status
core	servers, libraries, utilities	35	required
contrib-1	programs, demos, fonts	36	recommended
contrib-2	contributed toolkits	34	recommended

The compiled programs will need roughly half to two thirds as much space as the source code. Thus, you will need roughly 60 megabytes to hold the source and compiled versions of the programs in the core distribution.

Create a directory into which you will put all of the sources. In this directory, execute the appropriate operating system commands to read in the core tape. If your site is set up so that *tar* uses a 1600bpi tape drive by default, you will probably type something like:

```
% mkdir /usr/local/src/X
% cd /usr/local/src/X
% tar x
```

See your system administrator for help.

B.2.4 Using Symbolic Links

This release uses links (symbolic, on machines that support them) in several places to avoid duplication of certain files (mostly header files). If you are building this release on a system for which configuration files have not been supplied, you should check the LN configuration parameter in the appropriate *util/imake.includes/*.macros* file. If your operating system does not support soft links, LN should be set either to create hard links or to copy the source file.

If you need to move the release to another machine after it has been built, use *tar* instead of *cp* or *rcp* so that you preserve dates and links. This is usually done with a command of the form:

```
% (chdir /usr/local/src/X; tar cf - .) | \
rsh othermachine "(chdir /moredisk/X; tar xpBf -)"
```

See your system administrator for help.

B.2.5 Configuring the Release

This release makes extensive use of a utility called *imake* to generate machine-specific *Makefiles* from machine-independent *Imakefiles*. Another utility, called *makedepend* is used to generate *Makefile* dependencies for C language files. Sample *Makefiles* are provided, although you are strongly urged to use *imake* and *makedepend* if you have even the most remote interest in portability.

The configuration files for *imake* are located in the directory *util/imake.includes*. *Makefiles* are created from a template file named *Imake.tmpl*, a machine-specific *.macros* file, and a site-specific *site.def* file. With only a few exceptions, configuration parameters are *cpp* symbols that may be defined on a per-server basis or for all servers in a given site. The template file should *not* be modified.

The file *util/imake.includes/README* describes each of the build parameters and what value they should have. The defaults have been chosen to work properly on a wide range of machines and to be easy to maintain. Site-specific configurations should be described in the file *site.def* using the following syntax:

```
#ifndef BuildParameter
#define BuildParameter site-specific-value
#endif
```

B.2.6 Compiling the Release

Once the configuration parameters are set, you should be able to type the following at the top of the build tree to compile the core software:

```
% make World >& make.world &
```

Don't redirect the output to *make.log* as this particular file is deleted as part of the build process. This will take anywhere from 2 to 12 hours, depending on the machine used, and should complete without any significant errors on most machines.

If you need to restart the build after all of the *Makefiles* and dependencies have been created, type the following command at the top of the build tree:

```
% make -k >& make.out &
```

If you later decide to change any of the configuration parameters, you'll need to do another full *make World*.

B.2.7 Installing the Release

If everything compiles successfully, you may install the software by typing the following as root from the top of the build tree:

```
# make install
```

If you would rather not do the installation as root, make the necessary directories writable by you and do the install from your account. Then, check the ownership and protections on *xterm* and *xload* in the BINDIR directory (usually */usr/bin/X11/*). *Xterm* must be installed setuid to root so that it can set the ownership of its pseudoterminal and update */etc/utmp*. *Xload* needs to be setuid to root or setgid to the group owning the file */dev/kmem* so that it can get the system load average.

If your */etc/termcap* and */usr/lib/terminfo* databases don't have entries for *xterm*, sample entries are provided in the directory *clients/xterm/*. System V users will need to compile the *terminfo* entry with the *tic* utility.

If you plan to use the *xinit* program to run X, you might want to create a link named X pointing to the appropriate server program (usually named something like *Xmachine* in the directory */usr/bin/X11/*). However, *xinit* is not intended for novice users; instead, site administrators are expected to either use *xdm* or provide user-friendly interfaces.

If you would like to have manual pages installed, check the *ManDirectoryRoot*, *ManDir* and *LibManDir* configuration parameters in *util/imake.includes/* and type the following at the top of the build tree:

```
# make install.man
```

If you would like to have lint libraries created and installed, type the following at the top of the build tree:

```
# make install.ln
```

Finally, make sure that all users have the BINDIR (usually */usr/bin/X11/*) in their PATH environment variable.

B.2.8 Notes on Kernels and Special Files

On some machines, it may be necessary to rebuild the kernel with a new device driver, or to at least reconfigure it. If you have never run X before and are using a system not listed in these notes, you might need to verify that the CSR addresses in your kernel configuration file match your hardware. In addition, you should make sure that the kernel autoconfigures the display when booting.

You may need to create special devices for your display, mouse, or keyboard. For example,

```
# /etc/mknod /dev/bell c 12 2      # for bell on Sun
# MAKEDEV displays                 # for displays on the RT/PC
```

The protection modes on the display device files should be set so that only the server can open them. If the server is started by */etc/init*, the protections can be root read/write, everyone else no access; otherwise, they will have to be read/write for everyone or else your server will have to be setuid to root.

On a Digital QVSS (VAXstation II), you should use *adb* to make sure that the kernel variable *qv_def_scrn* is set to 2 so that the full width of the VR-260 monitor is used (otherwise there will be an unused black strip down the right edge of the screen). This can be done by changing the value either in */vmunix* directly or in */sys/vaxuba/qv.o* and relinking and reinstalling the kernel. You will need to reboot for the new value to take effect.

For more information, see the appropriate *README* files and manual pages in the *server/ddx/* directories.

B.2.9 Testing the Release

Even if you plan on using *xdm* to run X all the time, you should first run it by hand from another terminal to check that everything is installed and working properly. Error messages from the X server will then appear on your terminal, rather than being written to the *xdm-errors* or to */usr/adm/X?msgs* (where *?* is the number of the display).

The easiest way to test the server is to go to */usr/bin/X11* (or wherever you have installed the various X programs), and run *xinit* as follows:

```
% cd /usr/bin/X11
% xinit
```

If all is well, you should see a gray stipple pattern covering the screen, a cursor shaped like an "X" that tracks the pointer, and a terminal emulator window. Otherwise, check the following:

1. If the gray background doesn't appear at all, check the permissions on any special device files (usually stored in */dev/*) described in the *README* in the appropriate *server/ddx/* subdirectories.

2. If the background appears, but the cursor is a white square that doesn't change, make sure that the fonts have been installed (in particular, the font named *cursor.snf* in the directory */usr/lib/X11/fonts/misc/*; see the configuration parameter *DefaultFontPath*). Also make sure that there is a file named *fonts.dir* in each font directory. This file is created by the *mkfontdir* program and is used by the server to find fonts in a directory.

3. If the cursor appears but doesn't track the pointer, make sure that any special device files (often named something like */dev/mouse*) are installed (see the server's *README* file).

4. If the server starts up and then goes black a few seconds later, the initial client (usually *xterm* or *xdm*) is dying. Make sure that *xterm* is installed setuid to root and that you have created enough pseudoterminals. If you are running *xinit*, and have a file named *.xinitrc* in your home directory, make sure that it is executable and that the last program that it starts is run in the foreground (i.e. that there is no ampersand at the end of the line). Otherwise, the *.xinitrc* will finish immediately, which *xinit* assumes means that you are through.

Once you have the initial window working properly, try running some other programs from the *xterm*. To position a new window with the *uwm* window manager, press Button 1 (usually the left most button on the pointer) when the flashing rectangle appears:

```
% xclock -g 200x200-0+0 &
% uwm &
% xlogo &
% xeyes &
...
```

X should now be ready to use. Read the manual pages for the new programs, look at the new fonts, and have fun.

B.2.10 Creating Extra Pseudoterminals

Since each *xterm* will need a separate pseudoterminal, you should create a large number of them (you probably will want at least 32 on a small, multiuser system). Each pty has two devices, a master and a slave, which are usually named /dev/tty[pqrstu][0-f] and /dev/pty[pqrstu][0-f]. If you don't have at least the "p" and "q" lines configured (do an "ls /dev"), you should have your system administrator add them. This is often done by running the MAKEDEV script in */dev*:

```
# cd /dev
# ./MAKEDEV pty0
# ./MAKEDEV pty1
```

B.2.11 Starting X from /etc/rc

A new utility named *xdm* is provided in this release for running X servers from the system startup file */etc/rc*. It provides a portable, attractive alternative to running X from */etc/init* or *xinit*. Designed to be easily tailored to the needs of each specific site, *xdm* takes care of keeping the server running, prompting for username and password and managing the user's session. The sample configuration currently uses shell scripts to provide a fairly simple environment. This will be an area of continuing work in future releases.

The key to *xdm*'s flexibility is its extensive use of resources, allowing site administrators to quickly and easily test alternative setups. When *xdm* starts up, it reads a configuration file (the default is */usr/lib/X11/xdm/xdm-config* but can be specified with the *-config* command line flag) listing the names of the various datafiles, default parameters, and startup and shutdown programs to be run. Because it uses the standard X Toolkit resource file format, any parameters that may be set in the *xdm-config* file may also be specified on the command line using the standard *-xrm* option.

The default configuration contains the following lines:

```
DisplayManager.servers:      /usr/lib/X11/xdm/Xservers
DisplayManager.errorLogFile: /usr/lib/X11/xdm/xdm-errors
DisplayManager*resources:    /usr/lib/X11/xdm/Xresources
DisplayManager*startup:      /usr/lib/X11/xdm/Xstartup
DisplayManager*session:      /usr/lib/X11/xdm/Xsession
DisplayManager*reset:        /usr/lib/X11/xdm/Xreset
```

The *servers* file contains the list of servers to start. The *errorLogFile* is where output from *xdm* is redirected. The *resources* file contains default resources for the *xdm* login window. In particular, this is where special key sequences can be specified (in the *xlogin*login.translations* resource). The *startup* file should be a program or executable script that is run after the user has provided a valid password. It is a hook for doing site-specific initialization, logging, etc. The *session* entry is the name of a session manager program or executable script that is run to start up the user's environment. A simple version has been supplied that provides a simple *xterm* window and *uwm* window manager if the user does not have an executable *.xsession* file in his or her home directory. Finally, the *reset* program or executable script is run after the user logs out. It is a hook for cleaning up after the *startup* program.

To run *xdm* using the default configuration, add the following line to your system boot file (usually named */etc/rc* or */etc/rc.local*):

```
/usr/bin/X11/xdm &
```

Most sites will undoubtedly want to build their own configurations. We recommend that you place any site-specific *xdm-config* and other *xdm* files in a different directory so that they are not overwritten if somebody ever does a *make install*. If you were to store the files in */usr/local/lib/xdm*, the following command could be used to start *xdm*:

```
/usr/bin/X11/xdm -config /usr/local/lib/xdm/xdm-config &
```

Many servers set the keyboard to do non-blocking I/O under the assumption that they are the only programs attempting to read from the keyboard. Unfortunately, some versions of */etc/getty* (A/UX's in particular) will immediately see a continuous stream of zero-length reads which they interpret as end-of-file indicators. Eventually, */etc/init* will disable logins on that line until somebody types the following as root:

```
# kill -HUP 1
```

Under A/UX, one alternative is to disable logins on the console and always run *xdm* from */etc/inittab*. However, make sure that you save a copy of the old */etc/inittab* in case something goes wrong and you have to restore logins from over the network or from single-user mode.

Another less drastic approach is to set up an account whose shell is the *xdmshell* program found in *clients/xdm/*. This program is not installed by default so that site administrators will examine it to see if it meets their needs. The *xdmshell* utility makes sure that it is being run from the appropriate type of terminal, starts *xdm*, waits for it to finish, and then resets the console if necessary. If the *xdm* resources file (specified by the *DisplayManager*resources* entry in the *xdm-config* file) contains a binding to the *abort-display* action similar to the following

xlogin*login.translations: #override Ctrl<Key>R: abort-display()

the console can then by restored by pressing the indicated key (Control-R in the above example) in the *xdm* login window.

The *xdmshell* program is usually installed setuid to root but executable only by members of a special group, of which the account which has *xdmshell* as its shell is the only member:

```
% grep xdm /etc/passwd
x:aB9i7vhDVa82z:101:51:Account for starting up X: (contd.)
/tmp:/etc/xdmshell
% grep 51 /etc/group
xdmgrp:*:51:
% ls -lg /etc/xdmshell
-rws--x--- 1 root xdmgrp 20338 Nov 1 01:32 /etc/xdmshell
```

If the *xdm* resources have not been configured to have a key bound to the *abort-display()* action, there will be no way for general users to login to the console directly. Whether or not this is desirable depends on the particular site.

B.2.12 Obsolete Support for Starting X from /etc/init

Warning: the following is provided for compatibility with older systems and may not be supported in future releases.

Ultrix and 4.3bsd use a new, expanded format of the */etc/ttys* configuration file that allows you to specify a window system and initial program (usually a terminal emulator or session manager) to be run. Although it is preferable to use *xdm*, there is support in *xterm* for starting X and an initial *xterm* window from */etc/ttys*.

Creating the ttyv Terminals

Since most versions of */etc/init* require an actual terminal line per entry in */etc/ttys*, you will need to dedicate one pseudoterminal for each display. Although *xterm* normally allocates a pty dynamically, the *-L* option may be given to force it to use the pseudoterminal passed to it from */etc/init*.

By convention, the pseudoterminal pair with the highest minor device number is renamed *[pt]tyv0*, the next highest *[pt]tyv1*, and so on for as many login windows as will be needed. The highest are chosen instead of the lowest so that they don't get in the way of the normal low to high search that most programs do when allocating a pty. On a small system that only has "p" and "q" pseudoterminals, the following commands might be used to set up "v" terminals for two displays:

```
# cd /dev
# mv ttyqf ttyv0 ; mv ptyqf ptyv0
# mv ttyqe ttyv1 ; mv ptyqe ptyv1
```

See your system administrator for help.

Adding Window System Entries to /etc/ttys

Once you have renamed the pseudoterminals, you can add entries for them in */etc/ttys*. Again, this only works on systems that have the new 4.3bsd format for starting window systems, not on older systems that use the 4.2bsd small entry format and */etc/ttytype*. If your machine does not have the new format, rename the ttyv's and ptyv's back and go on to the next section.

The *Xserver* manual page gives a more detailed description of different ways to set up */etc/ttys* entries (also see your system documentation). Usually, the ttyv's are placed at the bottom of the file and look something like this:

ttyv0 "/usr/bin/X11/xterm -L -geometry 80x24+0+0 -display :0" *(contd.)*
xterm off window="/usr/bin/X11/X :0"

Note that unlike X10, the server number argument to the X server command must be preceeded by a colon. Additional comand line options may be specified on either the *xterm* command line or the *X* command line. However, many versions of *init* have fairly small program name buffers, limiting the length of the entry. Also, some versions don't allow pound signs within entries, meaning that arbitrary numeric color specifications cannot be given. This is why *xdm* was written.

Once you have added or changed any entries, you need to signal *init* to reread */etc/ttys* and restart. This can be done as root by typing the following command:

```
# kill -HUP 1
```

This will abort any existing processes on any changed lines before restarting, so it should only be done by a system administrator.

Appendix C Contents of the Release — MIT Core Distribution

This documentation is reproduced from sources included in the MIT distribution.[1]

This release contains roughly 100 megabytes of source code and documentation. Because no one site will probably need or want all of it, the release has been broken into 3 pieces of roughly equal size: one for the core software, one for various user-contributed toolkits, and one for the rest of the user-contributed software.

C.1 The Core Distribution

The core distribution, containing roughly 30 megabytes of software that is supported by the staff of the **X** Consortium, is made up of the directories listed below. If you find a reproducible bug in this section of the release, please fill out a copy of the form located in *doc/bugs/bug-report* and mail it to *xbugs@expo.lcs.mit.edu*.

./ The top level directory contains important notices, the general **X** manual page, and all of the subdirectories for building the release.

X11/ Copies of all public header files are either stored here or linked in during the *make all* build phase. This directory, and the bitmaps in the directory below it get copied to the directory specified by the IncDir configuration

---

[1] *X Window System* is a trademark of MIT.

parameter (by default, */usr/include/X11*) during the *make install* phase. Note that the final directory name should never be anything other than *X11* or else all X programs will fail to compile.

X11/bitmaps/ This directory contains a number of single plane images stored in *bitmap* format (read and written with the Xlib routines *XReadBitmapFile*, *XmuReadBitmapDataFromFile*, and *XWriteBitmapFile*). They are often #included in C programs and may be used as background tiles with *xsetroot* utility. Also, the X Toolkit allows users to specify the names of files in this directory to be used as cursors and icons. For more information, see the manual page for *bitmap* and the document *util/bm-convert/bm-convert.doc*.

clients/ This directory is the top of the user program source tree. There are other programs in the *demos/* and *examples/* trees, but they are for demonstration purposes only. A number of other very useful user-contributed programs can be found under *contrib/clients/*.

clients/bitmap/ This directory contains an editor for creating and modifying single plane bitmap images (such as the ones stored in *X11/bitmaps/*) used in defining two color tiles (for filling areas with stipples) and masks (for clipping and specifying cursor images). All resources can be specified both from the command line and in your defaults. Two new programs, *bmtoa* and *atobm* have been added that convert *bitmap* files to and from simple strings.

clients/uwm/ This directory contains one of the older window managers for X. A number of bugs have been fixed and several new features have been added.

clients/x10tox11/ This directory contains a rewrite of the X10 to X11 protocol translator. It masquerades as an X10 server, converting X10 requests into X11 requests and X11 events into X10 events (i.e. it is not a libnest implementation). The *x10tox11* program allows X10 programs to be run unmodified on an X11 server, making converting from X10 to X11 much easier. This new version should be substantially faster and give more accurate results than the last version.

clients/xbiff/ This directory contains a simple little program that displays a picture of a mailbox whose flag goes up when you get new mail. It uses the Mailbox widget in the Athena widget set.

clients/xcalc/ This directory contains a desktop calculator program that emulates a TI-30, an HP-10C, and a slide rule. This program needs to be rewritten.

clients/xclipboard/ This directory contains two programs for manipulating selections: *xclipboard* gathers text that is sent to the CLIP_BOARD from other clients (see *xterm* and the Athena Text widget), and *xcutsel* provides a bridge between older clients that can only deal with cut-buffers and newer clients that use selections.

clients/xclock/ This directory contains a simple little program that displays a clock. It can display the time in either analog or digital format, and uses the Clock widget in the Athena widget set.

clients/xdm/ This directory contains the new Display Manager. It is intended to replace *xterm -L* and most uses of *xinit*. Site administrators should study the documentation and sample configurations to tailor *xdm* to their particular environments. Several sample configurations are provided underneath the *config* subdirectory.

clients/xdpyinfo/ This directory contains a utility for printing information about a display's visuals and screens.

clients/xedit/ This directory contains a simple text editor built on top of the Athena Text widget and X Toolkit.

clients/xev/ This directory contains a program for examining the contents of events and how they are generated.

clients/xfd/ This directory contains a utility for displaying the characters in a font.

clients/xhost/ This directory contains a utility for controlling access to the display on a host by host basis.

clients/xinit/ This directory contains a utility for starting an X server and an initial client (usually a terminal emulator) on systems that don't have support for doing so from */etc/init*. Site administrators are expected to create user-friendly startup scripts as *xinit* isn't intended for novice users.

clients/xkill/ This directory contains a utility for getting rid of unwanted windows.

clients/xload/ This directory contains a program for monitoring machine load averages. It displays a histogram of the most recent load averages and is often used to monitor machines in a network. It uses the Load widget from the Athena widget set, which will need to be modified if you are porting X to a new operating system.

clients/xlogo/ This directory contains a program that uses the Logo widget from the Athena widget set to display the X Window System logo.

clients/xlsfonts/ This directory contains a utility for listing the fonts that are available on a given server. If you request long listings from a server with many compressed fonts, your display may pause for a long time.

clients/xlswins/ This directory contains a utility for listing windows on the display. It is useful for locating windows that might have popped off the screen for some reason.

clients/xmag/ This directory contains a utility for magnifying parts of the display when debugging graphics. It may not work properly if more than one type of visual is displayed on the screen at once.

clients/xman/ This directory contains a utility for displaying manual pages. A small amount of effort is required to add the appropriate emulation for the local operating system's *man* program.

clients/xmh/ This directory contains a visual interface to the MH mail handling system. It makes extensive use of the **X** Toolkit and the Athena widget set.

clients/xmodmap/ This directory contains a utility for displaying changing the keyboard, modifier, or pointer maps. It reads a scripts of commands and is usually run when you login or first start up **X**.

clients/xpr/ This directory contains utilities for printing screen dumps of images obtained with *xwd*.

clients/xprop/ This directory contains a utility for examining the properties attached to a given window.

clients/xpseudoroot/ This directory contains a prototype implementation of pseudo-root windows as described in the previous version of the *Inter-Client Communication Conventions Manual* (ICCCM). It is provided solely for experimentation and **is guaranteed to change** when the final ICCCM specification is adopted.

clients/xrdb/ This directory contains a utility for loading user-specified default resource definitions into the server. It is usually run when you login or first start up X.

clients/xrefresh/ This directory contains a simple utility for refreshing all or part of your screen.

clients/xset/ This directory contains a utility for setting various personal preferences for keyclick, pointer acceleration, etc. It now supports adding and deleting entries from the font path.

clients/xsetroot/ This directory contains a utility for setting the background of the root window.

clients/xterm/ This directory contains a VT102 and Tektronix 4014 terminal emulator. Many, many bugs have been fixed since the previous release. The VT102 mode now uses the X Toolkit translation manager (making arbitrary rebinding of keys possible), selections (see *xclipboard* and *xcutsel*), and sets its process group correctly.

clients/xwd/ This directory contains a utility for dumping images of windows. It is usually used to take a snapshop of a window for printing or for later displaying with the *xwud* program. Some servers still have problems with XY format images, and most run quite slowly.

clients/xwininfo/ This directory contains a utility for examining the various attributes of a window (such as size, placement, window manager information, etc.). It is frequently used with *xprop* to examine the window hierarchy.

clients/xwud/ This directory contains a utility for displaying images that were previously creating using the *xwd* utility.

demos/ This directory contains several programs that are fun to watch, but are not of much use beyond that.

demos/ico/ This directory contains a neat program that rolls a many-sided (you get to choose among several) object around the screen.

demos/maze/ This directory contains a rather attractive demonstration of maze solving.

demos/muncher, demos/plaid/ These directories contain programs for drawing cute pictures.

demos/puzzle/ This directory contains a "rearrange the tiles" puzzle game for X11. If you have a color display, try running *puzzle -picture mandrill.cm* from the directory in which it is built.

demos/xeyes/ This directory contains an attentive program inspired by a NeWS demo seen at SIGGRAPH '88.

doc/ This directory contains all of the documents describing the standard distribution. Manual pages for the various clients can be found in the individual program source directories.

doc/HelloWorld/ This directory contains David Rosenthal's USENIX '88 *Hello, World* paper on using toolkits.

doc/Protocol/ This directory contains the official specification of the X Protocol. This is the final authority of what is and is not part of the X protocol and is part of the X standard.

doc/Server/ This directory contains several guides to porting the X server to new platforms.

doc/Xaw/ This directory contains a guide for the Athena widget set.

doc/Xlib/ This directory contains the source for the Xlib programming guide and manual pages. There is an untested script called *doc/Xlib/Xman/expand.names* that will rename the manual pages to match the names of the routines that they describe.

doc/Xt/ This directory contains the Specification for the X Toolkit Intrinsics. The Intrinsics are now part of the X standard; any vendor that ships Xlib is expected to ship Xt as well.

doc/bdf/ This directory contains the Bitmap Distribution Format for describing fonts. BDF is now part of the X standard; all server vendors are expected to ship a program to convert fonts in this format to whatever internal formats they prefer.

doc/bugs/ This directory contains a template for submittings bugs reports (see *doc/bugs/bug-report*). Please use this form when reporting bugs in the supported distribution to *xbugs@expo.lcs.mit.edu.*

doc/extensions/ This directory contains documentation for possible extensions to the core protocol and base libraries. It currently includes the proposed PEX 3d graphics extension and an input synthesis extension.

doc/fontnames/ This directory contains the specification for font naming proposal under evaluation by the X Consortium. This is the format used in naming the fonts donated by Adobe Systems, Inc. and Digital Equipment Corporation and by Bitstream, Inc.

doc/releasenotes/ This directory contains the sources for this document.

doc/tutorials/ This directory contains essays on how to use particularly troublesome parts of the X Window System. Contributions are always welcome.

examples/ This directory contains various example programs that don't belong anywhere else.

examples/CLX/ This directory contains several samples of how to use the CLX Common Lisp X interface.

examples/Xaw/ This directory contains several small programs that test out the various Athena widgets.

extensions/ This directory tree contains the source code for several sample server extensions: a spline drawing request (*bezier*), a package for using live video in X (*plxvideo*), the beginnings of an extension for doing input recording and synthesis (*xtest1*), and a trapezoid drawing request (*zoid*).

extensions/include/ This directory contains header files for the sample extensions.

extensions/lib/ This directory contains the client library routines for communicating with the extension packages.

extensions/server/ This directory contains the server routines for implementing the extensions.

extensions/test/ This directory contains several example programs for testing the extensions.

fonts/ This directory tree contains the sources for various utilities for creating and manipulating font files. The user-contributed distribution has a variety of translators for converting fonts from various formats to BDF.

fonts/bdf/ This directory tree contains the source for a nice selection of fonts. Starting with this release, organizing fonts into directories is rather important given the length of the font names and the ability to have aliased and wildcarded names for fonts. As the BDF format is now part of the X standard, all server vendors are expected to ship compilers to convert BDF files to the appropriate packed font format for their servers. By default, the sample server will have all three of the font directories found here in the font path. If the resolution of the main display is less than 88 dots per inch (as set in the server's *.macros* file), the 75dpi fonts will preceed the 100dpi fonts in the path. Otherwise, the 100dpi fonts will appear first in the font path.

fonts/bdf/misc/ This directory contains the cursor and fixed width fonts from the previous releases. It is intended for fonts that should always be in the font path.

fonts/bdf/75dpi/ This directory contains fonts donated by Adobe Systems, Inc. and Digital Equipment Corporation and by Bitstream, Inc. designed for 75 dot per inch monitors. A nice selection of families, weights, and sizes is provided. These fonts follow the new font naming convention; most users will want to learn how to properly use wildcards.

fonts/bdf/100dpi/ This directory contains versions of the 75dpi fonts for 100 dot per inch monitors. Some families at this resolution were not ready in time for this release.

fonts/bdftosnf/ This directory contains the program used to compile fonts in BDF format into the packed Server Natural Format used by the sample server.

fonts/mkfontdir/ This directory contains a new utility for creating the font database that the server uses to map fontnames to filenames. Whenever fonts are added or removed from a directory, this program **must** be run in that directory to rebuild the database.

lib/ This directory contains all of the major libraries in the standard distribution.

lib/CLX/ This directory contains the CLX Common Lisp X package. This is a native Common Lisp interface to the X protocol (i.e. it doesn't use Xlib) that will be under review by the X Consortium for possible inclusion in the X standard.

lib/X/ This directory contains the Xlib C language programming library. The interface provided by this package is part of the X standard (i.e. any vendor that ships any C interface must ship Xlib in order to call its product X). Vendors are free to change the internals, but the interface must remain the same. Several new routines have been added since the last release to provide access to elements of opaque data structures.

lib/X/sysV/ This directory contains routines used to make Xlib work on System V-based machines.

lib/X/mips/ This directory contains routines used to make Xlib work on platforms manufactured by Mips Computer Systems.

lib/Xaw/ This directory contains the Athena widget set. It is the beginning of a growing collection of user interface objects built on top of the X Toolkit Intrinsics. Widgets are used in building higher-level applications, and should ideally provide as much mechanism and as little policy as possible (that is for user interface toolkits, user interface management systems, and applications to implement). A much more complete set developed by Hewlett-Packard is available in the user-contributed distribution (unfortunately, it has not yet been ported to the R3 standard X Toolkit Intrinsics).

lib/Xmu/ This directory contains a collection of miscellaneous routines for supporting the MIT applications. It is *not* part of the X standard; vendors are not required to ship this library. *Xmu* uses external interfaces to all libraries and should be portable to wide variety of systems. It is currently used by parts of the Athena widget set and by various clients.

lib/Xt/ This directory contains a sample implementation of the X Toolkit Intrinsics, a collection of resource, event, and object managers that provide a mechanism for building user interfaces objects called *widgets*. The Intrinsics have been adopted as part of the X standard. Any vendor that ships *Xlib* is expected to ship *Xt*.

lib/oldX/ This directory contains X11 implementations of the X10 *XDraw* (including spline support) and *AssocTable* routines.

rgb/ This directory contains a sample RGB color database and a program to compile it. A better database is sorely needed, but nobody has volunteered one yet. Gray levels and several new colors have been added.

server/ This directory contains a sample server for the core protocol. It should match the X Protocol Specification fairly closely, but the Specification is the final authority. Read the documentation in the *doc/Server* directory, any README files in the *server/ddx/* directories, and study the code very hard before trying to make any changes.

server/ddx/ This directory contains the device dependant libraries for a number of different platforms. Study any README files before building or installing any servers.

server/ddx/apollo/ This directory contains full sources for building a server that runs on monochrome and color Apollo displays. The README file gives hints and prerequisites for building this server.

server/ddx/cfb/ This directory contains a sample "color frame buffer" library for getting color ports off the ground. After a server is running, it should then be optimized to use any available hardware support. The cfb code is very slow, but very portable.

server/ddx/dec/ This directory contains full sources for building servers for both the monochrome (qvss) and color (qdss) displays on the VAXstation II, 2000, and 3000 series displays. It also contains routines for controlling and interpreting LK201 keyboards.

server/ddx/hp/ This directory contains full sources for building a server that runs on the HP 9000/300 series platforms with Topcat displays.

server/ddx/ibm/ This directory contains sources for building a server that runs on the APA16 and Megapel displays under IBM AOS (but not under AIX).

server/ddx/macII/ This directory contains sources for building a server than runs on the Apple Macintosh II under A/UX.

server/ddx/mfb/ This directory contains a portable driver for monochrome frame buffer displays. It is primarily intended for platforms that have no special graphics hardware and as an initial porting base. If hardware support is available, it should be used wherever possible.

server/ddx/mi/ This directory contains a machine independent implementation of the various graphics operations. It is frequently used with the mfb and cfb libraries in porting the server to new platforms and in manipulating in-memory pixmaps. It is designed to be very portable.

server/ddx/ndx/ This directory contains sources for building a server with no input or output devices. It uses the generic monochrome and color frame buffer code and is useful for testing the device-independent parts of the server.

server/ddx/plx/ This directory contains sources for building a server that runs on Parallax video graphics controllers attached to Suns or VAXes. It also uses the Parallax Video Extension in the *extensions/server/* directory.

server/ddx/snf/ This directory contains the routines for manipulating SNF fonts. Most servers use the SNF out of convenience, but there is no requirement that they do so.

server/ddx/sun/ This directory contains full sources for building a server that runs on Sun bw2 and various cg displays. It uses the cfb library instead of a lot of device specific routines and is therefore somewhat slower than some of the other color servers in the supported distribution. See the README file in this directory before building or installing the Sun server.

server/dix/ This directory contains the device independent portions of the sample **X** server. It is highly recommended that you not change any code in this directory as it will prevent you from upgrading to new versions. If you find problems or have a proposal for a change that would make porting to new platforms easier, please send in a bug report as described in Section 3.

server/include/ This directory contains header files that are used throughout the server.

server/os/ This directory contains the various operating system-dependent portions of the server.

server/os/4.2bsd/ This directory contains the routines needed to make the sample server run under operating systems that support the 4.2bsd socket interfaces.

server/os/bsdemul/ This directory contains emulations of commonly-used BSD routines. It is typically used by System V based servers.

util/ This directory contains various programs and scripts for building and configuring the release. The programs in this section should be the first ported when bringing up **X** on a new platform.

util/bm-convert/ This directory contains a filter for converting X10 format bitmap file to X11 format (see *bitmap* for additional information).

util/checkfn/ This directory contains a utility for checking for invalid file-names. It is typically used before preparing a distribution.

util/compress/ This directory contains the sources for the BSD *compress* program. It is provided for systems that don't already have it.

util/cpp/ This directory contains sources for a public domain C preprocessor derived from Martin Minow's DECUS *cpp*. It is provided for systems whose native *cpp* cannot handle the complexity of the server or the X Toolkit. Users of A/UX 1.0 will need to build and install as described in the file *server/ddx/macII/R3setup.sh* before attempting to build this release.

util/imake/ This directory contains the most important build utility. The *imake* program is used to generate the appropriate machine dependent Makefiles from machine independent descriptions called Imakefiles. It uses the C preprocessor so that symbolic names and macro functions may be defined. It has its own handcrafted Makefile, and a special program for determining the initial compilation flags. If you are porting the release to a new machine, you may need to edit *util/imake/ccflags.c* to add any compiler flags that your machine will need when compiling *imake*. *Imake* will be built automatically as part of *make World*.

util/imake.includes/ This directory contains the configuration files used to generate the various *Makefiles*. The README file describes which parameters can be set and where. Server-specific values may be given in the appropriate *.macros¡* files and site-wide values that differ from the defaults may be given in the file *site.def*. The file *Imake.tmpl* should **not** be changed. If you change any of these parameters, you will need to do a full rebuild to make them take effect. If you are porting X to a new machine, study the files in this directory *very* carefully.

util/makedepend/ This directory contains a program for automatically generating dependencies for Makefiles. It is used as part of the build process to ensure that the right files are recompiled whenever any source files are changed. If the configuration parameter *CppSourcesPresent* is set to *YES*, *makedepend* will have a copy of the C preprocessor built into it for speed. This is not necessary and is not done in this release. *Makedepend* is built automatically as part of the "make World" phase.

util/patch/ This directory contains Larry Wall's *patch* program, an extraordinarily useful program for patching diffs into source code. This program is not built automatically in this release; it is provided simply for the convenience of people who do not have access to the comp.sources.unix archives.

util/scripts/ This directory contains various useful scripts for tasks such as installing software and generating link trees.

util/soelim/ This directory contains a version of the *soelim* program for those systems that lack one.

Appendix D **Contents of the Release —
User-Contributed Software**

D.1 The User-Contributed Distribution

This documentation is reproduced from sources included in the MIT distribution.[1]   The
user-contributed distribution contains the directories listed below. Bugs in this section
of the release should be reported to the individual authors, not to *xbugs*.

contrib/ This directory is the top level of the user-contributed distribution. Its
layout is meant to roughly parallel the core distribution.

contrib/clients/ This directory tree contains a variety of generally useful programs.

contrib/clients/alertyorngs/ This directory contains several utilities for popping up dialog windows to tell or ask the user for various information.

contrib/clients/gsh/ This directory contains a graphical shell for novice users.

contrib/clients/hpxpr/ This directory contains a version of *xpr* that can print
on HP Laserjet printers.

contrib/clients/kterm/ This directory contains a version of *xterm* that can
work with Kanji fonts.

---

contrib/clients/magic/ This directory contains X drivers for the *magic* VLSI design system.

contrib/clients/pbm/ This directory contains Jef Poskanzer's Portable Bitmap Toolkit and a variety of utilities for converting bitmaps between different formats.

contrib/clients/splot/ This directory contains a plotting package.

contrib/clients/spy/ This directory contains a yet another magnifying glass utility.

contrib/clients/texx/ This directory contains a DVI previewer.

contrib/clients/x11startup/ This directory contains a collection of scripts and default configuration files that provide a nicer interface than plain *xinit*.

contrib/clients/xbgsun/ This directory contains a utility for loading a Sun raster image onto the root window background.

contrib/clients/xcalendar/ This directory contains a program for managing ones calendar.

contrib/clients/xdvi/ This directory contains yet another DVI previewing package.

contrib/clients/xdvorak/ This directory contains a utility for remapping the keyboard to use Dvorak-style bindings.

contrib/clients/xfig/ This directory contains a drawing package.

contrib/clients/xim/ This directory contains a program for displaying 8 and 24 bit images on 8 plane displays.

contrib/clients/xipr/ This directory contains a version of *xpr* for Imagen printers.

contrib/clients/xlock/ This directory contains a program for locking up a display when not in use.

contrib/clients/xmessage This directory contains another program for displaying messages. It is primarily used for error messages in X startup scripts and for leaving reminders on other people's displays.

contrib/clients/xmore/ This directory contains a version of the *more* pagination utility for X.

contrib/clients/xperfmon/ This directory contains a utility for collecting and displaying system statistics. It is operating system specific and will require porting to each particular platform.

contrib/clients/xpic/ This directory contains a *pic* previewer.

contrib/clients/xplaces/ This directory contains a tool for laying out and recording a user's initial session.

contrib/clients/xpref/ This directory contains a visual interface to several of the *xset* functions.

contrib/clients/xshell/ This directory contains an ancient program for invoking commands with single keystrokes.

contrib/clients/xshowcmap/ This directory contains a utility for displaying the colors in a colormap.

contrib/clients/xstring/ This directory contains a program for displaying a string on another user's display.

contrib/clients/xtools/ This directory contains yet another program for laying out a user's initial session.

contrib/clients/xtroff/ This directory contains a *troff* previewer.

contrib/clients/xwebster/ This directory contains a visual interface to the SRI-NIC *webster* dictionary database.

contrib/demos/ This directory tree contains a variety of somewhat amusing demo programs.

contrib/demos/paint/ This directory contains a very simple paint program.

contrib/demos/psycho/ This directory contains a multi-display version of *ico*.

contrib/demos/spaceout/ This directory contains another program for setting the root window background.

contrib/demos/worm/ This directory contains a program for investigating random slither patterns.

contrib/demos/xcolors/ This directory contains a program for displaying the available named colors.

contrib/demos/xfish/ This directory contains another program for setting the root window background.

contrib/demos/xgranite/ This directory contains still another program for setting the root window background.

contrib/demos/xphoon/ This directory contains a cute program for displaying the current phase of the moon (on the root window background, of course).

contrib/demos/xrotmap/ This directory contains a nasty program for rotating colormaps.

contrib/doc/ This directory tree contains additional documentation.

doc/SharedLibs/ This directory contains a proposed specification from AT&T on how to write shared versions of the major C language libraries. It is a proposal from AT&T and is not part of the X standard.

contrib/extensions/ This directory tree contains extension packages for the core protocol.

contrib/extensions/pex/ This directory contains the current documents and header files for the PEX proposed 3d graphics extension to X.

contrib/fonts/ This directory tree contains utilities for creating and editing font files along with an eclectic collection of fonts.

contrib/fonts/bdf/ This directory tree contains several collections of random fonts. Most of them are ugly.

contrib/fonts/bdf/bmug/ This directory contains fonts converted from the Berkeley Mac Users Group public domain software archives.

contrib/fonts/bdf/info-mac/ This directory contains fonts converted from the INFO-MAC software archives.

contrib/fonts/bdf/oldx10/ This directory contains BDF versions of many of the X10 fonts.

contrib/fonts/bdf/oldx11/ This directory contains the fonts that were shipped in previous releases of X11. Most of them are rather ugly.

contrib/fonts/utils/ This directory tree contains a variety of utilities for converting various font formats to BDF as well as a two versions of a rudimentary tool for splitting font files apart so that they can be edited.

contrib/games/ This directory tree contains several interesting games that are useful for getting people accustomed to X.

contrib/games/mazewar/ This directory contains an implementation of the ancient and honorable *mazewar*, the grandfather of most networked computer games.

contrib/games/qix/ This directory contains an X version of the video arcade games of the same name.

contrib/games/xhanoi/ This directory contains a program for solving the Tower of Hanoi problem.

contrib/games/xmille/ This directory contains a very pretty computer version of the card game Milles Bournes.

contrib/games/xpuzzle/ This directory contains yet another puzzle program.

contrib/games/xsol/ This directory contains an X version of the card game solitaire.

contrib/games/xtrek/ This directory contains the infamous *xtrek*. It requires System V shared memory interfaces in order to work.

contrib/hacks/ This directory tree contains several programs of questionable usefulness.

contrib/hacks/arctest/ This directory contains a simple program for testing arcs.

contrib/hacks/reborder/ This directory contains a little utility for resetting the borders of windows after an anti-social window manager dies.

contrib/hacks/xbounce/ This directory contains a program for dribbling windows on the screen.

contrib/hacks/xchcursor/ This directory contains a program for cycling the cursor through different patterns.

contrib/hacks/xsetsize/ This directory contains a utility for moving, resizing, and iconifying windows from the command line. It is the prime example of a program that violates the *Inter-Client Communications Conventions* and probably will not work with most window managers.

contrib/server/ This directory tree contains code and documentation for items that have not been integrated into the sample server.

contrib/server/sgi/ This directory tree contains patches to the sample server as well as the machine-specific drivers needed to make the R3 server run on Silicon Graphics workstations.

contrib/server/speedups/ This directory contains suggested ways of optimizing the sample server. The emphasis to date in the server has been on accuracy instead of performance. There are a great many places where substantial improvements could be made.

contrib/server/veryoldxpc/ This directory contains the results of an old attempt to port a very early version of the X11 server to the IBM-PC under MS-DOS. Substantial amounts of work will be necessary to make it at all useful. This package will not be included in future releases unless substantial progress is made on bringing it up to date.

contrib/toolkits/ This directory tree contains several native toolkits (i.e. not built on top of other toolkits).

contrib/toolkits/InterViews/ This directory contains a new version of the InterViews C++ toolkit from Stanford University.

contrib/toolkits/Xr11/ This directory contains a new version of the X-Ray toolkit from Hewlett-Packard.

contrib/toolkits/andrew/ This directory contains a new version of the Andrew toolkit from Carnegie-Mellon University.

contrib/toolkits/clue/ This directory contains a sample implementation of the Common Lisp User Environment from Texas Instruments.

contrib/widgets/ This directory tree contains a variety of widgets. Some of them are based on the R2 *Xt* Intrinsics and others are based on the current Intrinsics.

contrib/widgets/Dclock/ This directory contains a digital clock widget based on the R2 Intrinsics.

contrib/widgets/Mailwatch/ This directory contains a better mailbox widget based on the R2 Intrinsics.

contrib/widgets/MenuBox/ This directory contains a prototype of menu widget that will eventually become part of the Athena widget set. It is based on the R3 Intrinsics.

contrib/widgets/Xhp/ This directory contains a large, integrated widget set from Hewlett-Packard and a version of the R2 X Toolkit Intrinsics upon which these widgets are temporarily based.

contrib/widgets/Xsw/ This directory contains a collection of widgets from Sony which are also based on the R2 Intrinsics.

contrib/widgets/cpicker/ This directory contains a widget for selecting and modifying colors based on the R2 Intrinsics.

contrib/widgets/tblwidget/ This directory contains a geometry manager widget that uses *tbl*-style formatting commands to layout child windows based on the R2 Intrinsics.

contrib/widgets/widgeteditor/ This directory contains a simple widget editor based on the R2 Intrinsics.

contrib/widgets/widgetwrap/ This directory contains a utility routine for creating widgets and setting their arguments.

contrib/widgets/xpalette/ This directory contains a widget for displaying colors based on the R2 Intrinsics.

contrib/windowmgrs/ This directory tree contains several of the more popular window managers.

contrib/windowmgrs/awm/ This directory contains the *awm* window manager.

contrib/windowmgrs/rtl/ This directory contains the *rtl* tiling window manager.

contrib/windowmgrs/twm/ This directory contains the *twm* window manager.

contrib/windowmgrs/wm/ This directory contains the old *wm* window manager. It is provided primarily for historical reasons.

Appendix E **How to Obtain X**

E.1 In the USA

Complete sets of manuals only, or both manuals and tapes of the full MIT release are obtainable from:

> **MIT Software Center**
> Technology Licensing Office
> room E32-300
> 77 Massachusetts Avenue
> Cambridge, MA 02139
> USA

E.2 In Europe

Complete sets of manuals only, or both manuals and tapes, or tapes only (in a variety of formats) containing the full MIT release are obtainable from:

> **Unipalm Limited**
> 147 St. Neots Road
> Hardwick
> Cambridge CB3 7QJ
> England

Phone: +44 954 211797 international, (0954) 211797 in the UK.
Fax: +44 954 211244 international, (0954) 211244 in the UK.

E.3   How to Obtain GNU Emacs

GNU Emacs is produced and developed and distributed by:

> **Free Software Foundation**
> 1000 Mass Avenue
> Cambridge, MA 02138
> USA

The terms of the licence allow (and encourage) anybody with a copy of the system to distribute full source code and documentation free to anybody else.

If you can't find someone who already has a copy, you can obtain a full distribution of the system for the price of media and a handling fee, either from the **Free Software Foundation** or, in Europe, from **Unipalm** (address above).

Appendix F X Network and Electronic Mail Services

There are a number of **X**-related services available across the electronic mail and other networks. These include bulletin boards, "information servers", and facilities for obtaining **X** software, both the MIT release and other programs and software.

F.1 The xpert Mailing List

The xpert mailing list is a forum for discussion of aspects of **X**, including problems with existing software, plans for changes, possible improvements, and other general information. This is organised by the **X** people at MIT and is a source of much useful (and authoritative) information.

To join the list, send a mail message to:

> `xpert-request@athena.mit.edu`

asking to be added to the distribution list.

F.2 The xstuff Server

The xstuff server is a service which sends you program and/or documentation files across the mail network, in response to a request which you send to it by electronic mail. Primarily it contains "official" information from the **X**-Consortium, including newly released documentation and fixes to the MIT-released software.

The remainder of this section consists of the information you get from the server when you send it a "help" request.

This message comes to you from the xstuff server, xstuff@expo.lcs.mit.edu. *It received a message from you asking for help.*

The xstuff server is a mail-response program. That means that you mail it a request, and it mails back the response.

The xstuff server is a very dumb program. It does not have much error checking. If you don't send it the commands that it understands, it will just answer "I don't understand you".

The xstuff server has 4 commands. Each command must be the first word on a line. The xstuff server reads your entire message before it does anything, so you can have several different commands in a single message. The xstuff server treats the **Subject:** *header line just like any other line of the message. You can use any combination of upper and lower case letters in the commands.*

The archives are organized into a series of directories and subdirectories. Each directory has an index, and each subdirectory has an index. The top-level index gives you an overview of what is in the subdirectories, and the index for each subdirectory tells you what is in it.

If you are bored with reading documentation and just want to try something, then send the server a message containing the line

> **send index fixes**

When you get the index back, it will contain the numbers of all of the fixes and batches of fixes in the archive; send the server another message asking it to send you the fixes that you want:

> **send fixes 1 5 9 11–20**

etc. If you are using a mailer that understands "@" notation, send to xstuff@expo.lcs.mit.edu. If your mailer deals in "!" notation, try sending to some-place!eddie!expo.lcs.mit.edu!xstuff. For other mailers, you're on your own.

Here is some more documentation. The server has 4 commands:

help command *: The command* help *or* send help *causes the server to send you the help file. You already know this, of course, because you are reading the help file. No other commands are honored in a message that asks for help (the server figures that you had better read the help message before you do anything else).*

index command *: If your message contains a line whose first word is* index, *then the server will send you the top-level index of the contents of the archive. If there are other words on that line that match the name of subdirectories, then the indexes for those subdirectories are sent instead of the top-level index. For example, you can say* `index`

or   •

    `index fixes`

You can then send back another message to the xstuff server, using a send *command (see below) to ask it to send you the files whose name you learned from that list.*

(Footnote: index fixes *and* send index fixes *mean the same thing: you can use the* send *command instead of the* index *command, if you want, for getting an index.*

If your message has an index *or a* send index *command, then all other* send *commands will be ignored. This means that you cannot get an index and data in the same request. This is so that index requests can be given high priority.)*

send command *: If your message contains a line whose first word is* send, *then the xstuff server will send you the item(s) named on the rest of the line. To name an item, you give its directory and its name. For example:*

    `send fixes 1-10`

Once you have named a category, you can put as many names as you like on the rest of the line; they will all be taken from that category. For example:

    `send fixes 1-10 11-20 21-30`

Each send *command can reference only one directory. If you would like to get one fix and one of something else, you must use two* send *commands.*

You may put as many send *commands as you like into one message to the server, but the more you ask for, the longer it will take to receive. See "FAIRNESS", below, for an explanation. Actually, it's not strictly true that you can put as many* send *commands as you want into one message. If the server must use* uucp *mail to send your files, then it cannot send more than 100K bytes in one message. If you ask for more than it can send, then it will send as much as it can and ignore the rest.*

path command *: The* path *command exists to help in case you do not get responses from the server when you mail to it.*

Sometimes the server is unable to return mail over the incoming path. There are dozens of reasons why this might happen, and if you are a true wizard, you already know what those reasons are. If you are an apprentice wizard, you might not know all the reasons but you might know a way to circumvent them.

If you put in a path *command, then everything that the server mails to you will be mailed to that address, rather than to the return address on your mail. The server host expo.lcs.mit.edu does not have a direct* uucp *connection to anywhere; you must go through eddie or somewhere else.*

F.2.1 Notes

The xstuff server acknowledges every request by return mail. If you don't get a message back in a day or two you should assume that something is going wrong, and perhaps try a path *command.*

The xstuff server does not respond to requests from users named "root", "system", "daemon", or "mailer". This is to prevent mail loops. If your name is "Bruce Root" or "Joe Daemon", and you can document this, I will happily rewrite the server to remove this restriction. Yes, I know about Norman Mailer and Waverley Root. Norman doesn't use netmail and Waverley is dead.

F.2.2 Fairness

The xstuff server contains many safeguards to ensure that it is not monopolized by people asking for large amounts of data. The mailer is set up so that it will send no more than a fixed amount of data each day. If the work queue contains more requests than the day's quota, then the unsent files will not be processed until the next day. Whenever the mailer is run to send its day's quota, it sends the requests out shortest-first.

If you have a request waiting in the work queue and you send in another request, the new request is added to the old one (thereby increasing its size) rather than being filed anew. This prevents you from being able to send in a large number of small requests as a way of beating the system.

The reason for all of these quotas and limitations is that the delivery resources are finite, and there are many tens of thousands of people who would like to make use of the archive.

F.3 FTP and Other Network Servers

For those with access to the Internet (Arpanet), there are several sites which offer FTP access, allowing you to obtain software directly over the network. There are also other sites which allow access via uucp or other protocols. Details of these are published occasionally on the xpert mailing list.

Appendix G **Information You Need from your System Manager**

If you install **X** yourself, as we said before it is strongly recommended that you use the default configuration so that all the files are stored in the standard directories.

However, if the system has been installed with a non-standard configuration, you will need to obtain from your system manager at least the following information:

1. Directory for the **X** executable programs.
   (default: */usr/bin/X11/*).

2. Directory for the bitmaps library.
   (default: */usr/include/X11/bitmaps/*).

3. Directory for manual pages.
   (default: */usr/man/mann/*).

4. Directories for fonts.
   (default: */usr/lib/X11/fonts/misc/*, */usr/lib/X11/fonts/75dpi/* and */usr/lib/X11/fonts/100dpi/*).

5. Location of the RGB colour database.
   (default: */usr/lib/X11/*).

6. Name of the application-specific resources directory.
   (default: */usr/lib/X11/app-defaults/*).

Index

In this index, page numbers are shown in **bold** type to indicate a major source of information about the item being indexed. Page numbers in *italics* indicate a definition.